The Core of the Curriculum for Accounting Majors

The Core of the Curriculum
for Accounting Majors

by Richard E. Flaherty

American Accounting Association

American Accounting Association
5717 Bessie Drive
Sarasota, Florida 33583

CONTENTS

Project Advisory Committee

Elba F. Baskin, Oklahoma State University
Homer A. Black, Florida State University
Thomas R. Hofstedt, Stanford University
Charles W. Plum, Texas A&M University
Jay M. Smith, Jr., Brigham Young University
R.M. Sommerfeld, University of Texas
Doyle Z. Williams, University of Southern California
Leon E. Hay, Indiana University
Robert L. Grinaker, University of Houston
Robert J. Kaufmann, Price Waterhouse & Co.
Lewis F. Davidson, University of North Carolina
Paul L. Gerhardt, American Accounting Association

FOREWORD

The announced intention of the American Assembly of Collegiate Schools of Business to develop standards for accreditation of accounting programs, and renewed stress by the American Institute of Certified Public Accountants on the perceived need for a 150-credit-hour program of formal education for students preparing to enter a professional accounting career, make it particularly appropriate to publish Accounting Education Research Monograph No. 3, The Core of the Curriculum for Accounting Majors, *at this time.*

The research upon which the monograph is based was funded through the generosity of the Price Waterhouse Foundation. The present grant continued the support given by the Price Waterhouse Foundation which resulted in the 1971 publication of A New Introduction to Accounting *and the 1975 publication of* Accounting Education Research Monograph No.2, Researching The Accounting Curriculum: Strategies for Change, *edited by William L. Ferrara.*

The symposium reported upon in Accounting Education Research Monograph No. 2 set the objective of the present monograph as identifying the accounting topics which, in the opinion of accounting educators and practitioners, lie at the core of every curriculum for accounting majors. The questionnaires utilized by the author of this monograph were completed by the respondents in 1975. It is quite possible that some of the respondents would have different views of the importance of individual topics were they to complete the questionnaire in 1979, but it is probable that, to a large extent, topics deemed to be in the core in 1975 would also be placed in the core in 1979. Accordingly, the results of the research appear to be worth the serious consideration of persons presently concerned with evaluating the content of an existing curriculum for accounting majors, existing courses in certain areas of accounting specialization, or designing new courses or curricula.

Leon E. Hay
Director of Education
1977-78, 1978-79

April, 1979

ix

ACKNOWLEDGEMENTS

This study would not have been possible without the cooperation of the hundreds of accounting practitioners and educators who contributed to the study by spending valuable time responding to an overly long questionnaire. The dedication of these individuals to quality accounting education is obvious and their assistance is gratefully acknowledged.

My sincere appreciation is extended to the Price Waterhouse Foundation for the financial support which made this study possible. The Project Advisory Committee provided invaluable assistance, especially during the formative stages of the research effort. The members of the committee were Elba F. Baskin, Homer A. Black, Thomas R. Hofstedt, Charles W. Plum, Jay M. Smith, Ray M. Sommerfeld, Doyle Z. Williams, and Robert L. Grinaker. In addition, the three individuals who served as Director of Education for the American Accounting Association during this research effort, Robert L. Grinaker, Leon E. Hay and Doyle Z. Williams, provided much-needed support and encouragement. The author gratefully extends his appreciation to Lewis F. Davidson for his assistance with respect to the research methodology underlying this study.

Finally, to my wife, Ricci, and my daughters, Kristin and Erin, who were deprived of a husband and a father much too often during this study, go my heartfelt thanks for their understanding and support.

Richard E. Flaherty

Tempe, Arizona
May, 1979

1

Introduction

Objectives of the Study

The general objective of this study was to provide useful information for evaluating and developing accounting curricula in colleges and universities. The study attempts at least partially to meet the charge of the participants in a 1974 symposium which provided the impetus for this research. [1] Thus the specific objectives of the study were to identify a body of common accounting knowledge, to identify cores of accounting knowledge for various areas of specialization, to determine the degree of emphasis which ought to be placed upon conceptual knowledge and technical ability for various accounting topics and to determine the relative importance of various accounting topics. Also, the study compares the views of accounting educators and accounting practitioners both by area of specialization and on an overall basis with respect to various accounting topics.

The next section of this chapter describes the background of this project. Then, major findings are briefly summarized. Finally, the chapter concludes with a description of the organization of the remaining chapters.

Background

The present study had its genesis in the 1971-72 Advisory Committee to the Director of Education of the American Accounting Association (AAA). In 1972 Robert T. Sprouse, then President-elect of the AAA, requested funding from the Price Waterhouse Foundation for a symposium of leading accounting educators. The purpose of the symposium would be to consider needed changes in accounting education and to suggest possible fruitful areas of accounting education research. As a result of numerous discussions, the Price Waterhouse Foundation in 1973 announced a research grant to the AAA of $100,000.

The grant to the AAA was to be utilized for research in accounting education, with primary emphasis to be placed upon the accounting curriculum beyond introductory accounting. The reasons for specifying emphasis upon curriculum beyond the introductory level was that the Price Waterhouse Foundation had previously funded a study of introductory accounting. This earlier study led to the

---

[1] Ferrara *et al.*, editors, *Researching the Accounting Curriculum: Strategies for Change.* Education Series Number 2 (Sarasota, Florida: American Accounting Association, 1975).

1

publication of *A New Introduction to Accounting* in 1971 and, subsequently, to numerous innovative approaches at that level.

The first step toward achieving the objectives of the grant was a two-day symposium sponsored by the AAA in Chicago in May, 1974. [2] This symposium, chaired by William L. Ferrara and devoted to the subject "Researching the Accounting Curriculum: Strategies for Change," was designated as Phase I of the project, while this research project has been designated as Phase II. The first evening of the symposium was devoted to a panel discussion of "The Future of the Accounting Curriculum in a College of Business Administration." The morning and afternoon sessions during the two days of the symposium consisted of papers, critiques, small group discussions and summarizations. Papers presented dealt with advanced financial accounting, advanced managerial accounting, auditing, taxation, not-for-profit organizations and social measurements.

The primary objective of Phase I, the symposium, was to identify accounting curriculum problem areas and to suggest procedures for resolving the problems. While many problems were identified by the symposium participants, a clear consensus developed among the participants regarding the area most in need of research, as follows:

> It was the overwhelming majority opinion of the symposium participants that the greatest need and opportunity for curriculum research in accounting is in the area of the "accounting core," that is, the collection of courses, modules or study units that fits between the study of introductory accounting and the various accounting specialties . . . . [3]

The "core" was further defined in the symposium proceedings as "that collection of accounting subject matter which *every* accounting major should be required to take and be expected to understand." [4] An exhibit in the proceedings depicted the accounting core as follows: [5]

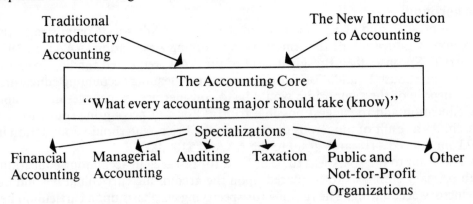

This notion of an "accounting core" as developed by the symposium participants served as the foundation for this study.

---

2   *Ibid.*
3   *Ibid.*, p. 224.
4   *Ibid.*
5   *Ibid.*, p. 225.

It was the consensus of those involved in formulating the proposal which gave rise to the grant that a full-time researcher should be hired to undertake the project, with assistance as required. Past efforts of AAA committees in the area of accounting education were hampered by meager financial resources and limited committee life. Thus, in late 1974 the author was hired as Project Director and an Advisory Committee was selected. Supervisory responsibility for the project was placed with the AAA Director of Education.

The immediate task confronting the Project Director and Advisory Committee was to decide which of the many potentially worthwhile projects suggested by the May 1974 symposium participants should be pursued. Relevant literature was reviewed, including not only publications dealing with various aspects of accounting education, but also material related to educational objectives, educational research, professional education in other fields and curriculum development. [6] This literature review provided many insights into researchable areas, educational research methods and potential payoffs from pursuing the various research avenues. This review also provided the basis for a more informed consideration of the recommendations of the symposium participants.

Several meetings involving the Project Director, Advisory Committee and AAA Director of Education were held during 1975 to discuss the possible research avenues and possible research methods. It was quickly decided that the consensus recommendation of the symposium participants was both a desirable and feasible avenue to pursue. After several meetings, the research methodology was settled and the research effort was underway. [7] The following months were devoted to development of a suitable questionnaire and identification of a set of desired responses. Questionnaires were ultimately mailed to our sample and responses were tabulated and analyzed. A brief overview of our research results is presented in the following section. Detailed analyses of the research findings were presented in subsequent chapters.

Overview of Research Results [8]

Using techniques described in Chapter 2, a body of common accounting knowledge, or "common core," was identified. [9] This common core includes those accounting topics which all accounting majors, regardless of their area of ultimate specialization, should be required to take. The common core consists of 105 of the 197 topics included in the questionnaire. [10]

---

6 A bibliography of relevant published works reviewed by the Project Director is included immediately following Chapter 9.

7 The research approach is described in detail in Chapter 2.

8 To avoid misinterpretation of the highlights presented in this section, the reader should, as a minimum, scan the overview of research methodology presented in Chapter 2.

9 Chapter 3 contains the detailed analysis of the common accounting core.

10 A sample questionnaire is presented in Appendix A.

The common core topics can be broken down as follows according to the section of questionnaire topics in which they were presented:

Questionnaire Section	Total Number of Topics	Number in Common Core	Percent in Common Core
Financial	65	42	64.6%
Managerial	51	24	47.1%
Auditing	50	33	66.0%
Taxation	31	6	19.4%
Total	197	105	

Significant differences (at the .05 level) in importance mean responses existed between educator and practitioner respondents for 54.5 percent (107 out of 197) of the topics, broken down into 53.3 percent (56 out of 105) of the common core topics and 55.4 percent (51 out of 92) of the non-core topics. In the vast majority of these instances involving significant disagreement, the mean educator response was higher than the mean practitioner response.

Questionnaire respondents, looked at as a group, almost invariably indicated that conceptual knowledge should receive more emphasis than technical ability.

Area accounting cores were also identified for managerial accounting, taxation, financial accounting, auditing, and generalists. Each of these area cores was identified based solely upon the responses of individuals within the respective areas.

The managerial accounting area core [11] consists of 156 (79.2 percent) of the 197 questionnaire topics. That is, the 105 common core topics plus an additional 51 topics constitute the managerial accounting area core. These topics may be analyzed as follows:

Questionnaire Section	Total Number of Topics	Number in Common Core	Percent in Common Core
Financial	65	52	80.0%
Managerial	51	50	98.0%
Auditing	50	42	84.0%
Taxation	31	12	38.7%
Total	197	156	

Significant differences (at the .05 level) between managerial accounting educator and practitioner mean importance responses existed for 36 (23.1 percent) of the 156 core area topics. The educator mean importance response exceeded the

---

[11] See Chapter 4 for the detailed analysis.

practitioner mean for 31 of these 36 topics. Practitioner respondents in the managerial accounting area considered the following area core topics to be significantly more important than did educators:

Foreign currency translation
SEC reporting
Business combinations: consolidation procedures
Internal control: description based on flowchart
Management letter

Managerial accounting respondents almost invariably indicated that more emphasis should be placed upon conceptual knowledge than upon technical ability. The technical ability mean response exceeded the conceptual knowledge mean response for only three of the 156 area core topics, as follows:

Fundamentals of Federal income tax determination
Internal control; description based on flowchart
Tax returns and accompanying schedules

Even in these three instances the technical ability mean was not significantly higher than the conceptual knowledge mean. Managerial accounting educators generally scaled topics higher on both conceptual knowledge and technical ability than did managerial accounting practitioners. However, managerial accounting practitioners placed considerably more emphasis on technical ability with respect to auditing topics than did managerial accounting educators.

The taxation area core [12] includes 162 (82.2 percent) of the 197 questionnaire topics, broken down as follows:

Questionnaire Section	Total Number of Topics	Number in Area Core	Percent in Area Core
Financial	65	58	89.2%
Managerial	51	27	52.9%
Auditing	50	46	92.0%
Taxation	31	31	100.0%
Total	197	162	

There was a significant difference (at the .05 level) between the taxation educator and taxation practitioner mean importance response for 63 (38.9 percent) of the 162 area core topics. It is interesting to note that 14 (45.2 percent) of the taxation topics are included in this group of topics on which significant differences existed. Educators tended to scale topics more highly with respect to importance than did practitioners, as indicated by the fact that the practitioner mean

---

12 See Chapter 5 for the detailed analysis.

exceeded the educator mean for only the following five out of the 63 topics on which significant differences were discovered:

Foreign currency translation
Audit administration: setting and collecting fees
Taxation for international operations
Complex tax provisions: foreign tax credit
State and local taxes

Taxation respondents generally placed more emphasis upon conceptual knowledge than upon technical ability. However, the technical ability mean exceeded the conceptual knowledge mean for 11 (35.5 percent) of the 31 taxation topics, indicating that taxation respondents believe a strong technical orientation is essential to prepare students for a career in taxation. Taxation educators generally scaled topics more highly with respect to both conceptual knowledge and technical ability than did taxation practitioners.

The financial accounting area core [13] consists of 168 (85.3 percent) of the 197 questionnaire topics, as follows:

Questionnaire Section	Total Number of Topics	Number in Area Core	Percent in Area Core
Financial	65	60	92.3%
Managerial	51	43	84.3%
Auditing	50	45	90.0%
Taxation	31	20	64.5%
Total	197	168	

Significant differences (at the .05 level) between educator and practitioner mean importance responses were found for 90 (53.6 percent) of the financial accounting area core topics. The educator mean exceeded the practitioner mean for 86 of these topics. The four exceptions were:

Foreign currency translation
Interim reporting
Business combinations: consolidation procedures
Complex tax provisions: consolidated corporate returns

Financial accounting respondents scaled conceptual knowledge higher than technical ability for all but the following four area core topics:

Tax returns and accompanying schedules
Complex tax provisions: individuals
Complex tax provisions: partners and partnerships
Complex tax provisions: subchapter S

---

[13] See Chapter 6 for the detailed analysis.

Financial accounting educators generally scaled topics more highly with respect to both conceptual knowledge and technical ability than did financial accounting practitioners.

Included in the auditing area core, [14] as determined by the responses of auditing educators and practitioners, are 145 (73.6 percent) of the 197 questionnaire topics, broken down as follows:

Questionnaire Section	Total Number of Topics	Number in Area Core	Percent in Area Core
Financial	65	51	78.5%
Managerial	51	37	72.5%
Auditing	50	44	88.0%
Taxation	31	13	41.9%
Total	197	145	

There was a significant difference (at the .05 level) between auditing educator and auditing practitioner mean importance response for 39 (26.9 percent) of the 145 area core topics. For all but seven of these 39 topics the educator mean exceeded the practitioner mean. The exceptions were:

Materiality
Legal responsibilities of auditor: classic cases
Auditing procedures: working papers
Management letter
Audit administration: client relations
Operational auditing: methodology
Recognition of tax opportunities

Auditing respondents, like those in other areas, almost invariably indicated that more emphasis should be placed upon conceptual knowledge than upon technical ability. Unlike the pattern found in other areas, auditing educators and auditing practitioners placed virtually the same emphasis upon conceptual knowledge on an overall basis. However, educators tended to scale topics slightly higher on an overall basis with respect to technical ability. It should be noted, though, that practitioners scaled 33 of the 50 auditing topics higher with respect to technical ability than did educators.

The responses of generalist educators and practitioners led to the inclusion of 171 (86.8 percent) of the 197 questionnaire topics in the generalist area core, [15] comprised as follows:

---

[14] See Chapter 7 for the detailed analysis.
[15] See Chapter 8 for the detailed analysis.

Questionnaire Section	Total Number of Topics	Number in Area Core	Percent in Area Core
Financial	65	59	90.8%
Managerial	51	44	86.3%
Auditing	50	48	96.0%
Taxation	31	20	64.5%
Total	197	171	

Significant differences (at the .05 level) between educator and practitioner mean importance responses were found for 74 (43.3 percent) of the 171 area core topics. Included in the 74 topics were 33 out of the 48 auditing area core topics, indicating a significant amount of disagreement between generalist educators and practitioners regarding the importance of various auditing topics. In the majority (44) of the 74 cases where significant differences were found, the practitioner mean exceeded the educator mean.

Generalist respondents tended to emphasize conceptual knowledge more than technical ability. There were only six topics out of the 171 area core topics for which the mean technical ability response exceeded the mean conceptual knowledge response, as follows:

Accruals and deferrals
Double-entry system
Cash
Tax returns and accompanying schedules
Error corrections
Statements from incomplete records

Generalist practitioners tended to scale topics slightly higher with respect to conceptual knowledge than did generalist educators. On the other hand, educators in general scaled topics higher with respect to technical ability than did practitioners, even though practitioners placed relatively more emphasis on technical ability for auditing and taxation topics than did educators.

In summary, the questionnaire results were employed to identify a common accounting core and five area cores. We discovered that, in the view of our respondents, conceptual knowledge should generally be emphasized more than technical ability. We also discovered that, within the common core and the five area cores, significant disagreement exists between educators and practitioners regarding the importance of a large number of topics. Identification of areas of agreement and disagreement, as well as establishment of the importance and the degree of emphasis on conceptual knowledge and technical ability for the various topics, should be of considerable interest to those charged with evaluating and developing accounting curricula.

Organization

Following this introductory chapter, Chapter 2 presents a discussion of the research methodology underlying this study. Chapter 3 is devoted to identification and discussion of the "common core" of accounting knowledge, that is, that accounting subject matter which every accounting major, regardless of area of ultimate specialization, should be required to take. Chapters 4 through 8 present and discuss the "area cores" of accounting subject matter for the various areas of specialization, that is, managerial accounting, taxation, financial accounting, auditing and generalists, respectively. Finally, conclusions and suggestions for further research are presented in Chapter 9. Appendices related to the various chapters are presented following Chapter 9.

2

Research Methodology

The purpose of this chapter is to describe the process whereby the data underlying chapters 3 through 8 were generated and analyzed. Rationale for approaches followed is presented, development of the questionnaire, topics list, mailing process and sample are described and statistical techniques employed are discussed.

The Research Approach: An Overview

The objective of the research effort was to gather data which could be utilized as a basis for making recommendations regarding the educational objectives and content of accounting curricula for individuals preparing to enter an accounting career. This overriding objective guided the selection of research methods and data analysis.

It was decided that, as a basis for making recommendations regarding accounting curricula content and objectives, the opinions of individuals with recognized expertise in accounting education or accounting practice would be sought. Expert opinion has long been recognized as a source of knowledge in the social sciences. As John Buckley stated in his study *In Search of Identity,* "In any societal effort, action will tend to begin with, and reflect, the ideas of its leaders." [1] Likewise, Gordon and Howell note that a synthesis of the best of current opinion represents a contribution. [2] Simon also recognizes the general usefulness of expert opinion in a variety of research situations. [3] Thus, support for expert opinion as a useful source of knowledge is widespread.

The method of data collection chosen was a questionnaire. [4] Given our objectives and constraints, the choice among possible data collection methods was fairly easy. The choice was essentially between questionnaire and interview, or

---

[1] John W. Buckley, *In Search of Identity — An Inquiry into Identity Issues in Accounting* (Los Angeles: California Certified Public Accountants Foundation for Education and Research, 1972), p. x.

[2] Gordon and Howell, op. cit., p. 10.

[3] Julian L. Simon, *Basic Research Methods in Social Science: The Art of Empirical Investigation* (New York: Random House, Inc., 1969), pp. 274-6.

[4] A sample questionnaire is included in Appendix 2A.

some combination thereof. Given that we wished to gather the views of a rather large number of individuals in accounting education and in accounting practice, an extensive interview approach was considered infeasible. Furthermore, it was felt that the input desired, primarily the three scalar responses for each of 197 topics, could be obtained much more economically and at least as effectively via a questionnaire. Thus, the desired sample size and the nature of the input being sought both strongly favored a questionnaire approach. [5]

Since this study was descriptive, *i.e.,* a survey of the views of leading accounting educators and practitioners, descriptive, statistics formed the basis for the data analysis. Standard statistics were computed based on the responses to each of the three scales for each topic. One of these statistics, the mean, forms the basis for most of the analysis in Chapters 3-8. In addition, analysis of variance were performed to test for the significance of differences in means among areas of specialization and between educators and practitioners. A more detailed description of the data analysis is presented at a later point in this chapter.

The Sample
The primary objective of an expert opinion survey is to gather and synthesize the views of individuals whose experience and insight make their views worth seeking. Thus, selection of the sample is obviously quite critical. As Simon stated, "The statements of a million people about the size of your feet will be less accurate than the statement of the man who just sold you a pair of shoes." [6]

The procedure utilized to arrive at the list of desired participants in the study was, first, to rely upon the collective judgement of the individuals involved in the research project. The advisory committee was selected carefully so that the various areas of specialization would be represented. Thus, knowledge of the leaders in the various areas of specialization was also present to a great extent within the advisory committee. Accounting educators and accounting practitioners, both in public accounting and in industry, were sought as desired participants. Members of the advisory committee, all but one being accounting educators, served as virtually the sole source of names for the educator sample. The public accounting sample was expanded primarily by soliciting suggestions from appropriate individuals within the American Institute of Certified Public Accountants. The industry sample was expanded primarily by relying upon the only industry member of the advisory committee and his contacts within the Financial Executives Institute.

---

[5] Many references detail the advantages and disadvantages of interview and questionnaire data collection methods. Thus, such an analysis is not repeated here. For example, see Claire Selltiz, *et al., Research Methods in Social Relations,* revised (New York: Holt, Rinehart and Winston, 1959), p. 238-43; Simon, *op. cit.,* pp. 249-51; and Max D. Engelhart, *Methods of Educational Research* (Chicago: Rand McNally and Company, 1972), pp. 95-115, *passim.*

[6] *Ibid.,* p. 276.

In addition to the views of selected individuals identified as described above, we wished to obtain the opinions of other knowledgeable individuals in various areas of specialization in accounting practice. This was accomplished by, in a sense, delegating the responsibility for selecting the individuals to previously-selected respondents. That is, multiple copies of the questionnaire were mailed to certain individuals who were asked to complete one questionnaire and distribute each of the others to individuals within their organization with recognized expertise in one of the areas of specialization. Selltiz *et al.* recognize this technique as being "perhaps the most direct method of selecting informants." [7]

The Questionnaire

The objective of the questionnaire survey was to gather and analyze the views of knowledgeable accounting educators and practitioners regarding various accounting topics. Thus, an early task confronting the researchers was development of a list of accounting topics.

It was decided that only accounting topics, albeit broadly defined, would be included in the questionnaire. That is, in contrast to the Roy and MacNeill study, this study did not address the non-accounting portion of an accounting major's education. Numerous sources were utilized to begin developing an acceptable list of accounting topics. Included among these sources were numerous AAA committee reports, textbooks and published articles. [8] An initial, tentative list of topics was distributed to the advisory committee. This list was then revised based upon comments received and the revised list was distributed to selected educators and practitioners for comment. After several iterations, it was decided that attempts to further refine the topics list would not be productive.

The final list of 197 topics [9] was classified into financial, managerial, auditing and taxation topics. Numerous subheadings were also used within these four categories, as it soon became apparent that attempts to produce an unclassified, randomly ordered list of topics, which was conceptually preferable from a research design standpoint, was simply not feasible. The degree of detail required to convey the meaning of each topic without classification would have been overwhelming.

The next step in the questionnaire development was to determine the most desirable approach to obtaining views of respondents with respect to the topics. We wished to have the respondents assess both the importance of the topics and also the educational objectives with respect to each topic, that is, the type of learning deemed desirable for each topic. Pretesting of a proposed questionnaire led us to adopt a five-point, equal-appearing interval scale with only the end points labeled to assess the importance of each topic. [10] However, identification of and presentation of appropriate educational objectives required considerably more effort.

---

7   Selltiz, *et al.*, *op. cit.*, p. 56.
8   See the selected bibliography.
9   See the sample questionnaire in Appendix 2A.
10 See the sample questionnaire in Appendix 2A.

Discussion of learning objectives and taxonomies of learning objectives are quite numerous in the educational psychology literature. This literature thus formed the starting point for our search for appropriate educational objectives. [11] Classification schemes presented by Bloom, Gagne, Ebel and Gronlund, among others, were examined for possible application to our research. [12] Unfortunately, none of these taxonomies enjoy anywhere near general support even within the field of educational psychology, including the Bloom taxonomy, which is probably the most familiar taxonomy of learning objectives to accountants since some accounting writers have publicized this taxonomy. Furthermore, discussions with educational psychologists eventually led us to the conclusion that we would be better off to develop our own educational objectives that were applicable to the accounting discipline rather than to attempt to fit an existing taxonomy to our needs. Thus, a significant preliminary effort involved the development of these educational objectives.

The first step in this process was a pooling of advisory committee suggestions regarding verbs which could be used to describe possibly desirable learning outcomes for accounting subject matter (*e.g.,* to solve, to understand, to identify, to describe, to recall, *etc.*). This initial list was then distributed to faculty colleagues, fellow employees, and other acquaintances for review. Based upon input from this distribution a list of 40 verbs was settled upon for subsequent analysis.

The next step in the development of educational objectives was a pair-wise comparison of the 40 verbs on the basis of the degrees of similarity. About 70 educators and practitioners participated in this research step. The purpose of the pair-wise comparisons was to provide the researchers with data which could be analyzed as a basis for reducing the set of verbs from 40 to a manageable number which could be utilized in our questionnaire.

The data reduction technique used was cluster analysis. [13] The objective of cluster analysis is to reduce the number of items in the set while maintaining as much information as possible from the original set. Thus, in this case, the goal was to combine verbs in a step-wise fashion based on similarity responses. The program used combined the two most similar verbs first, thus resulting in 39 items after the first iteration. Then the next two most similar verbs were combined and so on until eventually only one item remained in the set.

Due to the sheer magnitude of the task that we would be asking questionnaire respondents to carry out, we did not wish to have more than three or four educational objectives in the questionnaire. Thus, we analyzed the clusters in the hierarchy at the levels where 5, 4, 3, and 2 clusters remained. It was the judgement of

---

[11] See the selected bibliography for these references.

[12] *Ibid.*

[13] In particular, the program used was Multiple Ordered Cluster Analysis (MOCA) distributed by National Educational Resources, Inc., of Ann Arbor, Michigan. The program was run at the University of Illinois at Urbana-Champaign Center for Advanced Computation.

the researchers that the clearest and most useful level was at the point where only two clusters remained. It was at this level that the clusters could fairly easily be identified as what we chose to call conceptual knowledge and technical ability. [14] This is not necessarily the often-used theory-procedures dichotomy. As we indicated in the questionnaire, conceptual knowledge was defined as mental processes ranging from simple recall or awareness to creative thinking or evaluation. Technical ability was defined as skill in applying existing knowledge to the solution of problems and ranges from classification and definition to the application of complex theories in novel problem situations. The same type of scale was used to assess each of the two educational objectives as was used to assess importance, *i.e.*, five-point equal appearing interval scales with only the end points labeled.

A substantial amount of pretesting with a variety of possible formats and labels was conducted in order to minimize surprises during the pilot study and the main study. Several approaches which were considered attractive from a research design standpoint were eliminated from consideration at this stage due to feasibility problems. For example, as mentioned earlier, we had considered presenting an undifferentiated randomly-ordered list of topics to respondents. It soon became apparent that the amount of description required to delineate each topic under this approach would be overwhelming. Thus, the topics were classified. Likewise, many terminology problems were identified and minimized as a result of pretests. A tentative package including a cover letter, questionnaire and insert describing the project resulted from this pretesting.

A pilot study was then conducted using both accounting educators and practitioners who had not been involved in the project prior to that time. Only minor changes resulted from the pilot study. Also, time estimates for completion of the questionnaire were obtained and appropriate data analysis was decided upon.

The first portion of the questionnaire was designed to collect selected demographic data. The last section of the questionnaire addresses some more general issues related to accounting education.

A "frame of reference" was provided respondents at the beginning of Part II to the questionnaire. Respondents were asked to consider desired entry-level educational background for a career in their area of expertise. They were also asked to look ahead, rather than considering only past and current requirements. Lastly, they were reminded that tradeoffs are always necessary in terms of what can be done in a formal educational program, *i.e.*, that time and other resources are scarce commodities. However, they were not told to assume a particular number of years or credit hours of formal educational preparation. We did not want respondents to be constrained in this manner.

---

[14] The reliability of these results for the total sample was assessed by using a split-half technique. Results from each of these samples were consistent with those of the total sample.

Data Analysis

Descriptive statistics formed the foundation for much of the data analysis. [15] Statistics relating to the location and shape of the distribution of responses were computed for each of the three scales for each topic. In particular, the mean, standard deviation, variance, kurtosis and skewness were computed for responses for each scale for each topic. [16] This analysis was performed for all respondents, all educators, all practitioners, for each area of specialization and, within area, for educators and practitioners separately.

A core of common accounting knowledge, hereafter referred to as the common core, was identified based upon the importance responses. We used two statistics, the mean and standard deviation, to determine which topics should be included in the common core. Specifically, 95 percent confidence limits were computed separately for educators and for practitioners by area of specialization based upon importance responses. The upper limit of each of these confidence intervals was then compared to 2, the midpoint of the importance scale. If the upper limit of the confidence interval exceeded 2 for all intervals computed for a given topic, that topic was included in the common core. The implication is that since all educator and practitioner groups in all areas of specialization consider such topics to be at least moderately important, the topics passing this test may be thought of as a core of common accounting knowledge.

While this selection criterion is admittedly arbitrary, it is, in the opinion of the researchers, at least as appealing as any alternative criterion. It has the advantage of being objective. Also, both the location (mean) and shape (standard deviation) of the distribution of responses are considered in the criterion. Comparison with the midpoint of the importance scale, 2.00, also has a certain amount of intuitive appeal. Further, since much of the subsequent analysis encompasses all 197 topics rather than merely core topics, the selection of a cut-off criterion is not particularly critical.

Area cores of accounting knowledge were identified by using the same selection criterion but applying it only to the educator and practitioner groups for the particular area of specialization. Thus, the area cores include the comon core topics plus those additional topics meeting the cut-off criterion for educators and practitioners within the area of specialization.

In addition to rank orderings and identification of common and area cores, tests for significant differences between educator and practitioner responses, overall and by area of specialization, were performed. [17] Significant differences are identified and discussed in subsequent chapters.

---

15 The reader may find it helpful to peruse one of the chapters presenting the findings for an area of specialization in conjunction with this discussion.

16 The program used was STANDARD SCORES as described in *SOUPAC Program Descriptions* (Computing Services Office, University of Illinois, Urbana, Illinois, 1974).

17 The program used was BALANOVA 5, described in *SOUPAC Program Descriptions, op. cit.*

A significant amount of verbal analysis and discussion is also presented based upon the statistical results. This analysis is ordered for the most part in terms of financial, managerial, auditing, and taxation topic groups.

Conceptual knowledge and technical ability mean responses are presented in the exhibits where topics are rank-ordered by importance means. Also, responses on these two scales are compared for each topic and verbal analysis of the comparisons is presented. Educator-practitioner differences on each of these scales are also highlighted.

Summary

Thus, this study is an expert opinion survey. It was designed to elicit and analyze the views of a large number of competent accounting educators and practitioners representing the various areas of specialization. The research design is based on the premise that the accounting discipline is rapidly becoming a discipline of specialties and yet significant commonalities exist. As Lawler indicated nearly a decade ago:

. . . specialization is not only inevitable — and it is not only desirable. It is an imperative necessity if the profession is to be equipped to render the range and quality of service which is needed by the business community. [18]

The study is further based upon the presumption that it is essential to assess not only the importance of various accounting topics but also the type of learning that ought to occur with respect to those topics. Subsequent chapters present the results of the study.

---

[18] John L. Lawler, ''The Specter of Specialization,'' *California CPA Quarterly* (March 1969), p. 10.

3

The Body of Common Accounting Knowledge

The principal recommendation resulting from the symposium which provided the impetus for this study was that the study should be "designed to determine, develop and test the content of the 'accounting core'. . . ." [1] As a result, one of the primary objectives of this study was to identify the common core, *i.e.*, that accounting subject matter which should be required of all accounting majors, regardless of their area of ultimate specialization.

Exhibit 3-1 presents the 197 questionnaire topics, along with the mean responses on the importance, conceptual knowledge and technical ability scales, rank-ordered according to the importance means. The means in Exhibit 3-1 were computed using *all* questionnaire responses. The sample upon which Exhibit 3-1 is based was comprised of the following number of respondents by area of specialization and, further, according to whether respondents were educators or practitioners:

Area of	Number of	Educators	Practitioners
Managerial accounting	96	33	63
Information systems	55	1	54
Taxation	95	14	81
Financial accounting	141	53	88
Auditing	123	13	110
Generalist	66	14	52
Other	10	2	8
Total	586	130	456

Due to incomplete responses by some participants, it was not possible to associate all respondents with an area of specialization. However, as the above tabulation

---

1 Ferrara *et. al., op. cit.,* p. 224.

indicates, the number of unclassifiable respondents is quite small and thus should not influence the reader's ability to interpret the responses. As is apparent from the preceding tabulation, practitioners (456 respondents) have much more influence on the means presented in Exhibit 3-1 than do educators (130 respondents).

Selected demographic information is presented in Appendix 3A. It may be useful to point out some aspects of our sample. Of particular interest is the fact that at least (data not available for some respondents) 413 (70.5 percent) of the 586 questionnaire respondents are certified public accountants. Also, 77 (59.2 percent) of the educator respondents have had administrative experience in education. Slightly more than two-thirds of the respondents (69.6 percent) have had public accounting experience, while almost one-half (45.9 percent) have had corporate accounting experience.

Within the educator group, 93 (71.5 percent) of the 130 respondents are affiliated with public universities. Also, 114 (87.7 percent) of the educator respondents are affiliated with universities which offer an undergraduate accounting degree, and 116 (89.2 percent) are affiliated with universities which offer a master's degree with an accounting emphasis. Within the practitioner sample are 205 public accounting respondents and 251 industry respondents.

The symbol "#" immediately preceding an importance mean in Exhibit 3-1 indicates that there was a statiscially significant difference (at the .05 level) between educator and practitioner mean responses for that topic. [2] Means computed separately on educators and practitioners are presented in Appendices 3B and 3C respectively. A brief discussion of these results on an overall basis is presented at a later point in this chapter.

The letter in the Area column of Exhibit 3-1 indicates that the topics were presented in the questionnaire under the heading of financial (F), managerial (M), auditing (A), or taxation (T). The common core topics are those topics which do not have an asterisk immediately to the left of the topic name. That is, an asterisk is used to denote non-core topics. Using the approach described in Chapter 2 to dichotomize the topics into core and non-core topics, we identified 105 out of the 197 topics as common core topics, that is, topics which every accounting major should be required to take.

---

2   This analysis and other analyses presented in subsequent chapters which involve comparisons of means were performed using BALANOVA 5, an analysis of variance program described in *SOUPAC Program Descriptions* (Computing Services Office, University of Illinois, Urbana, Illinois, 1974). The reader should note that this program compares unweighted means, that is, it eliminates the effect of different sample sizes in the groups being compared. Due to the lack of an adequate sample for systems educators, systems educators and practitioners were excluded from all ANOVA analyses.

EXHIBIT 3-1

RANK ORDERING ON IMPORTANCE MEANS:
ALL RESPONDENTS

			Means	
Area	Topic	Importance	Conceptual Knowledge	Technical Ability
F	Balance sheet	#3.27	3.21	2.84
A	Internal control: principles	3.20	3.09	2.18
F	Revenue and expense recognition	#3.16	3.18	2.73
F	Income statement	#3.14	3.12	2.77
A	Internal control: evaluation	3.12	2.96	2.22
F	U.S. financial accounting and reporting standards	#3.09	3.00	2.50
F	Double-entry system	3.08	3.05	2.89
F	Theoretical framework: current structure	#3.08	3.04	2.49
A	Internal control: audit exposure due to weaknesses	#3.04	2.87	2.04
T	Fundamentals of Federal income tax determination	#3.04	2.76	2.62
A	Internal control in an EDP environment	3.02	2.80	2.05
A	Audit evidence: types	2.99	2.87	2.51
F	Accruals and deferrals	#2.98	3.02	2.67
F	Transaction analysis	#2.97	2.96	2.65
F	Deferred taxes	2.96	2.96	2.43
F	Statement of changes in financial position	#2.93	2.93	2.57
F	Information needs of financial statement users	#2.92	2.87	2.12
A	Internal control: modifications in audit program based on evaluation	2.90	2.72	1.80
F	Regulatory influences	#2.86	2.77	2.17
A	Audit evidence: relative strength of types	2.85	2.73	1.98
F	Financial statement analysis	2.84	2.84	2.42
T	Recognition of tax opportunities	#2.80	2.61	1.59
T	Capital gains and losses	#2.79	2.48	2.37
F	Inventories	#2.79	2.84	2.47
F	Theoretical framework: alternatives to current structure	#2.79	2.86	2.12
M	Tax considerations in managerial decisions	2.78	2.74	2.26
A	Modifications of the standard short-form audit report	2.78	2.57	2.03
M	Accounting information requirements for management decisions	#2.78	2.77	2.18
M	Standard costs	#2.77	2.81	2.33
F	Materiality	2.77	2.80	2.18
A	Audit evidence: post-statement events	2.76	2.66	2.53
F	Business combinations: consolidation procedures	2.76	2.82	2.32
A	Standard short-form audit report	2.75	2.50	1.95
T	Tax planning	2.75	2.49	2.02

EXHIBIT 3-1
(continued)

Area	Topic	Importance	Conceptual Knowledge	Technical Ability
			Means	
M	Management information systems: internal control aspects	2.74	2.68	2.19
A	Internal control: description based on narrative	#2.73	2.66	1.98
A	Legal responsibilities of auditors: under the securities acts	2.72	2.48	1.74
A	Generally accepted auditing standards	#2.72	2.72	2.31
F	Leases	#2.71	2.71	2.22
F	Accounting for income taxes	#2.70	2.74	2.33
F	Present value and future worth concepts	#2.69	2.78	2.27
T	Non-taxable exchanges	2.68	2.38	2.08
A	Statistical inference in auditing: statistical sampling	#2.67	2.58	2.52
F	Error corrections	2.66	2.71	2.47
A	Statistical inference in auditing: judgmental sampling	2.65	2.49	2.05
M	Process costing	#2.65	2.75	2.26
A	Internal control: description based on questionnaire	#2.65	2.56	2.17
M	Budgeted financial statements	#2.62	2.65	2.22
F	Contingencies	2.62	2.64	2.09
M	Full costing	#2.62	2.71	2.24
M	Variable costing	#2.62	2.70	2.22
M	Short-range planning	#2.61	2.63	2.14
M	Flexible budgets	#2.61	2.65	2.19
M	Long-range planning	#2.60	2.64	2.15
F	Business combinations: purchase vs. pooling of interest	2.60	2.74	2.11
F	Long-term liabilities	#2.59	2.66	2.28
A	*Internal control: relationship of GAAS	2.59	2.38	2.26
M	Capital budgeting	#2.59	2.64	2.13
F	Fixed assets	#2.58	2.64	2.32
F	Depreciation, depletion and amortization	#2.58	2.66	2.30
F	SEC reporting	2.58	2.57	2.03
M	Cash management	2.57	2.59	2.14
M	Job order costing	#2.57	2.68	2.26
F	Short-term liabilities	#2.56	2.63	2.27
A	Influence of professional and regulatory bodies on auditing	#2.56	2.50	1.77
A	Auditing procedures: tests of account balances	2.56	2.38	2.28
M	Performance evaluation: return on investment	#2.55	2.64	2.06
A	Auditing procedures: tests of transactions	2.55	2.38	2.28
T	*Complex tax provisions: Corporations and shareholders	#2.54	2.39	1.95

EXHIBIT 3-1
(continued)

Area	Topic	Importance	Conceptual Knowledge	Technical Ability
			Means	
A	Auditing procedures: review of operations	2.54	2.47	2.24
M	Cost-volume-profit analysis	#2.53	2.55	2.20
F	*Corporate equity	#2.53	2.62	2.20
A	Legal responsibilities of auditors: classic cases	2.52	2.38	1.67
M	Performance evaluation: divisional performance	#2.52	2.59	2.07
F	*Earnings-per-share	2.51	2.57	2.12
M	Performance evaluation: responsibility accounting	#2.51	2.55	2.01
F	Interim reporting	2.51	2.54	2.00
F	Intangibles (excluding goodwill)	#2.51	2.61	2.09
A	Internal control: description based on flowchart	2.49	2.29	2.30
F	Investments in securities	#2.47	2.58	2.16
A	*Professional rules of conduct	#2.46	2.51	1.92
F	Research and development costs	2.46	2.58	2.07
A	Auditing procedures: compliance tests	2.46	2.34	2.24
F	Minority interest	2.45	2.59	2.11
F	Cash	#2.44	2.49	2.27
F	Receivables	#2.44	2.53	2.21
F	*Behavioral considerations in financial reporting	#2.42	2.48	1.76
A	Management letter	#2.42	2.33	1.86
M	Joint costs	#2.41	2.53	2.02
F	*Business combinations: unconsolidated subsidiaries	2.39	2.49	1.98
A	User's expectations regarding the auditor's role	2.39	2.44	1.52
A	*Auditing procedures: working papers	2.39	2.26	1.94
F	Convertible debt or equity	#2.38	2.51	2.05
T	*Tax research methodology	2.38	2.17	1.87
T	Taxation of deferred compensation	2.38	2.17	1.78
A	Long-form audit report	2.37	2.10	1.72
A	Audit administration: review	2.35	2.25	1.61
A	Extensions of the attest function: associated audit risk	2.35	2.08	1.38
A	Statistical inference in auditing: regression analysis	2.35	2.33	2.30
F	Statements from incomplete records	2.34	2.44	2.13
M	*Direct costing	#2.34	2.53	2.01
M	Management information systems: implementation	2.34	2.37	1.85

EXHIBIT 3-1
(continued)

			Means	
Area	Topic	Importance	Conceptual Knowledge	Technical Ability
T	*State and local taxes	#2.33	2.14	1.69
A	Legal responsibilities of auditors: exposure to criminal liability	#2.31	2.13	1.66
T	*Accumulated earnings tax	#2.29	2.20	1.38
M	Information economics	#2.29	2.38	1.78
M	*Management information systems: impact of external regulatory influences	2.28	2.28	1.76
M	Statistical analysis of cost variances	2.28	2.36	1.85
A	Statistical inference in auditing: other statistical methods	2.28	2.23	1.54
F	Price-level adjusted financial statements	#2.27	2.50	1.80
F	*Goodwill	#2.27	2.37	1.93
M	Spoilage, waste, defective units and scrap	2.27	2.35	1.92
A	*Legal responsibilities of auditors: at common law	#2.27	2.34	1.58
F	*Pensions	#2.27	2.35	1.79
A	*Requirements for professional certification (CPA)	2.26	2.25	1.91
A	Audit administration: planning	2.26	2.23	1.58
M	Organization theory	#2.26	2.31	1.70
F	Treasury stock	#2.26	2.36	2.00
T	*Theoretical framework of taxation: economic and social concepts	#2.25	2.15	1.02
F	Fund accounting: financial statements	2.24	2.32	1.82
M	*Performance evaluation: non-statistical variance analysis	#2.23	2.30	1.85
A	*Audit administration: client relations	#2.23	2.07	1.50
M	*Management information systems: administration	#2.22	2.23	1.76
M	*Learning curve models	2.21	2.33	1.76
F	Reporting forecasts	2.21	2.36	1.82
T	*Judicial doctrines in tax disputes	2.19	2.08	1.12
F	Installment sales	2.18	2.34	1.92
T	*Tax returns and accompanying schedules	2.18	1.88	2.23
F	*Foreign currency translation	2.17	2.32	1.79
T	*Administrative processes in tax matters	2.17	1.98	1.34
M	*Corporate planning models	#2.16	2.25	1.71
M	*Overhead control	#2.15	2.20	1.78
M	*Performance evaluation: non-financial performance measures	#2.13	2.22	1.68
F	*Fund accounting: types of organizations	2.13	2.22	1.71
M	*Computer science	#2.12	2.18	1.66
A	*Operational auditing: objectives	#2.12	1.96	1.66

EXHIBIT 3-1
(continued)

Area	Topic	Importance	Conceptual Knowledge	Technical Ability
			Means	
F	*Segment reporting	#2.09	2.22	1.67
T	*Social security taxes	2.09	1.90	1.49
M	*Performance evaluation: transfer pricing	#2.08	2.20	1.67
A	Audit administration: supervision	#2.08	2.00	1.45
F	*Development stage companies	#2.08	2.26	1.74
M	*Management information systems: design	#2.07	2.15	1.64
T	*Complex tax provisions: foreign tax credit	#2.05	1.89	1.39
T	*Taxation for international operations	#2.05	1.90	1.29
M	*Performance evaluation: common costs	#2.03	2.10	1.60
T	*Tax practice procedures	#2.03	1.83	1.51
A	*SEC filing requirements	2.02	2.05	1.57
T	*Complex tax provisions: DISC	#2.02	1.94	1.17
F	*Full costing vs. successful efforts costing	2.02	2.19	1.65
M	*Internal financial auditing	2.01	2.14	1.69
F	*Partnership financial statements	2.01	2.18	1.68
A	*Legal responsibilities of auditors: responses of the auditing profession to classic cases	#2.00	1.88	1.44
A	*Auditing procedures: audit practice case	#2.00	1.86	1.75
T	*Complex tax provisions: consolidated corporate returns	#2.00	1.85	1.61
A	*Operational auditing: methodology	#1.99	1.85	1.62
A	*Extensions of the attest function: possible areas	1.99	1.85	1.39
M	*Stimulation	#1.99	2.10	1.48
F	*International accounting standards	#1.99	2.09	1.52
M	*Statistical decision theory	#1.97	2.12	1.56
A	*Special considerations in auditing not-for-profit organizations	1.96	1.87	1.09
M	*Internal operational auditing	1.96	2.12	1.58
M	*Zero base budgeting	1.96	2.15	1.64
T	*Theoretical framework of taxation: alternatives to present framework	#1.96	1.86	1.22
T	*Complex tax provisions: individuals	1.96	1.78	1.95
M	*Performance evaluation: residual income	#1.96	2.05	1.59
F	*Consignments	#1.95	2.12	1.70
M	*Statistical cost estimation	#1.94	2.06	1.57
T	*Judicial processes in tax disputes	1.93	1.81	1.08
F	*Fund accounting: governmental units	#1.91	2.04	1.61
F	*National income accounting	1.90	2.03	1.49
M	*Network methods	#1.86	1.98	1.39
F	*Regulated industries	1.83	1.95	1.37

EXHIBIT 3-1
(continued)

Area	Topic	Importance	Conceptual Knowledge	Technical Ability
			Means	
T	*Complex tax provisions: partners and partnerships	1.81	1.66	1.92
M	*Behavioral considerations	#1.81	1.94	1.33
T	*Complex tax provisions: subchapter S	1.80	1.66	1.66
T	*Complex tax provisions: fiduciaries	#1.77	1.64	1.58
A	*Audit administration: setting and collecting fees	#1.77	1.62	1.02
F	*Fund accounting: hospitals	1.74	1.90	1.49
F	*Fund accounting: colleges and universities	1.73	1.87	1.48
A	*Comparative accounting and auditing standards among nations	#1.72	1.59	.76
T	*Federal gift tax	#1.72	1.55	1.31
A	*Audit administration: accounting firm organization	1.72	1.60	1.05
F	*Fiduciary accounting: bankruptcy	1.71	1.98	1.40
T	*Federal estate tax	#1.70	1.55	1.33
F	*Fiduciary accounting: receivership	1.69	1.94	1.37
M	*Planning and control of international operations	1.68	1.78	1.29
M	*Sensitivity analysis	#1.67	1.84	1.33
F	*Human resource accounting	1.67	1.83	1.35
M	*Special considerations in non-manufacturing concerns	#1.64	1.76	1.31
M	*Linear programming	#1.64	1.84	1.22
A	*Historical development of auditing	1.58	1.72	1.02
T	*Preparation of tax communications	1.53	1.35	1.66
M	*Social accounting	#1.49	1.67	1.07
T	*Natural resource taxation	1.48	1.41	1.32
F	*Fiduciary accounting: estates and trusts	1.48	1.68	1.24
T	*Personal holding company tax	1.45	1.38	1.26
M	*Requirements for professional certification (CMA)	1.45	1.57	1.23

* ➝ non-core topic.
\# ➝ significant difference (p < .05) between educator and practitioner importance mean responses.

The reader is reminded that the fact that the sample in a particular area of specialization was larger than that in another area does not mean that the larger sample had more influence in determining whether a topic should be included in the common core. The topic had to pass a cut-off criterion for each area of specialization and, within area, for educators and practitioners separately. Thus, all areas of specialization, and educators and practitioners within each area, were equally important in identifying the common core.

However, as indicated earlier, the fact that different sample sizes existed by area and between educators and practitioners does mean that the mean responses in Exhibit 3-1 are more heavily weighted by the views of practitioners than educators and also more by some areas of specialization than by others. Thus, the figures in Exhibit 3-1 must be interpreted carefully. Chapters Four through Eight present some more easily interpreted data since in those chapters we are looking at the input from only the respondents within the appropriate area of specialization.

It may also be helpful to the reader, in attempting to grasp the significance of the questionnaire results, to consider the overall importance attached to the set of questionnaire topics by various groups of respondents. The overall mean importance response (over all 197 topics) for all respondents, for all educators and for all practitioners were as follows:

Respondent Group	Importance Mean
All Respondents	2.34
Educators	2.54
Practitioners	2.27

Thus, educators, on an overall basis, tended to scale topics more highly with respect to importance than did practitioners.

Analysis of Common Core

The 105 common core topics can be analyzed as follows according to the section of the questionnaire in which they were presented:

Questionnaire Section	Total Number of Topics	Number in Common Core	Percent in Common Core
Financial	65	42	64.6%
Managerial	51	24	47.1%
Auditing	50	33	66.0%
Taxation	31	6	19.4%
Total	197	105	

Thus, the section of the questionnaire with the largest proportion of topics included in the common core was auditing, followed closely by financial, and then managerial and taxation in that order.

Numerous additional observations may be made regarding topics included in and excluded from the common core. The following is a summary of some of the more worthwhile and interesting observations related to Exhibit 3-1.

Importance Analysis

Financial Accounting Topics

As indicated in Exhibit 3-1, the following financial topics (listed in order of decreasing importance per the mean responses) were considered by respondents to be among the most important topics:

Balance sheet
Revenue and expense recognition
Income statement
U.S. financial accounting and reporting standards
Double-entry system
Theoretical framework: current structure
Accruals and deferrals
Transaction analysis
Deferred taxes
Statement of changes in financial position
Information needs of financial statement users

While some financial topics were deemed sufficiently unimportant by respondents from several areas of specialization to exclude them from the common core, others were excluded because of only one response group. In other words, they were considered sufficiently important to be included in the common core by both educators and practitioners in five of the six areas of specialization. The following topics were excluded because of the low importance responses of only the group indicated:

Topic	Respondent Group
Corporate equity	Systems-practitioners
Earnings per share	Systems-practitioners
Behavioral considerations in financial reporting	Auditing-practitioners
Business combinations: unconsolidated subsidiaries	Systems-practitioners
Goodwill	Systems-practitioners
Foreign currency translation	Generalist-practitioners
Fund accounting: types of organizations	Auditing-practitioners
Full costing vs. successful effort costing	Auditing-practitioners
Partnership financial statements	Systems-practitioners
Consignments	Financial-educators

Thus, were it not for the low importance responses of the group indicated, these 10 topics would be included in the common core. In the 10 cases where financial topics were excluded from the common core due to responses of only one group, systems or auditing practitioners accounted for nine of these exclusions. Only one of the exclusions was due to educator responses.

It should be noted also that none of the fiduciary accounting topics (*bankruptcy, receivership,* and *estates and trusts*) were included in the common core. Also excluded were the relatively recently developed topics of *international accounting standards, segment reporting, human resource accounting, development stage companies,* and *national income accounting*. Likewise, four of the five fund accounting topics were excluded from the common core. The only other financial topic excluded was *regulated industries*. While several of these topics may be relatively important for particular areas of specialization, their importance was not sufficiently pervasive to qualify them for the common core.

Managerial Topics

The managerial topics considered to be most important by respondents were (in order of decreasing importance):

Tax considerations in managerial decisions
Accounting information requirements for management decisions
Standard costs
Management information systems: internal control aspects

While these topics were considered to be more important than other topics in the managerial area, none of these topics were scaled as highly as the most important financial topics listed in the preceding section. [3] In general, as one can see by glancing through the managerial area indicators (M) in Exhibit 3-1, the managerial topics tended to show up in the middle and lower portion of the rank-orderings.

As noted earlier, 27 (52.9 percent) of the managerial topics were excluded from the common core. Of those topics not in the common core, the following were excluded due to the responses of only one group as indicated:

Topic	Respondent Group
Direct costing	Taxation-practitioners
Management information systems: impact of external regulatory influences	Taxation-practitioners
Management information systems: administration	Generalist-educators
Corporate planning models	Auditing-practitioners
Overhead control	Taxation-practitioners
Computer science	Taxation-practitioners
Performance evaluation: transfer pricing	Taxation-practitioners
Management information systems: design	Taxation-practitioners
Performance evaluation: common costs	Taxation-practitioners

3   Keep in mind that the mean responses in Exhibit 3-1 are weighted in favor of responses of financial accounting and auditing respondents, our most populous sample areas. Thus, one would expect the financial accounting and auditing topics to show up more favorably in general than topics from managerial accounting and taxation.

It is evident from the preceding tabulation that the views of taxation practitioners are not in accord with those of the other groups on most of the topics listed. As could be said for all topics which were excluded from the common core due to the responses of only one group, the vast majority of respondent groups consider such topics to be at least minimally important.

Zero base budgeting and *social accounting,* two topics which have received more than passing attention in recent years, were excluded from the common core. Also, eight of the nine quantitative techniques listed in the managerial section of the questionnaire were excluded from the common core. Those topics excluded were *simulation, network methods, linear programming, sensitivity analysis, statistical decision theory, statistical cost estimation, learning curve models* and *corporate planning models.* Among the other eight managerial topics excluded from the common core were *internal financial auditing* and *internal operational auditing.*

Auditing Topics

Perhaps one of the most surprising results of this study, in the view of the researchers, was that the proportion of auditing topics in the common core (66 percent) was greater than the proportion included from any other section. This is surprising because in some colleges and universities accounting major are not required to take an auditing course. A partial explanation for the inclusion of a high proportion of auditing topics is that eight of the nine internal control topics in this section met the criterion for inclusion in the common core. These topics could perhaps just as logically have been included in the managerial section of the questionnaire, which would have increased the proportion of managerial topics (from 47.7 percent to 53.3 percent) in the common core and decreased the proportion of auditing topics (from 66 percent to 61 percent) in the common core.

The most important auditing topics in the common core (listed in order of decreasing importance) were as follows:

Internal control: principles
Internal control: evaluation
Internal control: audit exposure due to weaknesses
Internal control: in an EDP environment
Audit evidence: types
Internal control: modifications in audit program based on evaluation
Audit evidence: relative strength of types

As indicated in Exhibit 3-1, these topics are not only the most important auditing topics, but also, in the views of the respondents, among the most important of all common core topics.

The following auditing topics were excluded from the common core because of the responses of only the group indicated:

Topic	Respondent Group
Requirements for professional certification (CPA)	Systems-practitioners
Professional rules of conduct	Systems-practitioners
Legal responsibilities of auditors: at common law	Systems-practitioners
Legal responsibilities of auditors: responses of the auditing profession to classic cases	Systems-practitioners
Internal control: relation of GAAS	Systems-practitioners
Auditing procedures: working papers	Systems-practitioners
Audit administration: client relations	Managerial-educators

Thus, six of the seven topics listed above were excluded from the common core due solely to the responses of systems practitioners.

In addition to those topics listed above, 10 other auditing topics were excluded from the common core, with two or more response groups scaling them sufficiently low to exclude them. These topics were:

Historical development of auditing
SEC filing requirements
Auditing procedures: audit practice case
Audit administration: setting and collecting fees
Audit administration: accounting firm organization
Operational auditing: objectives
Operational auditing: methodology
Extensions of attest function: possible areas
Comparative accounting and auditing standards among nations
Special considerations in auditing not-for-profit organizations

The topic *auditing procedures: audit practice case,* which has been one of the more controversial curriculum issues for many years, was excluded due to the views of auditing educators, managerial educators and systems practitioners. The two operational auditing topics, which have been receiving increasing attention in recent years, were excluded by systems practitioners and taxation practitioners.

Taxation Topics
Only six of the 31 taxation topics are included in the common core. They are (in order of decreasing importance):

Fundamentals of Federal income tax determination
Recognition of tax opportunities
Capital gains and losses
Tax planning
Non-taxable exchanges
Taxation of deferred compensation

The topic *fundamentals of Federal income tax determination* ranked very high on importance (10 out of 197 topics) while the rankings of the other five topics ranged from 22 to 95.

Of the 25 taxation topics not included in the common core, the following seven topics were excluded because of the low importance responses of only the group indicated:

Topic	Respondent Group
Accumulated earnings tax	Managerial-educators
Complex tax provisions: corporations and shareholders	Managerial-educators
Social security taxes	Auditing-practitioners
State and local taxes	Auditing-educators
Tax research methodology	Managerial-educators
Tax returns and accompaning schedules	Systems-practitioners
Theoretical framework of taxation: economic and social concepts	Auditing-practitioners

Thus, substantial importance is attached not only to the six common core topics, but also, except for one group in each case, to these seven topics.

The 18 taxation topics for which two or more response groups scaled them sufficiently low to exclude them from the common core were:

Administrative processes in tax matters
Federal estate tax
Federal gift tax
Taxation for international operations
Judicial doctrines in tax disputes
Judicial processes in tax disputes
Complex tax provisions: consolidated corporate returns
Complex tax provisions: DISC
Complex tax provisions: foreign tax credit
Complex tax provisions: fiduciaries
Complex tax provisions: individuals
Complex tax provisions: subchapter S
Complex tax provisions: partners and partnerships
Natural resource taxation
Personal holding company tax
Preparation of tax communications
Tax practice procedures
Theoretical framework of taxation: alternatives to present framework

In general, then, as one would expect, the more basic taxation topics are included in the common core while the more complex, more specialized and more practice-oriented topics are excluded from the common core.

Educators vs. Practitioners

As mentioned earlier, the symbol "#" preceding an importance mean in Exhibit 3-1 indicates that there is a significant difference (at the .05 level) between educator and practitioner mean importance responses for that topic. Several observations may be made regarding the frequency and nature of these differences.

Significant differences in importance mean responses occurred for 54.3 percent (107 out of 197) of all topics, which can be broken down into 53.3 percent (56 of 105) of the common core topics and 55.4 percent (51 of 92) of the non-core topics. Thus, it appears that the extent of agreement (disagreement) between educators and practitioners with respect to importance is virtually the same for core and non-core topics.

On an overall basis, as indicated earlier, educators tended to scale topics more highly with respect to importance than did practitioners. Of the 56 common core topics on which significant differences existed between educators and practitioners on importance means, the practitioner mean exceeded the educator mean for only six topics, as follows:

Topic	Importance Mean	
	Educators	**Practitioners**
Internal control: description based on narrative	2.38	2.83
Internal control: description based on questionnaire	2.42	2.71
Internal control: audit exposure due to weaknesses	2.84	3.10
Management letter	2.32	2.45
Audit administration: supervision	1.91	2.13
Recognition of tax opportunities	2.52	2.88

Likewise, the practitioner mean exceeded the educator mean for only 17 of the 51 non-core topics on which a significant difference existed.

Conceptual Knowledge and Technical Ability Analysis

The importance scale responses were used to determine the content of the common core (in terms of topic identification) and also as a basis for the rank orderings in Exhibit 3-1 and Appendices 3B and 3C. The two educational objective scales, *i.e.*, conceptual knowledge and technical ability, tell us the degree to which these two objectives ought to be achieved as viewed by the respondents. As indicated in the questionnaire, we defined conceptual knowledge as mental processes ranging from simple recall or awareness to creative thinking or evaluation. Technical ability was defined as skill in applying existing knowledge to the solution of problems ranging from classification and definition to the application of complex theories in novel problem situations. Viewing the three scales together, we can assess not only how important each topic is, but also the type of learning that ought to take place with respect to each topic.

The respondents scaled conceptual knowledge higher than technical ability for all but one common core topic. The only exception was *internal control: description based on flowchart,* for which the conceptual knowledge mean was 2.29 and the technical ability mean was 2.30. Thus, on an overall basis respondents placed more emphasis upon conceptual knowledge (overall mean response = 2.33) that upon technical ability (overall mean response = 1.86).

The importance mean response was higher than the conceptual knowledge (and thus the technical ability) mean response for 54 (51.4 percent) of the 105 common core topics. The importance and conceptual knowledge mean responses were relatively close to each other for practically all common core topics. It also appears that, in general, the higher technical ability means tend to be associated with the higher conceptual knowledge (and thus importance) means and vice versa, although there are several exceptions to this generality.

Educators vs. Practitioners
    In general, educators tended to scale topics higher with respect to conceptual knowledge than did practitioners. The overall mean conceptual knowledge response for all 197 topics was 2.59 for educators and 2.25 for practitioners. The practitioner mean response exceeded the educator mean response on conceptual knowledge for only 12 (11.4 percent) of the common core topics and for 23 (25 percent) of the non-core topics. Those common core topics for which the practitioner mean conceptual knowledge response was higher were as follows:

| | Conceptual Knowledge Mean | |
Topic	Educators	Practitioners
SEC reporting	2.38	2.63
Error corrections	2.69	2.72
Management information systems: implementation	2.30	2.38
Internal control: description based on narrative	2.45	2.72
Internal control: description based on questionnaire	2.39	2.60
Internal control: evaluation	2.93	2.97
Internal control: audit exposure due to weakness	2.74	2.91
Internal control: in an EDP environment	2.78	2.81
Management letter	2.30	2.34
Audit administration: planning	2.21	2.23
Audit administration: review	2.20	2.27
Recognition of tax opportunities	2.47	2.65

Of the 23 non-core topics for which the practitioner mean response was higher than the educator mean response on conceptual knowledge, 11 were in the taxation area.

Educators also, in general, scaled topics more highly with respect to technical ability than did practitioners. The mean technical ability response over all 197 topics was 2.10 for educators and 1.79 for practitioners. The practitioner mean technical ability response exceeded the educator mean technical ability response for only nine (8.6 percent) of the common core topics, as follows:

Topic	Technical Ability Mean	
	Educators	Practitioners
SEC reporting	1.78	2.10
Management information systems: implementation	1.83	1.86
Internal control: description based on questionnaire	2.08	2.20
Internal control: description based on flowchart	2.25	2.31
Statistical inference in auditing:		
regression analysis	2.00	2.39
Audit evidence: types	2.45	2.52
Audit evidence: post-statement events	2.29	2.60
Management letter	1.77	1.91
Taxation of deferred compensation	1.70	1.82

Also, the practitioner technical ability mean exceeded the educator technical ability mean for 28 (30.4 percent) of the non-core topics, of which 12 were taxation topics.

Implications of Common Core Analysis

One useful result of this analysis is the identification of a group of 105 topics which, as indicated by the level and pervasiveness of their importance, should be required as a part of the curriculum for all accounting majors. The relative emphasis upon conceptual knowledge and technical ability is also indicated. Since readers may not agree with our cut-off criterion for identifying common core topics, results for all topics are presented.

A major implication of the analysis is that not only should certain financial and managerial topics continue to be required of all accounting majors, but so should a significant segment of the auditing topics and a small, but significant subset of the taxation topics. This suggests a change in those curricula which do not presently require an auditing course or a tax course. That is, regardless of the area of ultimate specialization, the responses to our questionnaire imply that there should be required subject matter in all areas.

Also, the analysis indicates that, in general, greater emphasis should be placed upon conceptual knowledge, as defined in the questionnaire, than upon technical ability. In other words, the general orientation in the common core should be conceptual rather than technical, even though for certain topics the relative emphasis upon conceptual knowledge and technical ability may be about the same. In no case was a technical ability mean response significantly greater than the corresponding conceptual knowledge mean for a common core topic.

Another implication is that there are significant differences between educators and practitioners regarding the importance of the majority of common core topics. Thus, educators attempting to utilize this information for curriculum evaluation must decide how to weight these differing views.

In the following chapters, attention is devoted to the five areas of specialized accounting knowledge, that is, managerial accounting, taxation, financial accounting, auditing, and generalist. [4] A chapter is devoted to an analysis of each of these areas. Based upon questionnaire responses of individuals within the area of specialization, rank-orderings of topics on importance means are presented, area cores of accounting knowledge are identified, and other analyses related to each area core are presented. Chapters 4 through 8 all follow basically the same format so that the reader may conveniently compare results across the various areas of specialization.

---

   [4]   While it may seem strange to speak of an area of specialization for generalists, what we are really referring to for this area, as for the other areas, is a body of common accounting knowledge adequate to prepare an individual to begin a career as an accounting generalist.

4

Managerial Accounting
and Information Systems

Introduction

In this chapter the managerial accounting area core, as determined by questionnaire respondents identifying managerial accounting as their primary area of expertise, is presented and analyzed. The composition of the managerial accounting sample, which forms the basis for the analysis in this chapter, was as follows:

Educators		33
Practitioners:		
Public Accounting	19	
Industry	44	63
Total		96

In the following section, a rank ordering of questionnaire topics based upon the mean importance responses of our managerial accounting sample is presented, which includes identification of the managerial accounting area core. General observations regarding this area core are followed by a more detailed analysis in the next section of the chapter. The chapter then concludes with a brief presentation and analysis of the questionnaire results relating to our information systems respondents.

The Managerial Accounting Area Core

Exhibit 4-1 consists of the 197 questionnaire topics rank-ordered by the mean importance responses of the managerial accounting respondents. All of the topics except those preceded by "*" are included in the managerial accounting area core. The "#" indicates those area core topics for which mean importance responses differed significantly (at the .05 level) between educators and practitioners. Likewise, the letter preceding each topic indicates the questionnaire section in which the topic was presented. Conceptual knowledge and technical ability mean responses are also included.

EXHIBIT 4-1

RANK ORDERING BY IMPORTANCE MEANS:
ALL MANAGERIAL ACCOUNTING RESPONDENTS

			Means	
			Conceptual	Technical
Area	Topic	Importance	Knowledge	Ability
M	Accounting information requirements			
	for management decisions	3.29	3.25	2.77
F	Balance sheet	3.20	3.17	2.62
M	Responsibility accounting	3.19	3.14	2.70
F	Income statement	3.17	3.14	2.74
M	Flexible budgets	3.15	3.09	2.50
M	Standard costs	3.14	3.10	2.59
A	Internal control principles	3.12	2.99	2.09
F	Revenue and expense recognition	3.09	3.16	2.60
M	Cost-volume-profit analysis	3.07	3.04	2.61
F	Statement of changes in financial position	3.07	3.10	2.66
M	Long-range planning	3.06	3.04	2.46
M	Budgeted financial statements	3.04	3.03	2.52
M	Performance evaluation: divisional			
	performances	3.04	3.18	2.61
M	Variable costing	3.03	3.06	2.50
M	Capital budgeting	3.03	3.07	2.54
M	Performance evaluation: return on investment	3.03	3.12	2.50
M	Short-range planning	3.01	2.99	2.45
M	Process costing	3.00	3.04	2.54
M	Tax considerations in managerial decisions	2.99	2.94	2.31
F	Theoretical framework: current structure	2.97	2.99	2.28
F	Present value and future worth concepts	#2.94	3.09	2.66
M	Full costing	2.94	3.06	2.39
F	Double entry system	2.93	2.99	2.86
F	Accruals and deferrals	2.92	2.96	2.62
M	Cash management	2.92	2.94	2.24
F	Regulatory influences	2.90	2.82	2.00
F	Financial statement analysis	#2.89	2.97	2.44
M	Job order costing	2.89	2.94	2.53
M	Management information systems:			
	internal control aspects	2.87	2.80	2.28
F	Information needs of financial statement users	2.86	2.79	2.00
F	Transaction analysis	2.85	2.88	2.68
F	U.S. financial accounting and reporting			
	standards	2.85	2.88	2.29
A	Internal control: evaluation	2.85	2.62	2.03
F	Theoretical framework: alternatives to			
	current structure	#2.84	2.87	2.04
M	Direct costing	2.82	2.88	2.39
M	Overhead control	2.82	2.84	2.45
M	Performance evaluation: transfer pricing	#2.71	2.83	2.23

EXHIBIT 4-1
(continued)

Area	Topic	Importance	Conceptual Knowledge	Technical Ability
			Means	
A	Internal control: audit exposure due to weaknesses	2.69	2.53	1.74
M	Information economics	2.69	2.75	2.09
F	Inventories	2.68	2.77	2.51
M	Management information systems: implementation	#2.67	2.68	2.01
M	Corporate planning models	2.66	2.66	2.06
A	Audit evidence: types	2.65	2.41	1.97
M	Performance evaluation: non-financial performance measures	2.64	2.64	2.14
M	Performance evaluation: common costs	2.63	2.65	2.18
M	Management information systems: impact of external regulatory influences	2.62	2.58	1.97
M	Joint costs	2.62	2.72	2.12
A	Internal control: in an EDP environment	2.62	2.49	1.78
F	Behavioral considerations in financial reporting	2.61	2.63	1.97
F	Earnings-per-share	2.61	2.74	2.14
M	Performance evaluation: non-statistical variance analysis	2.60	2.71	2.22
F	Deferred taxes	#2.60	2.59	1.90
M	Organization theory	#2.59	2.70	1.94
F	Leases	#2.59	2.64	2.00
T	Tax planning	2.58	2.34	1.61
F	Research and development costs	#2.58	2.68	1.97
F	Business combinations: consolidation procedures	#2.58	2.70	2.00
M	Behavioral considerations (managerial)	#2.57	2.66	1.93
T	Capital gains and losses	#2.57	2.35	1.96
M	Management information systems: design	#2.56	2.58	1.93
F	Cash	2.54	2.40	2.27
T	Fundamentals of Federal income tax determination	#2.54	2.38	2.39
T	Recognition of tax opportunities	2.53	2.48	1.36
F	Depreciation, depletion and amortization	#2.51	2.64	2.26
A	Internal control: description based on narrative	2.51	2.46	1.85
M	Statistical analysis of cost variances	2.51	2.53	1.99
A	Internal control: description based on questionnaire	2.50	2.34	1.97
F	Business combinations: purchase vs. pooling of interest	#2.49	2.62	1.84
F	Short-term liabilities	2.48	2.55	2.16
M	Management information systems: administration	2.48	2.51	1.76

EXHIBIT 4-1
(continued)

Area	Topic	Importance	Conceptual Knowledge	Technical Ability
			Means	
F	Materiality	2.47	2.59	1.79
A	Audit evidence: relative strength of types	2.47	2.33	1.38
F	Interim reporting	2.46	2.51	1.84
M	Learning curve models	2.46	2.61	1.81
M	Performance evaluation: residual income	#2.45	2.41	1.83
F	Segment reporting	2.44	2.52	1.97
F	Receivables	2.44	2.46	2.17
M	Spoilage, waste, defective units, scrap	2.43	2.55	1.90
F	Price level adjusted financial statements	#2.43	2.65	1.88
F	Long-term liabilities	2.42	2.57	2.10
M	Internal operational auditing	2.40	2.46	1.90
F	Accounting for income taxes	2.39	2.43	1.93
A	Generally accepted auditing standards (GAAS)	2.39	2.33	1.76
F	Fixed assets	#2.39	2.47	2.18
A	Operational auditing: objectives	2.38	2.24	1.78
M	Computer science	#2.38	2.38	1.83
A	Audit evidence: post-statement events	2.38	2.30	1.90
A	Internal control: relationship of GAAS	2.36	2.17	1.88
A	Influence of professional and regulatory bodies on auditing	2.35	2.38	1.40
A	Internal control: modification in audit program based on evaluation	2.34	2.27	1.49
F	Reporting forecasts	2.34	2.49	1.96
M	Statistical cost estimation	#2.33	2.36	1.81
M	Simulation	2.33	2.47	1.65
M	Statistical decision theory	#2.33	2.42	1.73
A	Standard short-form audit report	2.33	2.12	1.47
A	Statistical inference in auditing: statistical sampling	2.33	2.21	2.15
F	Investments in securities	2.32	2.40	1.94
F	SEC reporting	#2.32	2.25	1.70
F	Corporate equity	2.32	2.40	1.95
T	State and local taxes	2.31	2.25	1.51
A	Requirements for professional certification (CPA)	2.29	2.18	1.67
F	Error corrections	2.29	2.51	1.94
M	Sensitivity analysis	#2.29	2.32	1.63
A	Professional rules of conduct	2.27	2.37	1.65
A	Statistical inference in auditing: judgmental sampling	2.27	2.17	1.63
A	Internal control: description based on flowchart	#2.27	2.08	2.12
A	Auditing procedures: review of operations	2.26	2.11	1.76
A	Modifications of the standard short-form audit report	2.26	2.11	1.44

EXHIBIT 4-1
(continued)

Area	Topic	Importance	Conceptual Knowledge	Technical Ability
			Means	
A	User's expectations regarding the auditor's role	2.26	2.29	1.33
F	Contingencies	2.24	2.20	1.66
M	Zero-base budgeting	2.24	2.31	1.69
A	Management letter	#2.23	2.06	1.71
⁻T	Taxation of deferred compensation	2.22	2.02	1.44
F	Business combinations: unconsolidated subsidiaries	2.21	2.35	1.75
F	Intangibles (excluding goodwill)	#2.21	2.30	1.80
A	Auditing procedures: tests of account balances	2.21	2.00	1.63
T	Non-taxable exchanges	2.19	1.97	1.42
A	Auditing procedures: tests of transactions	2.18	1.98	1.66
M	Special considerations in non-manufacturing concerns	#2.16	2.27	1.70
A	Operational auditing: methodology	2.15	2.10	1.87
M	Internal financial auditing	#2.14	2.35	1.83
F	Minority interest	#2.14	2.43	1.88
A	Legal responsibilities of auditors: under securities acts	2.13	1.98	1.46
F	Convertible debt or equity	2.13	2.31	1.83
M	Network methods	2.12	2.18	1.45
A	Long-form audit report	2.11	2.03	1.45
M	*Linear programming	2.10	2.16	1.34
F	*Pensions	2.10	2.20	1.54
A	SEC filing requirements	2.09	2.15	1.34
T	Social security taxes	2.08	2.02	1.44
T	Theoretical framework of taxation: economic and social concepts	2.08	2.09	.85
A	Statistical inference in auditing: regression analysis	#2.07	2.02	1.89
F	Goodwill	#2.04	2.25	1.68
A	Legal responsibilities of auditors: at common law	2.03	2.14	1.16
A	Extensions of attest function: associated audit risk	2.02	1.84	1.07
A	Legal responsibilities of auditor: exposure to criminal liability	2.00	1.89	1.23
F	Statements from incomplete records	2.00	2.30	1.72
A	Auditing procedures: compliance tests	1.98	1.91	1.53
M	Planning and control of international operations	1.97	2.10	1.39
F	Full costing vs. successful effort costing	1.97	2.12	1.55
F	Foreign currency translation	#1.96	2.12	1.51
A	Extensions of attest functions: possible areas	1.95	1.97	1.07

EXHIBIT 4-1
(continued)

Area	Topic	Importance	Conceptual Knowledge	Technical Ability
			Means	
A	Legal responsibilities of auditors: classic cases	1.91	1.83	1.27
A	Auditing procedures: working papers	1.91	1.86	1.55
A	Statistical inference in auditing: other statistical methods	1.91	1.87	1.33
F	Treasury stock	1.90	2.14	1.62
T	Taxation for international operations	#1.89	1.85	1.07
T	Complex tax provisions: corporations and shareholders	1.89	1.91	1.72
M	Social accounting	1.88	2.01	1.38
T	*Accumulated earnings tax	1.88	1.75	1.00
A	Audit administration: review	1.84	1.85	1.17
F	Installment sales	1.83	1.97	1.64
A	Audit administration: planning	1.82	1.78	1.22
F	Fund accounting: financial statements	#1.81	1.97	1.37
M	Requirement for professional certification (CMA)	1.79	1.96	1.46
F	Partnership financial statements	1.78	1.97	1.33
T	Theoretical framework of taxation: alternatives to present framework	1.76	1.79	1.00
A	*Auditing procedures: audit practice case	1.73	1.60	1.30
F	*Regulated industries	1.73	1.83	1.17
F	*International accounting standards	1.72	1.77	1.25
T	Tax returns and accompanying schedule	1.72	1.60	1.67
T	*Tax research methodology	1.70	1.55	1.04
A	*Audit administration: client relations	1.69	1.65	.98
F	*Consignments	1.69	1.93	1.59
F	*Development stage companies	1.67	1.78	1.23
F	*National income accounting	1.66	1.80	1.20
A	Audit administration: supervision	1.66	1.62	1.13
A	*Special considerations in auditing not-for-profit organizations	1.62	1.54	1.00
T	*Complex tax provisions: consolidated corporate returns	1.61	1.61	.93
A	*Legal responsibilities of auditors: responses of the auditing profession to classic cases	1.61	1.66	1.05
F	*Fund accounting: governmental units	1.60	1.75	1.28
F	Fund accounting: types of organizations	#1.59	1.80	1.26
T	*Tax practice procedures	1.59	1.56	.98
T	*Complex tax provisions: foreign tax credit	1.58	1.52	.93
T	*Administrative processes in tax matters	1.57	1.43	.87
T	*Complex tax provisions: DISC	1.54	1.60	.90
T	*Judicial doctrines in tax disputes	1.53	1.48	.69
A	*Audit administration: setting and collecting fees	1.51	1.46	.89

EXHIBIT 4-1
(continued)

Area	Topic	Importance	Conceptual Knowledge	Technical Ability
			Means	
F	*Human resource accounting	1.49	1.70	1.17
A	*Comparative accounting and auditing standards among nations	1.45	1.48	.61
F	*Fund accounting: hospitals	1.45	1.63	1.16
F	*Fund accounting: colleges and universities	1.41	1.54	1.06
T	*Complex tax provisions: individuals	1.39	1.27	1.09
F	*Fiduciary accounting: bankruptcy	1.39	1.59	.94
A	*Audit administration: accounting firm organization	1.36	1.35	.76
F	*Fiduciary accounting: receivership	1.36	1.56	.91
T	*Complex tax provisions: subchapter S	1.35	1.33	1.11
A	*Historical development of auditing	1.32	1.34	.68
T	*Natural resource taxation	1.27	1.37	1.10
T	*Judicial processes in tax disputes	1.25	1.29	.60
T	*Federal estate tax	1.21	1.13	.80
T	*Complex tax provisions: partners and partnerships	1.19	1.19	1.26
T	*Federal gift tax	1.19	1.10	.71
F	*Fiduciary accounting: estates and trusts	1.12	1.32	.86
T	*Complex tax provisions: fiduciaries	1.12	1.17	1.02
T	*Personal holding company tax	1.05	1.09	.93
T	*Preparation of tax communications	.88	.93	1.01

* → non-area core topics

\# → significant difference (p < .05) between educator and
practitioner importance mean responses

The managerial accounting area core consists of 156 (79.2 percent) of the 197 questionnaire topics. The 51 topics which are in this area core but which were not in the common core are presented, in descending order of importance, in Exhibit 4-2:

EXHIBIT 4-2

MANAGERIAL ACCOUNTING AREA CORE
TOPICS NOT IN COMMON CORE

Area	Topic	Importance Mean
M	Direct costing	2.82
M	Overhead control	2.82
M	Performance evaluation: transfer pricing	2.71
M	Corporate planning models	2.66
M	Performance evaluation: non-financial performance measures	2.64
M	Performance evaluation: common costs	2.63
M	Management information systems: impact of external regulatory influences	2.62
F	Behavioral considerations in financial reporting	2.61
F	Earnings-per-share	2.61
M	Performance evaluation: non-statistical variance analysis	2.60
M	Behavioral considerations	2.57
M	Management information systems: design	2.56
M	Management information systems: administration	2.48
M	Learning curve models	2.46
M	Performance evaluation: residual income	2.45
F	Segment reporting	2.44
M	Internal operational auditing	2.40
A	Operational auditing: objectives	2.38
M	Computer science	2.38
A	Internal control: relationship of GAAS	2.36
M	Statistical cost estimation	2.33
M	Simulation	2.33
M	Statistical decision theory	2.33
F	Corporate equity	2.32
T	State and local taxes	2.31
A	Requirements for professional certification (CPA)	2.29
M	Sensitivity analysis	2.29
A	Professional rules of conduct	2.27
M	Zero base budgeting	2.24
F	Business combinations: unconsolidated subsidiaries	2.21
M	Special considerations in non-manufacturing concerns	2.16
A	Operational auditing: methodology	2.15
M	Internal financial auditing	2.14
M	Network methods	2.12
A	SEC filing requirements	2.09
T	Social security taxes	2.08
T	Theoretical framework of taxation: economic and social concepts	2.08
F	Goodwill	2.04

EXHIBIT 4-2
(continued)

Area	Topic	Importance Mean
A	Legal responsibilities of auditors: at common law	2.03
M	Planning and control of international operations	1.97
F	Full costing vs. successful effort costing	1.97
F	Foreign currency translation	1.96
A	Extensions of the attest function: possible areas	1.95
A	Auditing procedures: working papers	1.91
T	Taxation for international operations	1.89
M	Social accounting	1.88
M	Requirements for professional certification (CMA)	1.79
F	Partnership financial statements	1.78
T	Theoretical framework of taxation: alternatives to present framework	1.76
T	Tax returns and accompanying schedules	1.72
F	Fund accounting: types of organizations	1.59

Thus, in order to prepare an individual to begin a managerial accounting career, the formal education should include some coverage of not only the 105 common core topics but also some exposure to the 51 topics identified in Exhibit 4-2.

Another way to analyze the composition of the managerial accounting area core is according to the section of the questionnaire in which the topics were presented, as follows:

Questionnaire Section	Total number of Topics	Number in Area Core	% in Area Core
Financial	65	52	80.0%
Managerial	51	50	98.0%
Auditing	50	42	84.0%
Taxation	31	12	38.7%
Total	197	156	

As indicated in the last column of the above presentation, the section of the questionnaire with the largest proportion of its topics in the managerial accounting area core was managerial accounting, followed by auditing, financial and taxation respectively.

It is also informative to take a look at the 41 topics excluded from the managerial accounting area core. These topics, presented in Exhibit 4-3, were excluded from the area core due to the low mean importance responses of either managerial accounting educators, practitioners, or both. The topics are listed by questionnaire section in order of decreasing mean importance responses (educators and practitioners combined) along with an indication of the group(s) responsible for their exclusion.

EXHIBIT 4-3

**TOPICS EXCLUDED FROM MANAGERIAL
ACCOUNTING AREA CORE**

Topic	Importance Mean	Excluded by
FINANCIAL:		
Pensions	2.10	P
Regulated industries	1.73	P
International accounting standards	1.72	E
Consignments	1.69	E,P
Development stage companies	1.67	E,P
National income accounting	1.66	P
Fund accounting: governmental units	1.60	E,P
Human resource accounting	1.49	E,P
Fund accounting: hospitals	1.45	E,P
Fund accounting: colleges and universities	1.41	E,P
Fiduciary accounting: bankruptcy	1.39	E,P
Fiduciary accounting: receivership	1.36	E,P
Fiduciary accounting: estates and trusts	1.12	E,P
MANAGERIAL:		
Linear programming	2.10	P
AUDITING:		
Auditing procedures: audit practice case	1.73	E
Audit administration: client relations	1.69	E
Special considerations in auditing not-for-profit organizations	1.62	P
Legal responsibilities of auditors: responses of auditing profession to classic cases	1.61	E,P
Audit administration: setting and collecting fees	1.51	E,P
Comparative accounting and auditing standards among nations	1.45	E,P
Audit administration: accounting firm organization	1.36	E,P
Historical development of auditing	1.32	E,P
TAXATION:		
Complex tax provisions: corporations and shareholders	1.89	E
Accumulated earnings tax	1.88	E
Tax research methodology	1.70	E
Complex tax provisions: consolidated corporate returns	1.61	E,P
Tax practice procedures	1.59	E
Complex tax provisions: foreign tax credit	1.58	E
Administrative processes in tax matters	1.57	E,P
Complex tax provisions: DISC	1.54	E,P
Judicial doctrines in tax disputes	1.53	E,P
Complex tax provisions: individuals	1.39	E,P
Complex tax provisions: subchapter S	1.35	E,P
Natural resource taxation	1.27	E,P
Judicial processes in tax disputes	1.25	E,P
Federal estate tax	1.21	E,P
Complex tax provisions: partners and partnerships	1.19	E,P

EXHIBIT 4-3
(continued)

Topic	Importance Mean	Excluded by
Federal gift tax	1.19	E,P
Complex tax provisions: fiduciaries	1.12	E,P
Personal holding company tax	1.05	E,P
Preparation of tax communications	.88	E,P

E ⟶ Educators
P ⟶ Practitioners

As Exhibit 4-3 indicates, only one of the 13 financial accounting topics excluded from the managerial accounting area core was excluded solely due to the managerial accounting educator importance responses. The other 12 were excluded by both managerial accounting educators and practitioners or by only practitioners. The only managerial accounting topic excluded from the managerial accounting core was *linear programming*. This exclusion was due to the low importance responses of managerial accounting practitioners. Of the eight auditing topics excluded from the area core, educator respondents scaled seven of them sufficiently low to exclude them, whereas practitioner respondents scaled six of them sufficiently low. Educators scaled all 19 of the taxation topics excluded from the area core sufficiently low to exclude them, while practitioners scaled 14 of them sufficiently low. Thus, one may conclude that, overall, there is substantial agreement between managerial accounting educators and practitioners with respect to these low-ranking topics.

Analysis of Managerial Accounting Area Core
IMPORTANCE ANALYSIS

Financial Accounting Topics

The most important financial accounting topics in the managerial accounting area core, as indicated in Exhibit 4-1, were as follows (listed in order of decreasing importance means):

Balance sheet
Income statement
Revenue and expense recognition
Statement of changes in financial position
Theoretical framework: current structure
Present value and future worth concepts
Double-entry system
Accruals and deferrals
Regulatory influences
Financial statement analysis
Information needs of financial statement users
Transaction analysis
U.S. financial accounting and reporting standards
Theoretical framework: alternatives to current structure

While this list of most-important financial topics does not differ significantly from the list prepared for all respondents combined (see Chapter 3), there are a few differences. *Deferred taxes* appeared in the most-important financial topics list for all respondents combined, but it does not appear to be quite as important for individuals preparing to enter a managerial accounting career. On the other hand, the topics *present value and future worth concepts, regulatory influences, financial statement analysis* and *theoretical framework: alternatives to current structure* are apparently more important for managerial accounting specialists than they are for all respondents combined. These latter four topics do not receive a significant amount of attention in most existing textbooks, even though they are apparently quite important for managerial accounting students.

As indicated in Exhibit 4-3, 13 financial accounting topics were excluded from the managerial accounting area core. Some of these exclusions appear to be consistent with current emphasis in accounting curricula. However, practically all accounting graduates obtain a reasonable background in *pensions* in intermediate accounting. Also, most intermediate and/or advanced accounting textbooks devote some attention to *consignments, fund accounting* and *fiduciary accounting*.

Looking at the financial accounting topics that fall in between the most important list and the list of such topics excluded from the area core, there appear to be few differences between suggested importance and existing emphasis as indicated by textbook coverage. One difference might be *full costing vs. successful effort costing,* which is an area core topic but currently receives virtually no textbook attention. Also, *SEC reporting* in an area core topic which is not currently included in the curriculum of most accounting graduates. Likewise, *reporting forecasts* and *segment reporting* do not currently receive the attention that managerial accounting respondents indicate is desirable. *Behavioral considerations in financial reporting* appears to be ranked fairly high by managerial accounting respondents compared with the current degree of emphasis on the topic.

Managerial Accounting Topics

Managerial accounting respondents scaled the following managerial accounting topics most highly (listed in decreasing order of importance means):

Accounting information requirements for management decisions
Responsibility accounting
Flexible budgets
Standard costs
Cost-volume-profit analysis
Long-range planning
Budgeted financial statements
Performance evaluation: divisional performance
Variable costing
Capital budgeting
Performance evaluation: return on investment
Short-range planning
Process costing
Tax considerations in managerial decisions

As one might expect, these managerial accounting topics dominated the top of the rank ordering by importance means (see Exhibit 4-1). That is, one would expect managerial accounting respondents to scale managerial accounting topics, in general, more highly than financial accounting, auditing and taxation topics.

Included in this list of most important managerial accounting topics are three of the four managerial topics scaled most highly by all respondents combined (see Exhibit 3-1):

Accounting information requirements for management decisions
Standard costs
Taxation considerations in managerial decisions

The fourth most important managerial accounting topic for all respondents combined, *management information systems: internal control aspects,* was only the eighteenth most important managerial topic as viewed by managerial accounting respondents.

It is rather apparent, when one compares this list of important managerial topics to existing popular textbooks and existing curricula, that there are substantial differences between what is currently being done and what managerial accounting respondents believe should be done. In particular, several topics which apparently receive very little emphasis currently are deemed quite important in preparing an individual for a managerial accounting career. The obvious implication is that inadequate attention, in the minds of our managerial accounting respondents, is given to meeting the needs of individuals interested in a managerial accounting career. This is consistent with the following observation by DeCoster:

> The development of a management accounting curriculum is one of the biggest challenges that accounting educators face. It is my impression that while accountants have given lip service over the years to developing and expanding the management accounting curriculum, there has been little positive action . . . The expansion of the management accountant's role in our society has not been met with corresponding curriculum advances. [1]

As perhaps the prime example of underemphasized topics, based on questionnaire responses, consider the highest ranking of the 197 topics, *accounting information requirements for management decisions.* While this topic undoubtedly receives some attention in practically all accounting curricula, it is highly unlikely that it receives the degree of emphasis indicated desirable by questionnaire respondents in more than a handful of existing curricula.

---

[1] Don T. DeCoster, "The Advanced Managerial Accounting Curriculum — Interaction with Other Disciplines: Quantitative, Behavioral, the Business Administration Core," a critique in Ferrara *et al., op. cit.,* p. 97.

Other topics which appear to receive substantially less attention currently than that deemed desirable include *long-range planning, budgeted financial statements, performance evaluation: division performance, capital budgeting, short-range planning* and *tax considerations in managerial decisions.* While one or more of these topics may be adequately emphasized in a few curricula with appropriate selection of electives, only rarely would one find an accounting graduate preparing to enter a managerial accounting career well-tooled in all of these topics.

For the most part, the low- and middle-ranking managerial accounting topics in the area core appear to receive the desired emphasis in existing curricula. However, the current emphasis upon *cash management, information economics, corporate planning models, management information systems: impact of external regulatory influences, organization theory* and *behavioral considerations* may be less than that deemed desirable by managerial accounting questionnaire respondents.

Auditing Topics
The managerial accounting respondents considered the following auditing topics to be most important in preparing an individual to enter a managerial accounting career (listed in decreasing order of importance means):

Internal control: principles
Internal control: evaluation
Internal control: audit exposure due to weaknesses
Audit evidence: types
Internal control: in an EDP environment

Thus, internal control topics, in general, are considered to be relatively important. This finding is not surprising since these topics could perhaps just as logically have been classified as managerial accounting topics. These topics were also among the most important auditing topics for all respondents combined, as evidenced in Exhibit 3-1. Given the pervasive nature of the high importance responses, it is not surprising that these topics apparently receive a substantial amount of attention in existing curricula.

As indicated in Exhibit 4-3, only eight of the 50 auditing topics were excluded from the managerial accounting area core. Among these excluded topics was the controversial topic *auditing procedures: audit practice case,* with mean importance responses of 1.97 for managerial accounting practitioners and 1.36 for managerial accounting educators. The other excluded topics currently appear to receive little, if any, attention in accounting curricula.

Most other auditing topics also appear to be currently receiving about the degree of emphasis indicated as desirable by our questionnaire respondents. One possible exception is *operational auditing: objectives,* with an importance mean of 2.38, which does not appear to receive much attention in existing curricula. As Grinaker stated:

> . . . inasmuch as all auditors (public, internal and governmental) are now significantly involved in operational auditing, operational auditing and its criteria can no longer be ignored in the auditing curriculum. [2]

Also, *operational auditing, methodology* had an importance mean of 2.15, which indicates that it should probably receive more emphasis than it does currently in preparing students for a managerial accounting career.

Taxation Topics

The following taxation topics were considered most important by managerial accounting respondents (listed in decreasing order of importance):

Tax planning
Capital gains and losses
Fundamentals of Federal income tax determination
Recognition of tax opportunities

While these are the most important taxation topics, it is apparent from Exhibit 4-1 that none of these topics rank among the most important considering all 197 topics. In fact, 54 topics are scaled more highly on importance than is the highest-ranking taxation topic, *tax planning*.

In general, managerial accounting respondents consider the same taxation topics to be highly important as do all respondents combined. One difference, however, is that managerial accounting respondents place relatively more importance on *tax planning*. Likewise, while *fundamentals of Federal income tax determination* was the third highest ranking taxation topic in the managerial accounting area core, it was not ranked nearly as high here as it was for all respondents combined, where it was tenth out of 197 topics.

Those taxation topics included in the managerial accounting area core but excluded from the common core are as follows:

Tax returns and accompanying schedules
Theoretical framework of taxation: alternatives to present
 framework
Taxation for international operations
Theoretical framework of taxation: economic and social
 concepts
Social security taxes
State and local taxes

---

[2] Robert L. Grinaker, "The Auditing Curriculum — Is There a Need for Change?" in Ferrara, *et al., op. cit.*, p. 140.

Thus, while these topics are not sufficiently pervasive in importance to be required of all accounting students, those students planning to pursue a managerial accounting career should have a background which includes these topics. Perhaps the only surprising topics in this group are the two theoretical framework topics, as the other four topics are all pragmatic issues of direct concern to managerial accountants.

Educators vs. Practitioners

Appendices 4A and 4B present the rank-ordering of topics by importance means for managerial accounting educators and practitioners, respectively. In general, managerial accounting educators tended to scale topics more highly with respect to importance than did managerial accounting practitioners. The overall importance mean was 2.36 for managerial accounting educators and 2.16 for managerial accounting practitioners.

As indicated in Exhibit 4-1, significant differences (at the .05 level) between educator and practitioner mean importance responses existed for 36 (23.1 percent) of the 156 managerial accounting area core topics. Included in the 36 topics were 18 (34.6 percent) of the 52 financial accounting topics in the area core, 12 (24.0 percent) of the 50 managerial accounting topics in the area core, three (7.1 percent) of the 42 auditing topics in the area core, and three (25.0 percent) of the 12 taxation topics in the area core.

The practitioner mean importance response exceeded the educator mean importance response for only five of the 36 topics for which significant differences between means existed, as follows:

> Foreign currency translation
> SEC reporting
> Business combinations: consolidation procedures
> Internal control: description based on flowchart
> Management letter

For the other 31 topics, the educator mean was significantly higher than the practitioner mean. Thus, most of the significant differences were in the expected direction, since educators generally scaled topics more highly with respect to importance than did practitioners.

CONCEPUTAL KNOWLEDGE AND TECHNICAL ABILITY ANALYSIS

Exhibit 4-1 includes the conceptual knowledge and technical ability mean responses for each topic, computed on all managerial accounting respondents. Appendices 4A and 4B include these means for managerial accounting educators and practitioners, respectively. In this section we first discuss conceptual knowledge and technical ability responses for all managerial accounting respondents. We then present a comparison of the responses of managerial accounting educators and practitioners on these two learning objectives.

It is apparent by scanning Exhibit 4-1 that managerial accounting respondents almost invariably believe that more emphasis should be placed upon conceptual knowledge than upon technical ability. The technical ability mean response exceeded the conceptual knowledge mean for only three of the 156 managerial accounting area core topics, as follows:

	Mean	
	Conceptual Knowledge	Technical Ability
Fundamentals of Federal income tax determination	2.38	2.39
Internal control: description based on flowchart	2.08	2.12
Tax returns and accompanying schedules	1.60	1.67

As is apparent, even in these three instances the technical ability mean does not significantly exceed the conceptual knowledge mean. As another indication of the greater emphasis upon conceptual knowledge, the overall mean conceptual knowledge response (across all topics) for managerial accounting respondents was 2.27, whereas the overall mean technical ability response was only 1.72.

Educators vs. Practitioners

In general, managerial accounting educators scaled topics more highly with respect to conceptual knowledge than did managerial accounting practitioners. The overall mean conceptual knowledge response for managerial accounting educators was 2.44, while that for managerial accounting practitioners was 2.13. The practitioner conceptual knowledge mean exceeded the educator conceptual knowledge mean for 23 (14.7 percent) of the managerial accounting area core topics, as follows:

Topic	Conceptual Knowledge Mean	
	Educators	Practitioners
Foreign currency translation	1.97	2.23
SEC reporting	1.84	2.56
Error corrections	2.48	2.53
Management information systems: implementation	2.66	2.70
Management information systems: administration	2.41	2.59
Statistical analysis of cost variances	2.52	2.54
User's expectations regarding the auditor's role	2.28	2.30
SEC filing requirements	2.14	2.16
Requirements for professional certification (CPA)	2.15	2.21
Internal control: description based on narrative	2.00	2.74
Internal control: description based on questionnaire	1.91	2.59
Internal control: evaluation	2.36	2.78
Internal control: audit exposure due to weaknesses	2.33	2.65
Internal control: modifications in audit program based on evaluation	2.24	2.28
Audit evidence: types	2.34	2.45
Audit evidence: relative strength of types	2.20	2.42
Audit evidence: post-statement events	2.04	2.47
Management letter	1.96	2.13
Audit administration: review	1.78	1.90
Recognition of tax opportunities	2.44	2.51
Social security taxes	2.00	2.03
Taxation of deferred compensation	1.79	2.15
State and local taxes	1.96	2.45

Also, the practitioner mean response was greater than the educator mean response for 16 (39.0 percent) of the 41 topics not in the managerial accounting area core.

The educator-practitioner relationship followed a similar pattern on the technical ability responses. Again, managerial accounting educators generally scaled topics higher with respect to technical ability (overall mean response of 1.83) than did managerial accounting practitioners (overall mean response of 1.63). Note that both educator and practitioner overall means are lower for technical ability than they were for conceptual knowledge. However, practitioners did scale 41 (26.3 percent) of the 156 managerial accounting area core topics more highly, considering mean responses, with respect to technical ability than did their educator counterparts, as follows:

	Technical Ability Means	
Topic	**Educators**	**Practitioners**
Foreign currency translation	1.35	1.63
Behavioral consideration in financial reporting	1.90	2.03
SEC reporting	1.32	2.00
Reporting forecasts	1.93	1.97
Management information systems: administration	1.76	1.77
Learning curve models	1.77	1.85
Statistical analysis of cost variances	1.94	2.02
Internal financial auditing	1.83	1.84
Planning and control of international operations	1.37	1.41
User's expectations regarding the auditor's role	.96	1.56
Influence of professional and regulatory bodies on auditing	1.15	1.58
SEC filing requirements	1.21	1.43
Requirements for professional certification (CPA)	1.52	1.77
Legal responsibilities of the auditor: classic cases	.81	1.59
Legal responsibilities of the auditor: exposure to criminal liability	.89	1.49
Modifications of the standard short-form audit report	1.36	1.50
Long-form audit report	1.43	1.47
Internal control: relationship of GAAS	1.71	2.00
Internal control: description based on narrative	1.52	2.05
Internal control: description based on questionnaire	1.52	2.24
Internal control: description based on flowchart	1.70	2.38
Internal control: evaluation	1.84	2.15
Internal control: audit exposure due to weaknesses	1.46	1.92
Internal control: modifications in audit program based on evaluation	1.44	1.53
Statistical inference in auditing: statistical sampling	1.93	2.32
Statistical inference in auditing: regression analysis	1.68	2.06

(continued)

Topic	Technical Ability Means	
	Educators	Practitioners
Audit evidence: types	1.58	2.24
Audit evidence: post-statement events	1.27	2.35
Auditing procedures: compliance tests	1.50	1.57
Auditing procedures: tests of transactions	1.62	1.71
Auditing procedures: tests of account balances	1.60	1.67
Auditing procedures: review of operations	1.67	1.86
Management letter	1.36	2.15
Audit administration: review	1.11	1.25
Operational auditing: objectives	1.56	2.11
Operational auditing: methodology	1.69	2.11
Extensions of the attest function: possible areas	.92	1.25
Extensions of the attest function: associated audit risk	.88	1.32
Taxation of deferred compensation	1.30	1.59
State and local taxes	1.42	1.62
Tax returns and accompanying schedules	1.67	1.68

It is readily apparent in scanning the preceding list of topics that managerial accounting practitioners place considerable more emphasis on technical ability with respect to auditing topics than do managerial accounting educators since 29 (70.7 percent) of the topics listed are auditing topics. This represents 69.1 percent of the auditing topics in the managerial accounting area core. It should also be noted that the practitioner mean response exceeded the educator mean response for 25 (61.0 percent) of the topics not in the area core.

The Information Systems Area Core

As indicated earlier, we were unable to obtain an adequate sample of information systems educators. Thus, the following tabulations and analyses relate only to the 54 information systems practitioner respondents. Exhibit 4-4 consists of the 197 questionnaire topics rank ordered by the mean importance responses of our information systems practitioner sample. As in other similar exhibits, the "*" preceding a topic identifies that topic as a non-area core topic. The letter preceding each topic indicates the questionnaire section in which the topic was presented.

Included in the information systems area core are 152 (77.2 percent) of the 197 questionnaire topics. These 152 area core topics were comprised as follows:

EXHIBIT 4-4

RANK ORDERING BY IMPORTANCE MEANS:
INFORMATION SYSTEMS PRACTITIONERS

Area	Topic	Importance	Conceptual Knowledge	Technical Ability
			Means	
A	Internal control: in an EDP environment	3.04	2.71	1.94
A	Internal control: evaluation	2.95	2.71	2.05
A	Internal control: audit exposure due to weaknesses	2.92	2.67	1.64
A	Internal control: principles	2.89	2.82	1.60
M	Management information systems: implementation	2.79	2.83	2.43
M	Accounting information requirements for management decisions	2.77	2.82	2.22
F	Balance sheet	2.73	2.72	2.26
M	Management information systems: administration	2.73	2.74	2.33
F	Error corrections	2.70	2.68	2.27
F	Information needs of financial statement users	2.69	2.71	2.21
M	Process costing	2.67	2.77	2.21
A	Internal control: description based on narrative	2.65	2.56	1.62
F	Income statement	2.64	2.65	2.25
M	Learning curve models	2.62	2.66	2.10
F	Theoretical framework: current structure	2.62	2.53	1.97
F	Double-entry system	2.60	2.56	2.19
M	Budgeted financial statements	2.60	2.59	2.24
A	Internal control: description based on questionnaire	2.59	2.42	2.12
F	Behavioral considerations in financial reporting	2.59	2.61	2.06
M	Management information systems: internal control aspects	2.55	2.58	2.19
A	Audit evidence: types	2.55	2.40	2.29
M	Long-range planning	2.54	2.55	2.27
F	Revenue and expense recognition	2.54	2.51	2.10
A	Internal control: modifications in audit program based on evaluation	2.54	2.28	1.26
A	Statistical inference in auditing: judgmental sampling	2.52	2.18	1.58
F	Deferred taxes	2.51	2.51	1.97
F	SEC reporting	2.49	2.53	2.08
M	Statistical analysis of cost variances	2.49	2.50	2.11
M	Performance evaluation: divisional performance	2.49	2.58	2.04
M	Information economics	2.49	2.55	2.11
M	Performance evaluation: responsibility accounting	2.48	2.60	2.11
F	Financial statement analysis	2.48	2.53	2.09

EXHIBIT 4-4
(continued)

Area	Topic	Importance	Conceptual Knowledge	Technical Ability
			Means	
M	Flexible budgets	2.48	2.53	2.21
F	Fund accounting: financial statements	2.48	2.44	1.95
M	Job order costing	2.47	2.62	2.09
M	Short-range planning	2.46	2.47	2.06
T	Recognition of tax opportunities	2.42	2.13	.44
M	Cash management	2.42	2.49	2.09
F	Statement of changes in financial position	2.38	2.53	2.01
M	Variable costing	2.37	2.41	2.04
F	Theoretical framework: alternatives to current structure	2.36	2.49	1.92
T	State and local taxes	2.35	1.95	1.76
A	Audit evidence: relative strength of types	2.35	2.15	1.33
A	Audit evidence: post-statement events	2.35	2.15	2.40
F	Transaction analysis	2.35	2.34	1.87
F	U.S. financial accounting and reporting standards	2.35	2.40	1.78
M	Standard costs	2.35	2.49	1.95
T	Complex tax provisions: corporations and shareholders	2.34	2.09	.23
A	Legal responsibilities of auditors: classic cases	2.33	2.04	1.47
M	Capital budgeting	2.33	2.43	1.89
M	Performance evaluation: return on investment	2.33	2.49	1.89
A	Legal responsibilities of auditors: under securities acts	2.33	1.86	1.26
F	Development stage companies	2.32	2.36	2.03
M	Joint costs	2.31	2.44	1.96
F	Fund accounting: types of organizations	2.30	2.28	1.81
F	Accruals and deferrals	2.30	2.33	1.82
M	Corporate planning models	2.29	2.42	1.91
F	Statements from incomplete records	2.29	2.30	1.86
F	Minority interest	2.28	2.30	1.79
M	Full costing	2.28	2.37	2.04
A	Statistical inference in auditing: regression analysis	2.27	2.16	2.86
T	Theoretical framework of taxation: economic and social concepts	2.27	1.96	.50
A	Statistical inference in auditing: statistical sampling	2.27	2.13	2.43
M	Tax considerations in managerial decisions	2.27	2.26	1.83
A	Modifications of the standard short-form audit report	2.25	1.77	1.41
A	Standard short-form audit report	2.24	1.81	1.17
F	Leases	2.24	2.29	1.78
M	Organization theory	2.23	2.26	1.82
T	Judicial doctrine in tax disputes	2.23	1.99	.30
F	Short-term liabilities	2.23	2.23	1.80

EXHIBIT 4-4
(continued)

Area	Topic	Importance	Means Conceptual Knowledge	Technical Ability
T	Accumulated earnings tax	2.22	1.94	.52
M	Performance evaluation: non-financial performance measures	2.22	2.26	1.80
M	Management information systems: design	2.22	2.32	1.96
F	National income accounting	2.22	2.26	1.89
T	Non-taxable exchanges	2.21	1.80	1.00
T	Social security taxes	2.19	1.88	1.39
T	Fundamentals of Federal income tax determination	2.18	1.95	1.29
F	Research and development costs	2.18	2.25	1.83
M	Cost-volume-profit analysis	2.17	2.14	1.79
F	Intangibles (excluding goodwill)	2.17	2.22	1.68
A	Statistical inference in auditing: other statistical methods	2.16	2.03	1.42
A	Audit administration: review	2.16	1.99	1.22
M	Performance evaluation: non-statistical variance analysis	2.16	2.22	1.84
A	Internal control: description based on flowchart	2.15	1.79	2.26
F	Present value and future worth concepts	2.14	2.29	1.74
M	Simulation	2.13	2.21	1.62
F	Inventories	2.12	2.09	1.59
T	Taxation of deferred compensation	2.12	1.79	1.59
A	Long-form audit report	2.11	1.49	1.43
F	Interim reporting	2.10	2.14	1.51
T	Tax planning	2.09	1.73	.71
A	Audit administration: client relations	2.09	1.85	1.22
F	Materiality	2.08	2.06	1.69
F	Long-term liabilities	2.08	2.13	1.71
A	Management letter	2.08	1.95	1.36
T	Tax practice procedures	2.06	1.66	1.27
M	Direct costing	2.06	2.22	1.82
A	Auditing procedures: tests of transactions	2.06	1.77	1.17
M	Network methods	2.05	2.15	1.67
T	Capital gains and losses	2.05	1.68	.95
F	International accounting standards	2.05	2.11	1.58
A	Auditing procedures: tests of account balances	2.04	1.76	1.26
F	Installment sales	2.03	2.04	1.62
T	Tax research methodology	2.03	1.62	1.32
F	Cash	2.01	2.17	1.74
A	Special considerations in auditing not-for-profit organizations	2.01	1.71	.50
F	Business combinations: consolidation procedures	2.01	2.13	1.61
F	Foreign currency translation	2.01	2.10	1.54
F	Reporting forecasts	2.00	2.04	1.64

EXHIBIT 4-4
(continued)

Area	Topic	Importance	Conceptual Knowledge	Technical Ability
			Means	
A	Auditing procedures: review of operations	2.00	1.88	1.17
M	Spoilage, waste, defective units and scrap	1.99	2.13	1.73
A	Extensions of the attest function: associated audit risk	1.99	1.47	.84
F	Fiduciary accounting: receivership	1.98	2.08	1.53
A	Audit administration: planning	1.98	1.94	1.09
T	Complex tax provisions: DISC	1.97	1.68	.80
M	Zero base budgeting	1.97	2.10	1.73
F	Fund accounting: governmental units	1.96	2.07	1.73
M	Statistical cost estimation	1.95	2.13	1.62
F	Accounting for income taxes	1.95	1.97	1.53
F	Contingencies	1.95	2.00	1.47
F	Fund accounting: colleges and universities	1.95	2.05	1.67
F	Convertible debt or equity	1.95	2.08	1.53
T	Taxation for international operations	1.95	1.68	.86
A	Legal responsibilities of the auditor: exposure to criminal liability	1.94	1.60	1.43
F	Fixed assets	1.94	1.96	1.52
F	Investments in securities	1.94	2.04	1.47
F	Consignments	1.93	1.96	1.43
M	Computer science	1.93	2.02	1.59
F	Fiduciary accounting: bankruptcy	1.92	2.07	1.53
F	Depreciation, depletion, and amortization	1.92	1.89	1.44
F	Regulatory influences	1.90	2.04	1.56
A	Auditing procedures: compliance tests	1.90	1.70	1.17
A	Comparative accounting and auditing standards among nations	1.90	1.60	.45
F	Full costing vs. successful effort costing	1.89	1.92	1.51
F	Price-level adjusted financial statements	1.89	2.04	1.53
F	Receivables	1.88	1.96	1.51
M	Statistical decision theory	1.88	2.05	1.56
A	Generally accepted auditing standards(GAAS)	1.87	1.97	1.68
A	Influence of professional and regulatory bodies upon the auditing function	1.87	1.92	1.43
F	Fund accounting: hospitals	1.87	1.99	1.63
A	User's expectations regarding the auditor's role	1.86	1.92	1.44
T	Complex tax provisions: foreign tax credit	1.86	1.55	.90
F	Treasury stock	1.85	1.96	1.50
A	Audit administration: supervision	1.84	1.71	1.13
F	Business combinations: purchase vs. pooling of interest	1.84	2.00	1.37
M	Management information systems: impact of external regulatory influences	1.83	1.86	1.47
T	Judicial processs in tax disputes	1.82	1.58	.30
M	Performance evaluation: residual income	1.81	1.97	1.64
M	Overhead control	1.81	1.99	1.62

EXHIBIT 4-4
(continued)

Area	Topic	Importance	Conceptual Knowledge	Technical Ability
			Means	
M	Performance evaluation: common costs	1.79	1.96	1.42
F	Human resource accounting	1.78	1.86	1.69
M	Performance evaluation: transfer pricing	1.77	1.95	1.41
F	*Corporate equity	1.77	1.91	1.45
T	*Administrative processes in tax matters	1.75	1.52	.52
A	*Auditing procedures: working papers	1.75	1.63	1.56
F	*Earnings-per-share	1.75	1.87	1.43
M	*Internal operational auditing	1.75	1.91	1.47
A	*Audit administration: setting and collecting fees	1.74	1.51	.86
M	*Internal financial auditing	1.73	1.95	1.54
T	*Theoretical framework of taxation: alternatives to present framework	1.73	1.40	1.18
T	*Tax returns and accompanying schedules	1.73	1.39	1.96
A	*Internal control: relationship of GAAS	1.72	1.39	1.86
T	*Complex tax provisions: fiduciaries	1.72	1.40	1.78
A	*Audit administration: accounting firm organization	1.68	1.53	.71
F	*Business combinations: unconsolidated subsidiaries	1.67	1.83	1.36
F	*Partnership financial statements	1.66	1.81	1.25
A	*Professional rules of conduct	1.65	1.74	1.16
F	*Regulated industries	1.64	1.73	1.26
F	*Goodwill	1.63	1.67	1.25
T	*Complex tax provisions: consolidated corporate returns	1.61	1.27	1.00
A	*Requirements for professional certification (CPA)	1.61	1.77	1.39
M	*Behavioral considerations	1.59	1.77	1.26
A	*SEC filing requirements	1.57	1.68	1.32
A	*Auditing procedures: audit practice case	1.57	1.38	.91
A	*Operational auditing: methodology	1.53	1.39	1.41
A	*Legal responsibilities of the auditor: responses of the auditing profession to classic cases	1.53	1.32	1.12
M	*Linear programming	1.53	1.72	1.20
A	*Operational auditing: objectives	1.52	1.38	1.45
A	*Legal responsibilities of the auditor: at common law	1.49	1.60	1.06
F	*Pensions	1.49	1.55	1.07
A	*Historical development of auditing	1.48	1.54	1.15
M	*Planning and control of international operations	1.48	1.69	1.22
M	*Sensitivity analysis	1.45	1.66	1.29
M	*Requirements for professional certification (CMA)	1.45	1.63	1.27

EXHIBIT 4-4
(continued)

Area	Topic	Importance	Means Conceptual Knowledge	Technical Ability
M	*Special considerations in non-manufacturing concerns	1.44	1.59	1.22
F	*Segment reporting	1.44	1.61	1.15
A	*Extension of the attest function: possible areas	1.40	1.15	.89
T	*Federal gift tax	1.34	1.10	.62
T	*Federal estate tax	1.32	.99	.62
T	*Complex tax provisions: subchapter S	1.29	1.11	1.85
T	*Complex tax provisions: partners and partnerships	1.27	1.05	1.91
F	*Fiduciary accounting: estates and trusts	1.24	1.26	.86
T	*Complex tax provisions: individuals	1.23	.99	1.96
M	*Social accounting	1.22	1.42	.97
T	*Natural resource taxation	1.16	.97	1.43
T	*Personal holding company tax	1.10	.87	.30
T	*Preparation of tax communications	1.02	.74	1.11

* ➔ non-area core topic

Questionnaire Section	Total Number of Topics	Number in Area Core	Percent in Area Core
Financial	65	56	86.2%
Managerial	51	42	82.4%
Auditing	50	36	72.0%
Taxation	31	18	58.1%
Total	197	152	

Thus, the financial accounting section had the greatest proportion of its topics in the information systems area core, followed closely by managerial and then auditing and taxation.

Looking at Exhibit 4-4, one can see that, as expected, internal control and management information systems topics dominate the upper portion of the rank-ordering. Also, many of the more traditional, fundamental managerial and financial accounting topics appear in the upper portion of the rank-ordering. The overall mean importance response for information systems practitioners was 2.06.

Conceptual knowledge and technical ability mean responses are also presented in Exhibit 4-4. Information systems practitioners tended to place more emphasis upon conceptual knowledge than upon technical ability. The overall mean conceptual knowledge response was 2.01, whereas the overall mean technical ability response was only 1.56.

5

Taxation

Introduction

The analysis in this chapter is based solely on the questionnaire responses of individuals identifying taxation as their primary area of expertise. The taxation sample had the following composition:

Educators		14
Practitioners:		
Public Accounting	46	
Industry	35	81
Total		95

The taxation area core is identified in the following section along with the rank-ordering on importance means and some general observations regarding the area core. The remainder of the chapter, like the preceding chapter, contains a more detailed analysis of the area core.

The Taxation Area Core

The 197 questionnaire topics are presented in Exhibit 5-1, rank-ordered by importance mean responses of taxation respondents. The non-core topics are indicated by the symbol "*", importance means are preceded by the symbol "#" on those topics for which a significant difference existed between taxation educator and taxation practitioner responses, and the letter preceding each topic indicates the questionnaire section in which the topic was presented.

EXHIBIT 5-1

RANK ORDERING BY IMPORTANCE MEANS:
TAXATION RESPONDENTS

Area	Topic	Importance	Conceptual Knowledge	Technical Ability
			Means	
T	Fundamentals of Federal income tax determination	3.37	3.01	3.42
F	Deferred taxes	3.31	3.21	2.70
T	Recognition of tax opportunities	3.30	3.01	2.13
T	Non-taxable exchanges	3.23	2.88	3.05
T	Tax planning	3.17	2.83	3.03
T	Complex tax provisions: corporations and shareholders	3.16	2.93	2.95
F	Double-entry system	3.16	3.12	2.82
F	Balance sheet	3.15	3.10	2.60
T	Tax research methodology	3.10	2.78	2.82
F	Accruals and deferrals	3.06	3.06	2.51
T	Capital gains and losses	3.04	2.69	3.15
T	Judicial doctrines in tax disputes	2.98	2.79	2.11
F	Transaction analysis	2.97	2.98	2.55
A	Internal control: evaluation	2.94	2.77	1.81
F	Income statement	2.93	2.91	2.44
T	Administrative processes in tax matters	2.90	2.58	2.42
A	Internal control: principles	2.90	2.90	1.68
F	Accounting for income taxes	2.90	2.94	2.49
F	Revenue and expense recognition	#2.89	2.93	2.50
A	Internal control: audit exposure due to weaknesses	2.89	2.73	1.66
M	Tax considerations in managerial decisions	2.87	2.85	2.44
F	U.S. financial accounting and reporting standards	2.86	2.83	2.18
T	Taxation of deferred compensation	2.85	2.53	2.37
A	Legal responsibilities of auditors: under securities acts	#2.83	2.44	1.68
A	Audit evidence: types	#2.82	2.68	2.39
A	Internal control: in an EDP environment	2.81	2.53	1.57
F	Error corrections	#2.79	2.73	2.39
A	Legal responsibilities of the auditor: classic cases	#2.79	2.48	1.81
T	Tax practice procedures	2.77	2.44	2.47
F	Business combinations: consolidation procedures	2.77	2.81	2.22
A	Modification of the standard short-form audit report	2.76	2.48	1.71
F	Theoretical framework: current structure	#2.76	2.71	2.25
F	SEC reporting	2.75	2.73	2.06
A	Internal control: description based on narrative	2.74	2.61	1.70

EXHIBIT 5-1
(continued)

Area	Topic	Importance	Means Conceptual Knowledge	Technical Ability
A	Internal control: description based on questionnaire	#2.74	2.60	1.93
T	Accumulated earnings tax	#2.73	2.58	1.96
A	Internal control: modification in audit program based on evaluation	2.73	2.56	1.26
T	Judicial processes in tax disputes	2.67	2.40	1.98
T	State and local taxes	#2.65	2.37	2.03
F	Financial statement analysis	2.64	2.58	2.15
A	Audit evidence: relative strength of types	#2.64	2.50	1.87
F	Business combinations: purchase vs. pooling of interests	2.63	2.76	2.06
T	Tax returns and accompanying schedules	2.62	2.26	3.05
F	Leases	2.61	2.55	2.09
T	Theoretical framework of taxation: economic and social concepts	#2.61	2.33	1.40
F	Statements from incomplete records	#2.61	2.59	2.23
T	Complex tax provisions: foreign tax credit	#2.61	2.33	2.31
A	Audit evidence: post-statement events	#2.60	2.46	2.51
F	Information needs of financial statement users	2.60	2.52	2.05
F	Contingencies	2.59	2.55	1.93
F	Materiality	2.59	2.66	1.95
A	Standard short-form audit report	2.58	2.24	1.63
F	Inventories	2.58	2.66	2.12
F	Regulatory influence	2.58	2.57	1.96
F	Theoretical framework: alternatives to current structure	#2.57	2.56	1.95
F	Statement of changes in financial position	#2.53	2.47	2.03
F	Corporate equity	#2.52	2.06	1.78
A	Long-form audit report	2.52	2.06	1.78
T	Complex tax provisions: DISC	2.50	2.33	1.73
A	Audit administration: review	2.50	2.27	1.71
F	Minority interest	#2.49	2.48	2.04
F	Development stage companies	2.49	2.57	2.10
F	Research and development costs	2.49	2.54	2.13
F	Fixed assets	2.49	2.50	2.10
T	Preparation of tax communications	2.48	2.07	2.78
A	Extensions of the attest function: associated audit risk	2.47	1.99	1.37
F	Intangibles (excluding goodwill)	2.46	2.42	1.86
T	Taxation for international operations	#2.46	2.17	2.08
F	Present value and future worth concepts	2.45	2.49	2.00
A	Auditing procedures: tests of account balances	2.44	2.13	2.09
F	Depreciation, depletion and amortization	2.44	2.47	2.10
A	Audit administration: client relations	#2.44	2.23	1.80

EXHIBIT 5-1
(continued)

Area	Topic	Importance	Means Conceptual Knowledge	Technical Ability
A	Audit administration: planning	2.44	2.30	1.63
F	Installment sales	2.43	2.42	2.00
A	Statistical inference in auditing: judgmental sampling	2.42	2.16	1.48
T	Complex tax provisions: consolidated corporate returns	#2.42	2.18	2.53
T	Complex tax provisions: individuals	#2.41	2.19	2.44
F	Fund accounting: financial statements	#2.41	2.44	1.95
M	Standard costs	2.41	2.45	1.93
F	Behavioral considerations in financial reporting	#2.40	2.37	1.78
F	Long-term liabilities	#2.40	2.36	2.00
A	Auditing procedures: working papers	2.39	2.15	1.80
T	Theoretical framework of taxation: alternatives to present framework	#2.38	2.08	1.76
M	Short-range planning	2.38	2.41	1.99
T	Social security taxes	2.37	2.04	1.70
A	Auditing procedures: tests of transactions	2.37	2.11	2.02
A	Auditing procedures: review of operations	2.37	2.28	2.02
A	Legal responsibilities of the auditor: exposure to criminal liability	#2.36	2.04	1.78
M	Long-range planning	#2.35	2.38	2.06
F	Business combinations: unconsolidated subsidiaries	2.34	2.40	1.81
A	Management letter	2.34	2.17	1.53
F	Short-term liabilities	#2.33	2.35	1.98
F	Convertible debt or equity	2.33	2.33	1.92
F	Pensions	2.33	2.32	1.65
M	Learning curve models	#2.32	2.32	1.86
A	Statistical inference in auditing: statistical sampling	2.31	2.20	2.41
T	Complex tax provisions: partners and partnerships	#2.31	2.07	2.46
F	Fund accounting: types of organizations	#2.31	2.35	1.82
A	Generally accepted auditing standards	2.31	2.31	1.93
A	Statistical inference in auditing: regression analysis	2.30	2.19	2.50
M	Cash management	2.30	2.42	2.06
F	Interim reporting	2.30	2.20	1.58
A	Professional rules of conduct	#2.29	2.42	1.69
F	Treasury stock	#2.28	2.26	1.89
T	Complex tax provisions: fiduciaries	#2.28	2.08	1.80
F	Foreign currency translation	#2.28	2.35	1.88
M	Budgeted financial statements	#2.27	2.35	1.91

EXHIBIT 5-1
(continued)

Area	Topic	Importance	Conceptual Knowledge	Technical Ability
			Means	
A	Statistical inference in auditing: other statistical methods	2.26	2.14	1.38
M	Variable costing	2.25	2.33	1.90
F	Investments in securities	#2.25	2.34	1.83
T	Complex tax provisions: subchapter S	#2.25	2.01	2.00
M	Process costing	2.25	2.37	1.93
A	Auditing procedures: compliance tests	2.24	2.01	2.04
M	Performance evaluation: return on investment	2.24	2.30	1.70
A	Internal control: description based on flowchart	#2.24	1.91	1.95
F	*International accounting standards	2.23	2.27	1.66
A	Audit administration: supervision	2.23	2.02	1.52
F	Earnings-per-share	#2.23	2.22	1.61
M	Full costing	2.23	2.39	1.87
M	Accounting information requirements for management decisions	2.22	2.29	1.66
A	Influence of professional and regulatory bodies upon the auditing function	2.22	2.16	1.57
M	Spoilage, waste, defective units and scrap	2.19	2.23	1.79
T	Federal gift tax	#2.19	1.87	2.10
M	Performance evaluation: divisional performance	2.18	2.21	1.67
F	Reporting forecasts	2.18	2.25	1.76
A	Audit administration: setting and collecting fees	#2.18	1.91	1.47
F	Partnership financial statements	#2.18	2.21	1.63
M	Job order costing	2.16	2.26	1.95
A	Auditing procedures: audit practice cases	2.16	1.88	1.84
M	Capital budgeting	#2.15	2.25	1.76
M	Flexible budgets	#2.15	2.27	1.88
F	Goodwill	2.14	2.09	1.73
A	Special considerations in auditing not-for-profit organizations	2.12	1.91	.86
M	Joint costs	#2.11	2.25	1.78
M	Statistical analysis of cost variances	#2.11	2.18	1.75
F	Cash	#2.09	2.26	1.84
A	Legal responsibilities of auditors: at common law	#2.08	2.23	1.47
A	User's expectations regarding the auditor's role	2.07	2.23	1.50
T	Federal estate tax	#2.06	1.89	2.10
M	Management information systems: implementation	#2.05	2.10	1.53
F	Receivables	#2.05	2.18	1.76
A	Internal control: relationship of GAAS	2.03	1.80	1.91

EXHIBIT 5-1
(continued)

Area	Topic	Importance	Conceptual Knowledge	Technical Ability
			Means	
F	Full costing vs. successful effort costing	2.03	2.11	1.66
F	National income accounting	#2.02	2.13	1.72
F	Fiduciary accounting: bankruptcy	2.02	2.14	1.60
T	Personal holding company tax	#2.02	1.81	2.09
A	Requirements for professional certification (CPA)	2.01	2.10	1.90
F	Fiduciary accounting: receivership	1.98	2.07	1.54
M	Management information systems: internal control aspects	#1.98	1.97	1.42
A	Legal responsibilities of the auditor: responses of the auditing profession to classic cases	#1.98	1.68	1.45
M	Performance evaluation: responsibility accounting	#1.97	2.05	1.53
A	Comparative accounting and auditing standards among nations	1.96	1.67	.67
M	Cost-volume-profit analysis	#1.95	1.98	1.72
A	Audit administration: accounting firm organization	1.95	1.72	1.43
M	Management information systems: administration	#1.95	2.01	1.48
F	Price-level adjusted financial statement	#1.94	2.03	1.44
F	Regulated industries	1.93	2.03	1.37
M	Corporate planning models	#1.92	2.06	1.65
F	Consignments	1.92	2.03	1.55
M	Organization theory	1.90	1.97	1.44
T	Natural resource taxation	1.89	1.72	1.64
A	Extensions of the attest function: possible areas	1.88	1.51	1.38
M	*Direct costing	1.87	2.06	1.58
F	*Human resource accounting	1.87	1.87	1.48
M	Information economics	#1.83	1.92	1.43
M	*Performance evaluation: non-statistical variance analysis	1.82	1.87	1.48
F	*Fiduciary accounting: estates and trusts	1.82	1.85	1.48
A	*Operational auditing: objectives	1.80	1.46	1.34
M	*Performance evaluation: residual income	1.80	1.85	1.44
F	*Fund accounting: governmental units	1.79	1.87	1.51
A	*SEC filing requirements	1.78	1.82	1.41
A	*Operational auditing: methodology	1.77	1.41	1.24
M	*Performance evaluation: non-financial performance measures	1.77	1.84	1.43
F	*Fund accounting: hospitals	1.75	1.86	1.47
M	*Management information systems: impact of external regulatory influences	1.75	1.85	1.32

EXHIBIT 5-1
(continued)

Area	Topic	Importance	Conceptual Knowledge	Technical Ability
			Means	
M	*Performance evaluation: transfer pricing	1.75	1.85	1.29
M	*Simulation	1.73	1.72	1.22
F	*Segment reporting	1.73	1.81	1.20
F	*Fund accounting: colleges and universities	1.73	1.82	1.49
M	*Internal financial auditing	1.72	1.80	1.43
M	*Network methods	1.72	1.71	1.16
M	*Computer science	1.71	1.85	1.34
M	*Planning and control of international operations	1.66	1.79	1.31
M	*Statistical decision theory	1.65	1.74	1.25
M	*Zero base budgeting	1.62	1.80	1.43
A	*Historical development of auditing	1.56	1.67	1.17
M	*Performance evaluation: common costs	1.56	1.61	1.11
M	*Statistical cost estimation	1.51	1.60	1.13
M	*Overhead control	1.49	1.59	1.17
M	*Management information system: design	1.45	1.51	1.09
M	*Internal operational auditing	1.44	1.54	1.15
M	*Special considerations in non-manufacturing concerns	1.42	1.58	1.19
M	*Sensitivity analysis	1.37	1.43	1.03
M	*Requirements for professional certification (CMA)	1.35	1.47	1.11
M	*Behavioral considerations	1.31	1.47	1.02
M	Linear programming	1.27	1.40	.89
M	*Social accounting	1.23	1.41	.94

* → non-area core topic

\# → significant difference ($p < .05$) between
     educator and practitioner importance mean responses.

The means in Exhibit 5-1 are heavily weighted toward the views of taxation practitioners, since there were nearly six times as many practitioner respondents as there were educator respondents in the taxation area. Separate rank-orderings on importance means by educators and practitioners are presented in Appendices 5A and 5B, respectively.

There are 162 topics in the taxation area core, or 82.2 percent of the questionnaire topics. Included in the area core are not only the 105 common core topics but also 57 additional topics, which are presented in Exhibit 5-2, rank-ordered by importance means (educators and practitioners combined).

EXHIBIT 5-2

TAXATION AREA CORE TOPICS
NOT IN COMMON CORE

Area	Topic	Importance Mean
T	Complex tax provisions: corporations and shareholders	3.16
T	Tax research methodology	3.10
T	Judicial doctrines in tax disputes	2.98
T	Administrative processes in tax matters	2.90
T	Tax practice procedures	2.77
T	Accumulated earnings tax	2.73
T	Judicial processes in tax disputes	2.67
T	State and local taxes	2.65
T	Tax returns and accompanying schedules	2.62
T	Theoretical framework of taxation: economic and social concepts	2.61
T	Complex tax provisions: foreign tax credit	2.61
F	Corporate equity	2.52
T	Complex tax provisions: DISC	2.50
F	Development stage companies	2.49
T	Preparation of tax communications	2.48
T	Taxation for international operations	2.46
A	Audit administration: client relations	2.44
T	Complex tax provisions: consolidated corporate returns	2.42
T	Complex tax provisions: individuals	2.41
F	Behavioral considerations in financial reporting	2.40
A	Auditing procedures: working papers	2.39
T	Theoretical framework of taxation: alternatives to present framework	2.38
T	Social security taxes	2.37
F	Business combinations: unconsolidated subsidiaries	2.34
F	Pensions	2.33
M	Learning curve models	2.32
T	Complex tax provisions: partners and partnerships	2.31
F	Fund accounting: types of organizations	2.31
A	Professional rules of conduct	2.29
T	Complex tax provisions: fiduciaries	2.28
F	Foreign currency translation	2.28
T	Complex tax provisions: subchapter S	2.25
F	Earnings-per-share	2.23
T	Federal gift tax	2.19
A	Audit administration: setting and collecting fees	2.18
F	Partnership financial statements	2.18
A	Auditing procedures: audit practice case	2.16
F	Goodwill	2.14
A	Special considerations in auditing not-for-profit organizations	2.12
A	Legal responsibilities of the auditor: at common law	2.08
T	Federal estate tax	2.06

EXHIBIT 5-2
(continued)

Area	Topic	Importance Mean
A	Internal control: relationship of GAAS	2.03
F	Full costing vs. successful effort costing	2.03
F	National income accounting	2.02
F	Fiduciary accounting: bankruptcy	2.02
T	Personal holding company tax	2.02
A	Requirements for professional certification (CPA)	2.01
F	Fiduciary accounting: receivership	1.98
A	Legal responsibilities of the auditor: responses of the auditing profession to classic cases	1.98
A	Comparative accounting and auditing standards among nations	1.96
A	Audit administration: accounting firm organization	1.95
M	Management information systems: administration	1.95
F	Regulated industries	1.93
M	Corporate planning models	1.92
F	Consignments	1.92
T	Natural resource taxation	1.89
A	Extensions of the attest function: possible areas	1.88

The taxation area core can also be analyzed as follows in terms of the section of the questionnaire in which the topics were presented:

Questionnaire Section	Total Number of Topics	Number in Area Core	% in Area Core
Financial	65	58	89.2%
Managerial	51	27	52.9%
Auditing	50	46	92.0%
Taxation	31	31	100.0%
Total	197	162	

Thus, as anticipated, the section of the questionnaire which had the largest proportion of its topics in the taxation area core was taxation, then auditing, followed closely by financial and, lastly, managerial.

Only 35 (17.8 percent) of the 197 questionnaire topics were excluded from the taxation area core. Exhibit 5-3 is a listing of these 35 topics, rank-ordered by importance mean responses (educators and practitioners combined) by questionnaire section. The last column in Exhibit 5-3 indicates whether the topic was excluded because of taxation educator responses, taxation practitioner responses, or both.

EXHIBIT 5-3

TOPICS EXCLUDED FROM
TAXATION AREA CORE

Topic	Importance Mean	Excluded by
FINANCIAL:		
International accounting standards	2.23	E
Human resource accounting	1.87	E
Fiduciary accounting: estates and trusts	1.82	P
Fund accounting: governmental units	1.79	P
Fund accounting: hospitals	1.75	P
Segment reporting	1.73	P
Fund accounting: colleges and universities	1.73	P
MANAGERIAL:		
Direct costing	1.87	P
Performance evaluation: non-statistical variance analysis	1.82	P
Performance evaluation: residual income	1.80	P
Performance evaluation: non-financial performance measures	1.77	P
Management information systems: impact of external regulatory influences	1.75	P
Performance evaluation: transfer pricing	1.75	P
Simulation	1.73	P
Internal financial auditing	1.72	P
Network methods	1.72	P
Computer science	1.71	P
Planning and control of international operations	1.66	E,P
Statistical decision theory	1.65	P
Zero base budgeting	1.62	P
Performance evaluation: common costs	1.56	P
Statistical cost estimation	1.51	P
Overhead control	1.49	P
Management information systems: design	1.45	P
Internal operational auditing	1.44	P
Special considerations in non-manufacturing concerns	1.42	P
Sensitivity analysis	1.37	P
Requirements for professional certification (CMA)	1.35	E,P
Behavioral considerations	1.31	P
Linear programming	1.27	P
Social accounting	1.23	P
AUDITING:		
Operational auditing: objectives	1.80	P
SEC filing requirements	1.78	P
Operational auditing: methodology	1.77	P
Historical development of auditing	1.56	P

E ➔ Educators
P ➔ Practitioners

A very obvious conclusion that may be drawn from Exhibit 5-3 is that virtually all (31 of 35) of the topics excluded from the area core were excluded due to the low importance response of taxation practitioners. An assessment of the significance of the difference between educators and practitioner mean responses is presented at a later point in this chapter.

Analysis of Taxation Area Core

IMPORTANCE ANALYSIS

Financial Accounting Topics
   As indicated in Exhibit 5-1, taxation respondents considered the following topics to be the most important financial accounting topics for an individual preparing for a taxation career (listed in decreasing order of importance):

   Deferred taxes
   Double-entry system
   Balance sheet
   Accruals and deferrals
   Transaction analysis
   Income statement
   Accounting for income taxes
   Revenue and expense recognition
   U.S. financial accounting and reporting standards

   The topic *accounting for income taxes,* as one might suspect, is considered relatively more important by taxation respondents than it was by all respondents combined (see Exhibit 3-1). On the other hand, the topics *statement of changes in financial position* and *information needs of financial statement users* are not considered as important by taxation respondents as by all respondents combined. Other than these differences, taxation respondents appear to be pretty much in agreement with the overall respondent group as to the most important financial accounting topics. However, the financial topics, relatively speaking, are not considered as important by taxation respondents as by all respondents combined.
   The seven financial accounting topics excluded from the taxation area core currently appear to receive very little emphasis in accounting curricula. Likewise, those financial accounting topics in the area core but at a relatively low level of importance, for the most part, apparently receive only limited attention in most existing curricula. Exceptions to this generalization include the topics *goodwill, cash, receivables,* and *price-level adjusted financial statements,* all of which currently receive more than passing attention in most curricula, even though they are considered of only minimal importance by taxation respondents. Also, current graduates may receive a more thorough background in the *fiduciary accounting* topics and *consignments* than that deemed desirable by taxation respondents.

Some financial accounting topics appear to receive less emphasis in most existing curricula than that indicated as desirable by taxation respondents. Included in this category are the topics *SEC reporting, theoretical framework: current structure, information needs of financial statement users, regulatory influences, theoretical framework: alternatives to current structure* and *development stage companies.* The views of taxation respondents appear to be reasonably consistent with the status quo on the remaining financial accounting topics.

Managerial Accounting Topics

As is evident in Exhibit 5-1, managerial accounting topics, in general, were not considered very important in preparing individuals for a career in taxation. In fact, only one managerial accounting topic, *tax considerations in managerial decisions,* was among the top 78 topics ranked in order of importance.

As indicated earlier, almost half (47.1 percent) of the 51 managerial accounting topics were excluded from the taxation area core, primarily due to the low importance responses of taxation practitioners (see Exhibit 5-3). For the most part, these excluded topics currently receive, at most, only limited coverage in most accounting curricula. Exceptions might include *computer science, statistical decision theory* and *overhead control.*

Auditing Topics

Auditing topics considered most important by taxation respondents, which were generally consistent with those considered most important by all respondents combined, were as follows (listed in decreasing order of importance):

Internal control: evaluation
Internal control: principles
Internal control: audit exposure due to weaknesses
Legal responsibilities of auditors: under the securities acts
Audit evidence: types
Internal control: in an EDP environment
Legal responsibilities of auditors: classic cases
Modifications of the standard short-form audit report
Internal control: description based on narrative
Internal control: description based on questionnaire
Internal control: modifications in audit program based on evaluation

In general, taxation respondents considered auditing topics to be fairly important in preparing individuals for a career in taxation.

As indicated in Exhibit 5-3, only four of the 50 auditing topics failed to meet our cut-off criterion for inclusion in the taxation area core. None of these four topics appear to receive more than passing attention in most existing curricula, even though the topic *SEC filing requirements* seems to be receiving increasing attention in some curricula.

It should also be noted that taxation respondents considered three *audit administration* topics *(review, client relations* and *planning)* to be reasonably important. These topics do not generally appear to receive the degree of emphasis in existing curricula that is deemed desirable by taxation respondents. The other three *audit administration* topics *(supervision, setting and collecting fees* and *accounting firm organization),* none of which appear to receive a significant amount of emphasis in existing curricula, are also included in the taxation area core. The topic *audit practice case,* which is not in the common core, is included in the taxation area core, albeit at a relatively low level of importance (2.16).

Taxation Topics

As is apparent in Exhibit 5-1, taxation topics dominated the upper portion of the rank-ordering of topics according to the importance responses of our taxation sample. Those taxation topics considered most important by taxation respondents were as follows (listed in decreasing order of importance):

Fundamentals of Federal income tax determination
Recognition of tax opportunities
Non-taxable exchanges
Tax planning
Complex tax provisions: corporations and shareholders
Tax research methodology
Capital gains and losses
Judicial doctrines in tax disputes
Administrative processes in tax matters
Taxation of deferred compensation

In general, these topics were also considered to be the most important taxation topics by all respondents combined, even though, as one would expect, they were considered less important by the latter group. The topics *complex tax provisions: corporations and shareholders, tax research methodology, judicial doctrines in tax disputes* and *administrative processes in tax matters* are considered significantly more important for individuals preparing for a career in taxation than they are for other accounting graduates.

All 31 of the taxation topics met our cut-off criterion for inclusion in the taxation area core, providing further evidence of the relatively high degree of importance placed on these topics as a group of taxation respondents, since only six of the 31 topics were in the common core. The implication is that accounting students planning to pursue a career in taxation should have in their background some exposure to all 31 taxation topics, including the more specialized topics such as *personal holding company tax, natural resource taxation,* and *subchapter S provisions.* In fact, as a quick perusal of Exhibit 5-1 demonstrates, most of the taxation topics not only met our cut-off criterion for inclusion in the area core, but also ranked relatively high within the area core in terms of importance.

Educators vs. Practitioners

The rank orderings of topics by importance means for taxation educators and taxation practitioners are presented in Appendices 5A and 5B, respectively. These appendices follow the same format as used in previous rank-ordering presentations, including an indication of the questionnaire section in which the topic was presented and the associated mean responses on the conceptual knowledge and technical ability scales.

On an overall basis, taxation educators tended to scale topics more highly with respect to importance than did taxation practitioners. The importance mean over all topics for taxation educators was 2.72, while the importance mean over all topics for taxation practitioners was 2.24.

The "#" preceding the importance mean in Exhibit 5-1 indicates that the educator and practitioner mean importance response differed significantly (at the .05 level) for that topic. Significant differences were found for 63 (38.9 percent) of the 162 taxation area core topics. Among these 63 topics were 22 (37.9 percent) of the 58 financial accounting topics in the area core, 14 (51.9 percent) of the 27 managerial accounting topics in the area core, 13 (28.3 percent) of the 46 auditing topics in the area core and 14 (45.2 percent) of the 31 taxation topics in the area core. It is interesting to note that the extent of disagreement is no less on taxation topics than on other topics.

Out of the 63 topics for which significant differences between educator and practitioner mean importance responses were found, the educator mean exceeded the practitioner mean in 58 (*i.e.*, all but five) cases. The five exceptions, that is, significant difference cases in which the practitioner mean exceeded the educator mean, were as follows:

Foreign currency translation
Audit administration: setting and collecting fees
Taxation for international operations
Complex tax provisions: foreign tax credit
State and local taxes

CONCEPTUAL KNOWLEDGE AND TECHNICAL ABILITY ANALYSIS

Up to this point, the analysis in this chapter has been based solely upon the importance responses. We now turn to an analysis of the conceptual knowledge and technical ability scale responses of our taxation sample. The mean responses on these two scales for taxation educator and practitioner respondents combined were included in Exhibit 5-1, while educator and practitioner mean responses are shown separately in Appendices 5A and 5B, respectively.

In general, taxation respondents indicated that more emphasis should be placed upon conceptual knowledge than upon technical ability. The mean technical ability response exceeded the mean conceptual knowledge response for only 19 (11.7 percent) of the 162 taxation area core topics when looking at taxation educators and practitioners combined (see Exhibit 5-1). These 19 area core topics for which taxation respondents indicate that greater emphasis should be placed upon technical ability were as follows:

Topic	Mean Conceptual Knowledge	Technical Ability
Fundamentals of Federal income tax determination	3.01	3.42
Non-taxable exchanges	2.88	3.05
Tax planning	2.83	3.03
Tax research methodology	2.78	2.82
Capital gains and losses	2.69	3.15
Tax practice procedures	2.44	2.47
Tax returns and accompanying schedules	2.26	3.05
Audit evidence: post-statement events	2.46	2.51
Preparation of tax communications	2.07	2.78
Complex tax provisions: consolidated corporate returns	2.18	2.53
Complex tax provisions: individuals	2.19	2.44
Statistical inference in auditing: statistical sampling	2.20	2.41
Complex tax provisions: partners and partnerships	2.07	2.46
Statistical inference in auditing: regression analysis	2.19	2.50
Auditing procedures: compliance tests	2.01	2.04
Internal control: description based on flowchart	1.91	1.95
Federal gift tax	1.87	2.10
Federal estate tax	1.89	2.10
Internal control: relationship of GAAS	1.80	1.91

As is apparent from this list, these are, almost without exception, highly pragmatic topics, topics which one would expect to cover predominantly in a technical sense.

The overall mean conceptual knowledge response across all topics for taxation respondents was 2.24, while the overall mean technical ability response was 1.83, further evidencing a greater emphasis upon conceptual knowledge than upon technical ability in the taxation area core. However, it should be noted that a significant emphasis upon technical ability is deemed desirable for many taxation topics, as 13 of the 19 topics for which the technical ability mean exceeded the conceptual knowledge mean were taxation topics. Thus, it appears that taxation respondents place relatively more emphasis upon technical ability for topics related to their area of expertise than respondents in other areas do for topics in their particular area of expertise.

Educators vs. Practitioners

Taxation educators generally scaled topics higher with respect to conceptual knowledge than did taxation practitioners, as indicated by the overall conceptual knowledge mean response of 2.78 for taxation educators and 2.17 for taxation practitioners. The practitioner conceptual knowledge mean exceeded the educator conceptual knowledge mean for only nine (5.6 percent) of the 162 area core topics, as follows:

| | Conceptual Knowledge Mean | |
Topic	Educators	Practitioners
Foreign currency translation	2.33	2.36
SEC reporting	2.67	2.74
Fiduciary accounting: bankruptcy	2.08	2.15
Fiduciary accounting: receivership	2.00	2.08
Development stage companies	2.33	2.60
Statistical analysis of cost variances	2.00	2.20
Internal control: description based on narrative	2.50	2.62
Management letter	2.08	2.18
Complex tax provisions: DISC	2.29	2.33

The practitioner mean exceeded the educator mean with respect to conceptual knowledge for only two (5.7 percent) of the 35 topics excluded from the taxation area core.

Likewise, taxation educators generally tended to scale topics higher with respect to technical ability than did their practitioner counterparts, the educators having an overall technical ability mean response of 2.18 and the practitioners having an overall mean response of 1.78. However, the practitioner mean technical ability response did exceed the educator mean technical ability response for 29 (17.9 percent) of the 162 taxation area core topics, as follows:

| | Technical Ability Mean | |
Topic	Educators	Practitioners
Foreign currency translation	1.67	1.90
Behavioral considerations in financial reporting	1.75	1.78
SEC reporting	2.00	2.07
Fiduciary accounting: bankruptcy	1.45	1.62
Fiduciary accounting: receivership	1.36	1.56
Interim reporting	1.30	1.61
Contingencies	1.91	1.93
Materiality	1.82	1.97
Development stage companies	1.58	2.17
Learning curve models	1.40	1.92
Statistical analysis of cost variances	1.40	1.80
Accounting information requirements for management decisions	1.60	1.66
Users' expectations regarding the auditor's role	1.45	1.51
Internal control: description based on questionnaire	1.90	1.94
Statistical inference in auditing: regression analysis	1.91	2.57
Audit evidence: post-statement events	2.17	2.56
Administrative processes in tax matters	2.25	2.47
Taxation for international operations	1.58	2.21
Tax planning	2.83	3.09
Judicial doctrines in tax disputes	2.00	2.13
Judicial processes in tax disputes	1.83	2.02
Complex tax provisions: consolidated corporate returns	1.92	2.68

(continued)

Topic	Technical Ability Mean	
	Educators	Practitioners
Complex tax provisions: DISC	1.67	1.74
Complex tax provisions: foreign tax credit	2.00	2.38
Taxation of deferred compensation	2.18	2.41
State and local taxes	1.75	2.09
Tax practice procedures	1.92	2.59
Tax returns and accompanying schedules	2.58	3.15
Theoretical framework of taxation: alternatives to present framework	1.73	1.76

Thus, while educators, in general, scaled technical ability more highly than did practitioners, the practitioner mean response did exceed the educator mean response on 13 (41.9 percent) of the 31 taxation topics, as indicated in the preceding tabulation. The practitioner mean exceeded the educator mean on only four (11.4 percent) of the 35 topics excluded from the taxation area core.

6

Financial Accounting

Introduction
In this chapter the responses of individuals identifying financial accounting as their area of specialization are utilized to identify and analyze the financial accounting area core. The financial accounting sample, which is the source of all of the analyses in this chapter, was composed as follows:

Educators		53
Practitioners:		
Public Accounting	34	
Industry	54	88
Total		141

Some general observations regarding the responses of these individuals are presented in the next section, followed by a more detailed analysis of the financial accounting area core.

The Financial Accounting Area Core
The 197 questionnaire topics are rank-ordered in Exhibit 6-1 according to the mean importance responses of the financial accounting respondents. Topics excluded from the financial accounting area core, because they did not meet our cut-off criterion as described in Chapter 2, are preceded by the symbol "*". The symbol "#" preceding an importance mean indicates that a significant difference (at the .05 level) existed between the mean importance responses of financial accounting educators and financial accounting practitioners for that topic. The letter preceding each topic indicates the questionnaire section in which the topic was presented. Conceptual knowledge and technical ability mean responses for each topic are also included in Exhibit 6-1 as a basis for subsequent discussion.

77

EXHIBIT 6-1

RANK ORDERING BY IMPORTANCE MEANS:
FINANCIAL ACCOUNTING RESPONDENTS

| | | | Means | |
| | | | Conceptual | Technical |
Area	Topic	Importance	Knowledge	Ability
F	U.S. financial accounting and reporting standards	3.51	3.48	3.03
F	Revenue and expense recognition	#3.50	3.50	3.10
F	Balance sheet	3.49	3.45	3.23
T	Fundamentals of Federal income tax determination	3.41	3.11	2.53
F	Theoretical framework: current structure	#3.41	3.43	2.89
F	Regulatory influences	3.29	3.11	2.62
A	Internal control: principles	3.29	3.14	2.27
F	Business combinations: consolidation procedures	#3.23	3.26	2.79
F	Income statement	3.23	2.28	2.98
A	Internal control: evaluation	#3.21	3.09	2.30
F	Double-entry system	3.20	3.18	3.07
A	Audit evidence: types	#3.20	3.09	2.68
F	Theoretical framework: alternatives to current structure	#3.19	3.30	2.49
F	Information needs of financial statement users	#3.18	3.13	2.24
F	Materiality	3.17	3.07	2.52
F	Deferred taxes	3.16	3.21	2.66
A	Internal control: audit exposure due to weaknesses	#3.14	2.97	2.17
A	Internal control: modifications in audit program based on evaluation	#3.13	2.94	2.03
A	Internal control: in an EDP environment	3.13	2.92	2.10
F	Statement of changes in financial position	3.09	3.15	2.88
T	Capital gains and losses	3.09	2.74	2.36
F	Transaction analysis	#3.09	3.18	2.81
F	Business combinations: purchase vs. pooling of interests	3.09	3.20	2.60
F	Accruals and deferrals	3.08	3.26	2.90
A	Audit evidence: relative strength of types	#3.07	2.96	2.10
F	Contingencies	3.07	3.04	2.56
F	Present value and future worth concept	#3.07	3.10	2.51
F	Leases	3.04	3.01	2.55
A	Legal responsibilities of auditors: under the securities acts	#3.02	2.85	1.88
M	Standard costs	#3.02	3.04	2.63
F	Accounting for income taxes	3.01	3.09	2.71
F	Inventories	3.00	3.14	2.76
A	Standard short-form audit report	#3.00	2.76	2.21

EXHIBIT 6-1
(continued)

Area	Topic	Importance	Conceptual Knowledge	Technical Ability
			Means	
A	Modifications of the standard short-form audit report	#3.00	2.85	2.30
A	Audit evidence: post-statement events	#3.00	2.93	2.76
F	Earnings-per-share	2.99	2.96	2.64
M	Management information systems: internal control aspects	2.98	2.88	2.41
A	Generally accepted auditing standards (GAAS)	#2.98	2.98	2.48
T	Non-taxable exchanges	2.98	2.63	2.12
M	Tax considerations in managerial decisons	2.97	2.88	2.44
F	Interim reporting	#2.93	2.94	2.54
M	Capital budgeting	#2.92	2.87	2.39
M	Variable costing	#2.90	3.02	2.43
T	Tax planning	#2.89	2.64	2.01
F	Business combinations: unconsolidated subsidiaries	2.89	2.87	2.33
F	Long-term liabilities	2.89	2.98	2.57
F	Financial statement analysis	#2.88	2.99	2.56
T	Recognition of tax opportunities	2.88	2.69	1.55
A	Statistical inference in auditing: statistical sampling	#2.88	2.84	2.57
M	Cost-volume-profit analysis	#2.87	2.88	2.55
F	SEC reporting	2.87	2.82	2.37
A	Influence of professional and regulatory bodies upon the auditing function	2.86	2.77	1.98
M	Flexible budgets	#2.86	2.85	2.43
M	Accounting information requirements for management decisions	#2.86	2.81	2.25
F	Corporate equity	2.86	3.05	2.58
M	Full costing	#2.85	2.95	2.45
M	Process costing	#2.84	2.96	2.50
F	Fixed assets	#2.84	2.78	2.28
M	Long-range planning	#2.81	2.78	2.28
F	Depreciation, depletion and amortization	#2.81	2.95	2.59
A	Statistical inference in auditing: judgmental sampling	#2.80	2.64	2.16
M	Short-range planning	#2.79	2.78	2.34
M	Budgeted financial statements	#2.79	2.81	2.44
F	Error corrections	2.79	2.95	2.74
M	Performance evaluation: return on investment	#2.79	2.82	2.25
F	Investments in securities	2.77	2.97	2.54
A	Auditing procedures: tests of account balances	2.76	2.63	2.41
A	Internal control: relationship of GAAS	2.76	2.53	2.41
M	Job order costing	#2.76	2.90	2.50
F	Intangibles (excluding goodwill)	2.76	3.01	2.45

EXHIBIT 6-1
(continued)

			Means	
Area	Topic	Importance	Conceptual Knowledge	Technical Ability
A	Legal responsibilities of auditors: classic cases	#2.75	2.65	1.77
M	Performance evaluation: divisional performance	#2.75	2.78	2.26
M	Performance evaluation: responsibility accounting	#2.74	2.69	2.16
M	Cash management	2.74	2.69	2.30
A	Auditing procedures: tests of transactions	#2.74	2.60	2.43
A	Internal control: description based on narrative	2.73	2.72	1.98
F	Research and development costs	#2.73	2.85	2.37
A	Auditing procedures: compliance tests	#2.72	2.59	2.37
F	Convertible debt or equity	2.72	2.99	2.44
M	Joint costs	#2.71	2.79	2.35
F	Minority interest	2.71	2.96	2.38
A	Management letter	2.71	2.57	1.99
F	Short-term liabilities	2.70	2.86	2.45
A	Auditing procedures: review of operations	2.68	2.63	2.36
A	User's expectations regarding the auditor's role	#2.67	2.56	1.60
A	Internal control: description based on flowchart	#2.62	2.53	2.34
T	Complex tax provisions: corporations and shareholders	2.61	2.41	1.92
M	Management information systems: impact of external regulatory influences	#2.60	2.60	2.10
F	Behavioral considerations in financial reporting	2.60	2.67	1.76
A	Auditing procedures: working papers	2.60	2.52	2.14
A	Statistical inference in auditing: regression analysis	#2.58	2.60	2.18
F	Foreign currency translation	#2.58	2.75	2.20
F	Receivables	2.58	2.77	2.44
A	Statistical inference in auditing: other statistical methods	#2.57	2.50	1.63
M	Direct costing	#2.56	2.79	2.20
F	Cash	2.55	2.62	2.44
A	Professional rules of conduct	#2.55	2.53	2.02
F	Treasury stock	2.54	2.70	2.35
F	Pensions	2.54	2.74	2.15
M	Performance evaluation: non-statistical variance analysis	#2.54	2.59	2.08
F	Price-level adjusted financial statements	#2.53	2.89	2.05
A	Internal control: description based on questionnaire	2.53	2.57	2.25

EXHIBIT 6-1
(continued)

Area	Topic	Importance	Means Conceptual Knowledge	Technical Ability
F	Goodwill	2.50	2.68	2.26
M	Information economics	2.50	2.56	1.96
A	Extensions of the attest function: associated audit risk	2.49	2.27	1.48
A	Legal responsibilities of auditors: at common law	#2.48	2.45	1.68
A	Legal responsibilities of auditors: exposure to criminal liability	#2.48	2.31	1.70
A	Audit administration: review	2.48	2.44	1.58
A	Long-form audit report	#2.46	2.25	1.80
A	Requirements for professional certification (CPA)	2.45	2.36	2.04
F	Segment reporting	#2.43	2.61	1.96
M	Spoilage, waste, defective units and scrap	2.42	2.46	2.09
F	Fund accounting: financial statements	#2.41	2.49	1.98
T	Accumulated earnings tax	2.41	2.40	1.43
A	Audit administration: planning	2.40	2.35	1.62
F	Statements from incomplete records	2.40	2.57	2.31
M	Organization theory	#2.40	2.41	1.81
F	Reporting forecasts	2.39	2.51	2.02
T	Tax research methodology	#2.37	2.27	1.85
T	Administrative processes in tax matters	2.35	2.11	1.19
F	Fund accounting: types of organizations	#2.32	2.42	1.89
T	Taxation of deferred compensation	2.31	2.21	1.64
M	Statistical analysis of cost variances	#2.30	2.48	1.88
T	Judicial doctrines in tax disputes	#2.30	2.16	1.00
F	Full costing vs. successful effort costing	2.29	2.51	1.90
M	Performance evaluation: non-financial performance measures	#2.29	2.39	1.81
A	Operational auditing: objectives	#2.28	2.09	1.75
F	Development stage companies	#2.27	2.52	1.99
T	State and local taxes	2.26	2.10	1.58
M	Management information systems: implementation	#2.26	2.31	1.89
A	Audit administration: client relations	2.25	2.08	1.47
T	*Complex tax provisions: DISC	2.25	2.18	1.18
M	Corporate planning models	2.25	2.33	1.82
T	Theoretical framework of taxation: economic and social concepts	#2.24	2.22	1.11
M	Zero base budgeting	2.24	2.50	1.93
A	SEC filing requirements	#2.24	2.16	1.77
F	International accounting standards	2.24	2.40	1.82
T	*Taxation for international operations	2.23	2.04	1.30
M	Management information systems: administration	2.21	2.17	1.85

EXHIBIT 6-1
(continued)

Area	Topic	Importance	Conceptual Knowledge	Technical Ability
			Means	
T	*Complex tax provisions: foreign tax credit	2.21	2.03	1.42
F	Installment sales	2.21	2.56	2.02
A	Audit administration: supervision	2.20	2.15	1.42
M	Overhead control	#2.19	2.23	1.77
M	Performance evaluation: transfer pricing	#2.19	2.26	1.77
A	Legal responsibilities of auditors: responses of the auditing profession to classic cases	#2.19	2.06	1.52
M	Performance evaluation: common costs	#2.16	2.23	1.74
M	Learning curve models	#2.15	2.39	1.81
F	Fund accounting: governmental units	#2.15	2.31	1.82
M	Performance evaluation: residual income	#2.15	2.24	1.79
A	Auditing procedures: audit practice case	2.15	2.09	1.87
T	Tax returns and accompanying schedules	2.14	1.85	1.96
M	Management information systems: design	2.12	2.22	1.66
F	Partnership financial statement	#2.11	2.40	1.85
A	Special considerations in auditing not-for-profit organizations	#2.10	2.02	1.20
F	National income accounting	#2.10	2.22	1.59
M	Internal financial auditing	#2.09	2.24	1.76
A	Operational auditing: methodology	2.09	1.94	1.71
F	*Consignments	2.07	2.26	1.83
F	Regulated industries	#2.07	2.13	1.63
T	Social security taxes	#2.05	1.97	1.54
A	*Comparative accounting and auditing standards among nations	2.04	1.84	1.01
M	Simulation	2.04	2.24	1.66
A	*Extensions of the attest function: possible areas	2.03	1.92	1.52
T	Complex tax provisions: individuals	#2.03	1.79	1.90
T	Theoretical framework of taxation: alternatives to present framework	#2.03	1.98	1.27
M	Internal operational auditing	2.02	2.28	1.65
M	Computer science	1.99	2.13	1.57
T	*Judicial processes in tax disputes	1.98	1.88	.95
T	Complex tax provisions: consolidated corporate returns	#1.97	1.78	1.53
M	*Statistical cost estimation	1.96	2.14	1.62
M	*Statistical decision theory	1.93	2.17	1.60
M	Network methods	1.92	2.15	1.58
F	Fund accounting: colleges and universities	#1.91	2.07	1.63
M	Planning and control of international operations	#1.91	1.93	1.53
F	Fund accounting: hospitals	#1.90	2.07	1.63
M	*Behavioral considerations	1.88	2.00	1.38

EXHIBIT 6-1

(continued)

Area	Topic	Importance	Means Conceptual Knowledge	Technical Ability
T	*Complex tax provisions: fiduciaries	1.86	1.73	1.44
T	*Tax practice procedures	1.84	1.68	1.23
F	*Human resource accounting	1.83	2.08	1.51
T	Complex tax provisions: partners and partnerships	1.83	1.63	1.88
T	Complex tax provisions: subchapter S	#1.83	1.63	1.77
A	*Audit administration: setting and collecting fees	1.80	1.67	.92
T	*Federal estate tax	1.78	1.55	1.22
M	*Linear programming	1.75	2.08	1.42
M	*Sensitivity analysis	1.74	2.03	1.50
T	*Federal gift tax	1.73	1.58	1.19
F	*Fiduciary accounting: bankruptcy	1.72	2.13	1.51
A	*Audit administration: accounting firm organization	1.71	1.57	1.05
A	*Historical development of auditing	1.70	1.90	1.08
F	*Fiduciary accounting: receivership	1.67	2.04	1.46
M	*Special considerations in non-manufacturing concerns	1.65	1.74	1.31
M	*Social accounting	1.60	1.75	1.19
M	*Requirements for professional certification (CMA)	1.50	1.59	1.32
T	*Natural resource taxation	1.49	1.42	1.28
F	*Fiduciary accounting: estates and trusts	1.43	1.73	1.26
T	*Preparation of tax communications	1.40	1.20	1.51
T	*Personal holding company tax	1.35	1.24	1.15

* ➝ non-area core topic

\# ➝ significant difference (p < .05) between educator and practitioner importance mean responses

The financial accounting area core includes 168 (85.3 percent) of the 197 questionnaire topics. Thus, this area core includes not only the 105 accounting topics that are common to all areas of specialization but also an additional group of 63 topics considered important for an individual preparing to enter a career in financial accounting.

The 63 financial accounting area core topics which are not in the common core are listed, in decreasing order of importance, in Exhibit 6-2.

EXHIBIT 6-2

**FINANCIAL ACCOUNTING AREA CORE TOPICS
NOT IN COMMON CORE**

Area	Topic	Importance Mean
F	Earnings-per-share	2.99
F	Business combinations: unconsolidated subsidiaries	2.89
F	Corporate equity	2.86
A	Internal control: relationship of GAAS	2.76
T	Complex tax provisions: corporations and shareholders	2.61
M	Management information systems: impact of external regulatory influences	2.60
F	Behavioral considerations in financial reporting	2.60
A	Auditing procedures: working papers	2.60
F	Foreign currency translation	2.58
M	Direct costing	2.56
A	Professional rules of conduct	2.55
F	Pensions	2.54
M	Performance evaluation: non-statistical variance analysis	2.54
F	Goodwill	2.50
A	Legal responsibilities of auditors: at common law	2.48
A	Requirements for professional certification (CPA)	2.45
F	Segment reporting	2.43
T	Accumulated earnings tax	2.41
T	Tax research methodology	2.37
T	Administrative processes in tax matters	2.35
F	Fund accounting: types of organizations	2.32
T	Judicial doctrines in tax disputes	2.30
F	Full costing vs. successful effort costing	2.29
M	Performance evaluation: non-financial performance measures	2.29
A	Operational auditing: objectives	2.28
F	Development stage companies	2.27
T	State and local taxes	2.26
A	Audit administration: client relations	2.25
M	Corporate planning models	2.25
T	Theoretical framework of taxation: economic and social concepts	2.24

EXHIBIT 6-2
(continued)

Area	Topic	Importance Mean
M	Zero base budgeting	2.24
A	SEC filing requirements	2.24
F	International accounting standards	2.24
M	Management information systems: administration	2.21
M	Overhead control	2.19
M	Performance evaluation: transfer pricing	2.19
A	Legal responsibilities of auditors: responses of the auditing profession to classic cases	2.19
M	Performance evaluation: common costs	2.16
M	Learning curve models	2.15
F	Fund accounting: governmental units	2.15
M	Performance evaluation: residual income	2.15
A	Auditing procedures: audit practice case	2.15
T	Tax returns and accompanying schedules	2.14
M	Management information systems: design	2.12
F	Partnership financial statements	2.11
A	Special considerations in auditing not-for-profit organizations	2.10
F	National income accounting	2.10
M	Internal financial auditing	2.09
A	Operational auditing: methodology	2.09
F	Regulated industries	2.07
T	Social security taxes	2.05
M	Simulation	2.04
T	Complex tax provisions: individuals	2.03
T	Theoretical framework of taxation: alternatives to present framework	2.03
M	Internal operational auditing	2.02
M	Computer science	1.99
T	Complex tax provisions: consolidated corporate returns	1.97
M	Network methods	1.92
F	Fund accounting: colleges and universities	1.91
M	Planning and control of international operations	1.91
F	Fund accounting: hospitals	1.90
T	Complex tax provisions: partners and partnerships	1.83
T	Complex tax provisions: subchapter S	1.83

Thus, given our cut-off criterion, these 63 topics are not sufficiently pervasive in importance to be included in the common core. However, financial accounting respondents perceive them to be sufficiently important that individuals planning to enter a career in financial accounting should include some coverage of these topics in their formal educational preparation. A financial accounting "track" in an accounting curriculum would thus include these topics. The type of coverage deemed necessary can be at least partially determined by analyzing the conceptual knowledge and technical ability responses. This analysis is presented in subsequent sections of this chapter.

The 168 area core topics can be analyzed as follows in terms of the section of the questionnaire in which they were presented.

Questionnaire Section	Total Number of Topics	Number in Area Core	% in Area Core
Financial	65	60	92.3%
Managerial	51	43	84.3%
Auditing	50	45	90.0%
Taxation	31	20	64.5%
Total	197	168	

Thus, as expected, the section of the questionnaire with the largest proportion of topics included in the financial accounting area core was financial accounting, followed closely by auditing and then managerial and taxation in that order.

Twenty-nine topics were excluded from the financial accounting area core because of sufficiently low importance responses by financial accounting educators, financial accounting practitioners, or both. These topics are presented in Exhibit 6-3, listed by questionnaire section in order of decreasing importance, along with an indication of the group(s) responsible for their exclusion from the area core. In the "Excluded By" column, "E" indicates financial accounting educators and "P" indicates financial accounting practitioners. The importance means in Exhibit 6-3 are the mean responses for financial accounting educators and financial accounting practitioners combined.

EXHIBIT 6-3

TOPICS EXCLUDED FROM FINANCIAL ACCOUNTING AREA CORE

Topic	Importance Mean	Excluded by
FINANCIAL:		
Consignments	2.07	E
Human resource accounting	1.83	E
Fiduciary accounting: bankruptcy	1.72	E
Fiduciary accounting: receivership	1.67	E
Fiduciary accounting: estates and trusts	1.43	E,P
MANAGERIAL:		
Statistical cost estimation	1.96	P
Statistical decision theory	1.93	P
Behavioral considerations	1.88	P
Linear programming	1.75	P
Sensitivity analysis	1.74	P
Special considerations in non-manufacturing concerns	1.65	P
Social accounting	1.60	P
Requirements for professional certification (CMA)	1.50	E,P
AUDITING:		
Comparative accounting and auditing standards among nations	2.04	E
Extensions of the attest function: possible areas	2.03	P
Audit administration: setting and collecting fees	1.80	E
Audit administration: accounting firm organization	1.71	P
Historical development of auditing	1.70	P
TAXATION:		
Complex tax provisions: DISC	2.25	E
Taxation for international operations	2.23	E
Complex tax provisions: foreign tax credit	2.21	E
Judicial processes in tax disputes	1.98	E
Complex tax provisions: fiduciaries	1.86	E
Tax practice procedures	1.84	E
Federal estate tax	1.78	P
Federal gift tax	1.73	P
Natural resource taxation	1.49	E,P
Preparation of tax communications	1.40	E,P
Personal holding company tax	1.35	E,P

It is interesting to note that four of the five financial accounting topics excluded from the area core were excluded because of low importance scalings by financial accounting educators. On the other hand, seven of the eight managerial topics excluded from the area core were excluded because of the low importance scalings of financial accounting practitioners. A more detailed discussion of education-practitioner differences is presented in subsequent sections of this chapter.

Analysis of Financial Accounting Area Core

IMPORTANCE ANALYSIS

Financial Accounting Topics

Referring to Exhibit 6-1, the most important financial accounting topics as viewed by financial accounting respondents were as follows (listed in order of decreasing importance per mean responses):

U.S. financial accounting and reporting standards
Revenue and expense recognition
Balance sheet
Theoretical framework: current structure
Regulatory influences
Business combinations: consolidation procedures
Income statement
Double-entry system
Theoretical framework: alternatives to current structure
Information needs of financial statement users
Materiality
Deferred taxes

While this list of most important financial accounting topics is quite similar to that presented in Chapter 3 for all respondents, the topics *regulatory influences* and *business combinations: consolidation procedures* appear in this list but they were not ranked as highly for all respondents combined. Thus, these topics are deemed relatively more important by financial accounting respondents than by all respondents combined. The implication is that these two topics should receive greater emphasis for individuals preparing for a financial accounting career.

Also, the questionnaire results seem to imply that a greater emphasis should be placed on *information needs of financial statement users* than that which currently exists in most accounting curricula. Only limited attention is given to this topic in most accounting curricula. Most existing textbooks reflect an emphasis upon preparation and presentation of financial information rather than upon the needs of users.

At the other end of the spectrum are those financial topics which ranked relatively low based on importance means. As indicated in Exhibit 6-3, five financial accounting topics were excluded from the area core. Thus, these five topics are not deemed sufficiently important to be required of individuals entering a career in financial accounting. However, the topic *consignments* and the three *fiduciary accounting* topics are presented in most intermediate and/or advanced accounting textbooks.

Most of the financial accounting topics which only minimally meet the cut-off criterion for inclusion in the area core currently appear to receive only a minimum amount of emphasis in accounting curricula. One exception appears to be *partnership financial statements,* which probably receives more emphasis in most existing curricula than the questionnaire respondents deem desirable. Another exception is *regulated industries,* which receives virtually no attention in most existing curricula, even though the questionnaire respondents, given our cut-off criterion, consider the topic important enough to be a part of the area core.

Several other financial accounting topics in the area core currently appear to receive very little attention in accounting curricula. The most obvious examples are *development stage companies, full costing vs. successful effort costing, reporting forecasts* and *segment reporting.* All of these topics could be categorized as problem areas that have been addressed recently by the profession. The fact that they have not yet been effectively incorporated into existing curricula provides some evidence of a time lag between the emergence of problems and issues in practice and the integration of such issues into accounting curricula. This research does indicate, however, that leading educators and practitioners believe that such topics should be integrated into the curricula.

Managerial Accounting Topics

Again referring to Exhibit 6-1, the most important managerial accounting topics in the financial accounting area core were as follows (listed in order of decreasing importance per mean responses):

Standard costs
Management information systems: internal control aspects
Tax considerations in managerial decisions
Capital budgeting
Variable costing
Cost-volume-profit analysis
Flexible budgets
Accounting information requirements for management decisions
Full costing
Process costing
Long-range planning
Short-range planning
Budgeted financial statements
Performance evaluation: return on investment

Not surprisingly, none of these topics were ranked as highly in terms of importance as the highest ranking financial accounting topics.

As was the case with financial accounting topics, this list appears to be somewhat consistent with the most heavily emphasized managerial accounting topics in existing accounting curricula. However, there are some apparent inconsistencies between those topics deemed most important by financial accounting respondents and those topics receiving the greatest emphasis in existing curricula. In particular, *tax considerations in managerial decisions, accounting information requirements for management decisions* and *management information systems: internal control aspects* currently do not appear to receive the emphasis deemed desirable by financial accounting respondents. Also, unless a student takes a capital budgeting course, it is likely that too little attention will be devoted to the topics *capital budgeting, long-range planning, short-range planning* and *budgeted financial statements* in preparing a student to enter a career in financial accounting.

Looking at the managerial topics ranked relatively low with respect to importance, it is obvious that financial accounting practitioners consider most quantitative techniques to be considerably less important than do their educator counterparts. As indicated in Exhibit 6-3, all eight of the managerial topics excluded from the financial accounting area core were ranked sufficiently low for exclusion by practitioners. Of these eight topics, four could be considered quantitative in nature, *i.e., statistical cost estimation, statistical decision theory, linear programming* and *sensitivity analysis.* It also appears that practitioners consider two of the other topics, *behavioral considerations* and *social accounting,* to be of limited usefulness, even though we have recently begun to emphasize these topics more in the educational setting.

The financial accounting respondents scaled a few managerial topics which appear to receive substantial emphasis in most existing curricula relatively low with respect to importance. In particular, *computer science, performance evaluation: common costs,* and *performance evaluation: transfer pricing* barely met our cut-off criterion for inclusion in the area core.

Other managerial topics were ranked fairly high by financial accounting respondents, even though they apparently receive very limited attention in most existing textbooks and curricula. Included in this group, in addition to those topics discussed in connection with the highest-ranking managerial topics, are *cash management, management information systems: impact of external regulatory influences* and *information economics.*

Auditing Topics

The most important auditing topics in the financial accounting area core were as follows (listed in order of decreasing importance):

Internal control: principles
Internal control: evaluation
Audit evidence: types
Internal control: audit exposure due to weaknesses
Internal control: modifications in audit program based on evaluation
Internal control: in an EDP environment
Audit evidence: relative strength of types
Legal responsibilities of auditors: under the securities acts
Standard short-form audit report
Modifications of the standard short-form audit report
Audit evidence: post-statement events
Generally accepted auditing standards (GAAS)

Clearly, financial accounting respondents consider *internal control* and *audit evidence* to be the most important auditing topics. This is consistent with the views of all respondents combined, as indicated in Exhibit 3-1. Of the topics listed above, perhaps the only one which receives less emphasis than that indicated as necessary by financial accounting respondents is *legal responsibilities of auditors under the securities acts.* The rest of the listed topics all appear to receive substantial attention in existing curricula.

A topic which has historically been the subject of much debate is *auditing procedures: audit practice case.* The importance mean for financial accounting respondents for this topic was 2.15, which when used in computing the confidence interval was sufficiently high to include the topic in the area core. However, the relatively low importance mean appears to indicate only a fairly minimal emphasis. Also included in the area core, albeit at relatively low levels, are the topics of *operational auditing objectives* (2.28), *operational auditing: methodology* (2.09) and *SEC filing requirements* (2.24).

Taxation Topics

The financial accounting respondents ranked the following tax topics as most important (listed in order of decreasing importance):

Fundamentals of Federal income tax determination
Capital gains and losses
Non-taxable exchange
Tax planning
Recognition of tax opportunities

The high ranking of these topics is generally consistent with the typical tax background of accounting graduates not specializing in taxation. Perhaps *tax planning* and *recognition of tax opportunities* are not currently emphasized quite as heavily as they should be according to financial accounting respondents. It is obvious that *fundamentals of Federal income tax determination* (importance mean of 3.41) is considered very important by financial accounting respondents.

Also, five of the *complex tax provisions* topics excluded from the common core are included in the financial accounting area core. With one exception, *corporation and shareholders* (mean of 2.61), these topics are scaled very close to the cut-off criterion. The remaining four complex tax provision topics included in the area core are *individuals, consolidated corporate returns, partners and partnerships,* and *subchapter S.* This implies that financial accounting graduates should have some knowledge of these topics.

Educators vs. Practitioners

Questionnaire topics are rank-ordered according to mean importance responses of financial accounting educators and financial accounting practitioners in Appendices 6A and 6B, respectively. The same notation and symbolism is used in these appendices as was used in prior rank-orderings.

From an overall standpoint, financial accounting educators tended to scale topics more highly with respect to importance than did financial accounting practitioners. The overall mean importance response was 2.61 for financial accounting educators and 2.45 for financial accounting practitioners.

Significant differences (at the .05 level) between educator and practitioner mean importance responses occurred for 90 (53.6 percent) of the financial accounting area core topics. These topics were identified in Exhibit 6-1 by the symbol "#" preceding the mean importance response of educators and practitioners combined. Included in the 90 topics were 24 (40.0 percent) of the financial accounting topics in the area core, 30 (69.8 percent) of the managerial accounting topics in the area core, 27 (60.0 percent) of the auditing topics in the area core and nine (45.0 percent) of the taxation topics in the area core.

As one would expect, in practically all cases where significant differences existed between educator and practitioner mean importance responses, the educator mean was higher than the practitioner mean. The practitioner mean exceeded the educator mean for only the following four area core topics (out of the 90 on which significant differences were found):

Foreign currency translation
Interim reporting
Business combinations: consolidation procedures
Complex tax provisions: consolidated corporate returns

Conceptual Knowledge and Technical Ability Analysis

The conceptual knowledge and technical ability mean responses, computed on financial accounting respondents, are included in Exhibit 6-1. The mean responses for financial accounting educators and financial accounting practitioners are presented in Appendices 6A and 6B, respectively. As indicated previously, it is not enough to deterine how important the various topics are. We also need to know what type of coverage is deemed desirable. The two educational objectives assist us in making this assessment.

Financial accounting respondents scaled conceptual knowledge higher than technical ability for all but four area core topics. The four exceptions, all taxation topics, were:

	Mean	
	Conceptual Knowledge	Technical Ability
Tax returns and accompanying schedules	1.85	1.96
Complex tax provisions: individuals	1.79	1.90
Complex tax provisions: partners and partnerships	1.63	1.88
Complex tax provisions: subchapter S	1.63	1.77

The overall mean conceptual knowledge response (over all 197 topics) was 2.52 for financial accounting respondents. The overall mean technical ability response was 2.01. Thus, it is apparent that the financial accounting respondents, as a group, feel that conceptual knowledge should receive greater emphasis than technical ability.

Educators vs. Practitioners

In general, financial accounting educators scaled topics more highly on conceptual knowledge than did their practitioner counterparts. The overall mean conceptual knowledge response was 2.69 for financial accounting educators and 2.41 for financial accounting practitioners. However, the practitioner conceptual knowledge mean exceeded the educator conceptual knowledge mean on 35 (20.8 percent) of the 168 financial accounting area core topics, as presented in Exhibit 6-4.

EXHIBIT 6-4

**FINANCIAL ACCOUNTING AREA CORE TOPICS FOR WHICH
PRACTITIONER CONCEPTUAL KNOWLEDGE MEAN EXCEEDS
EDUCATOR CONCEPTUAL KNOWLEDGE MEAN**

Topic	Conceptual Knowledge Mean	
	Educators	Practitioners
Internal accounting standards	2.18	2.53
SEC reporting	2.63	2.93
Installment sales	2.52	2.58
Error corrections	2.94	2.95
Statements from incomplete records	2.54	2.59
Minority interest	2.86	3.01
Partnership financial statements	2.35	2.43
Interim reporting	2.90	2.96
Contingencies	2.92	3.12
Fund accounting: colleges and universities	2.02	2.10
Spoilage, waste, defective units and scrap	2.41	2.49
Cash management	2.65	2.71
Budgeted financial statements	2.78	2.83
Management information systems: implementation	2.07	2.44
Management information systems: administration	1.93	2.30
Performance evaluation: non-statistical variance analysis	2.54	2.62
Requirements for professional certification (CPA)	2.30	2.39
Internal control: principles	3.11	3.16
Internal control: description based on narrative	2.55	2.81
Internal control: description based on questionnaire	2.54	2.59
Internal control: audit exposure due to weaknesses	2.90	3.01
Internal control: in an EDP environment	2.83	2.96
Auditing procedures: audit practice case	2.00	2.14
Audit administration: planning	2.24	2.41
Audit administration: supervision	2.07	2.19
Audit administration: review	2.33	2.49
Accumulated earnings tax	2.06	2.56
Administrative processes in tax matters	1.97	2.18
Fundamentals of Federal income tax determination	3.02	3.15
Judicial doctrines in tax disputes	1.82	2.33
Complex tax provisions: corporations and shareholders	2.13	2.54
Recognition of tax opportunities	2.49	2.80
Social security taxes	1.82	2.05
Taxation of deferred compensation	2.18	2.22
State and local taxes	1.73	2.30

Also, the practitioner mean exceeded the educator mean on conceptual knowledge for 13 (44.8 percent) of the 29 non-core topics.

Financial accounting educators also generally scaled topics more highly on technical ability than did their practitioner counterparts. The overall mean for educators was 2.22 and that for practitioners was 1.87 on the technical ability scale. The practitioner mean exceeded the educator mean on technical ability for only 27 (16.1 percent) of the 168 financial accounting area core topics, as presented in Exhibit 6-5.

EXHIBIT 6-5

FINANCIAL ACCOUNTING AREA CORE TOPICS FOR WHICH
PRACTITIONER TECHNICAL ABILITY MEAN EXCEEDS EDUCATOR
TECHNICAL ABILITY MEAN

| | Conceptual Knowledge Mean | |
Topic	Educators	Practitioners
Regulatory influences	2.57	2.65
International accounting standards	1.46	2.02
Foreign currency translation	1.98	2.34
Behavioral considerations in financial reporting	1.49	1.94
SEC reporting	2.00	2.59
Minority interest	2.36	2.39
Interim reporting	2.38	2.64
Contingencies	2.38	2.67
Materiality	2.46	2.55
Development stage companies	1.84	2.07
Reporting forecasts	1.94	2.07
Full costing vs. successful effort costing	1.87	1.91
Fund accounting: types of organizations	1.70	2.00
Fund accounting: hospitals	1.60	1.65
Fund accounting: colleges and universities	1.50	1.71
National income accounting	1.27	1.79
Zero base budgeting	1.79	2.00
Long-range planning	2.24	2.30
Management information systems: implementation	1.70	1.99
Management information systems: administration	1.57	2.00
Performance evaluation: non-statistical variance analysis	2.07	2.08
Requirements for professional certification (CPA)	1.84	2.15
Internal control: description based on flowchart	2.33	2.35
Audit evidence: post-statement events	2.66	2.82
Complex tax provisions: subchapter S	1.68	1.82
Complex tax provisions: partners and partnerships	1.66	2.04
State and local taxes	1.48	1.67

The mean practitioner response was also greater than the mean educator response on technical ability for 10 (34.5 percent) of the 29 non-core topics.

7

Auditing

Introduction

This chapter consists of various analyses based upon the responses of individuals identifying auditing as their primary area of specialization. The breakdown of auditing respondents was as follows:

Educators		13
Practitioners:		
Public Accounting	52	
Industry	58	110
Total		123

In the following section a rank-ordering of the 197 questionnaire topics based upon the mean importance responses of the auditing sample is presented, which includes identification of the auditing area core. Following some general observations regarding the rank-ordering results, a more detailed analysis of auditing responses is presented in the last section of the chapter.

The Auditing Area Core

In Exhibit 7-1, the 197 questionnaire topics are rank-ordered according to the mean importance responses of auditing respondents. Those topics preceded by the symbol "*" are not in the auditing area core. The symbol "#" preceding the importance mean for a topic indicates that the mean importance responses of auditing educators and auditing practitioners differed significantly (at the .05 level) on that topic. Conceptual knowledge and technical ability mean responses are included as a basis for subsequent discussion. The questionnaire section in which each topic was presented is indicated by the letter preceding the topic.

EXHIBIT 7-1

RANK ORDERING BY IMPORTANCE MEANS:
AUDITING RESPONDENTS

| | | | Means | |
| | | | Conceptual | Technical |
Area	Topic	Importance	Knowledge	Ability
A	Internal control: principles	3.74	3.58	3.26
A	Generally accepted auditing standards (GAAS)	3.68	3.65	3.28
A	Internal control: relationship of GAAS	3.67	3.54	3.12
F	Income statement	3.64	3.52	3.23
F	Balance sheet	3.61	3.47	3.17
A	Internal control: evaluation	3.59	3.51	2.87
F	U.S. financial accounting and reporting standards	3.58	3.17	2.85
A	Internal control: modifications in audit program based on evaluation	3.55	3.41	2.86
M	Management information systems: internal control aspects	3.54	3.41	2.93
A	Audit evidence: types	3.52	3.45	3.00
A	Internal control: audit exposure due to weaknesses	3.49	3.41	2.90
F	Statement of changes in financial position	3.48	3.33	3.03
F	Revenue and expense recognition	#3.45	3.55	2.95
F	Transaction analysis	3.44	3.40	3.25
A	Internal control: in an EDP environment	3.43	3.33	2.78
F	Double-entry system	3.41	3.26	3.38
A	Audit evidence: relative strength of types	3.40	3.35	2.94
F	Accruals and deferrals	3.40	3.38	3.32
F	Inventories	3.39	3.33	3.09
F	Theoretical framework: current structure	#3.38	3.24	2.58
A	Statistical inference in auditing: statisical sampling	#3.35	3.20	2.86
F	Regulatory influences	3.33	3.03	2.37
F	Materiality	#3.28	3.25	2.58
A	Professional rules of conduct	3.26	3.19	2.65
A	Auditing procedures: tests of transactions	3.25	3.19	2.84
A	Standard short-form audit report	#3.24	3.25	2.90
T	Fundamentals of Federal income tax determination	3.24	3.05	2.53
A	Modifications of standard short-form audit report	#3.23	3.25	2.88
A	Influence of professional and regulatory bodies upon auditing	3.19	3.09	2.09
A	Auditing procedures: tests of account balances	3.19	3.14	2.84
F	Receivables	3.19	3.16	2.95
F	Financial statement analysis	3.18	3.04	2.62
A	Audit evidence: post-statement events	#3.16	3.13	2.59

EXHIBIT 7-1
(continued)

Area	Topic	Importance	Conceptual Knowledge	Technical Ability
			Means	
A	Internal control: description based on flowchart	3.14	3.03	2.77
A	Auditing procedures: review of operations	3.14	3.13	2.64
A	Auditing procedures: compliance tests	3.13	3.13	2.80
A	Statistical inference in auditing: judgmental sampling	3.09	3.12	2.75
F	Long-term liabilities	3.03	3.05	2.78
A	Auditing procedures: working papers	#3.01	2.88	2.51
F	Business combinations: consolidation procedures	2.98	2.97	2.64
F	Cash	2.97	2.95	2.91
F	Depreciation, depletion and amortization	2.97	3.04	2.82
F	Accounting for income taxes	#2.97	2.98	2.59
F	Fixed assets	2.95	3.00	2.79
F	Contingencies	2.95	2.92	2.40
A	Internal control: description based on narrative	2.94	2.93	2.68
F	Short-term liabilities	2.94	2.98	2.71
A	User's expectations regarding the auditor's role	2.93	2.97	1.45
F	Information needs of financial statement users	#2.92	2.79	1.70
F	Deferred taxes	#2.91	2.95	2.51
M	Standard costs	2.89	3.02	2.45
F	Investments in securities	2.86	2.89	2.68
F	Leases	#2.85	2.83	2.38
A	Internal control: description based on questionnaire	2.81	2.75	2.38
M	Accounting information requirements for management decisions	2.81	2.72	2.03
A	Legal responsibilities of auditors: under securities acts	#2.80	2.79	2.04
T	Capital gains and losses	#2.79	2.57	2.23
A	Legal responsibilities of auditors: at common law	#2.78	2.85	2.01
F	Corporate equity	#2.76	2.85	2.47
M	Computer science	2.73	2.64	2.02
M	Full costing	2.73	2.77	2.26
M	Management information systems: impact of external regulatory influences	2.73	2.56	1.89
F	Present value and future worth concepts	2.70	2.85	2.31
F	Business combinations: purchase vs. pooling of interests	2.69	2.80	2.20
F	Earnings-per-share	2.69	2.73	2.34
M	Job order costing	2.68	2.79	2.15
M	Tax considerations in managerial decisions	2.68	2.71	1.95

EXHIBIT 7-1
(continued)

| | | | Means | |
| | | | Conceptual | Technical |
Area	Topic	Importance	Knowledge	Ability
F	Business combinations: unconsolidated subsidiaries	2.68	2.75	2.38
F	Theoretical framework: alternatives to current structure	2.67	2.81	1.88
F	Goodwill	#2.66	2.75	2.31
M	Process costing	#2.66	2.76	2.15
M	Internal financial auditing	2.66	2.59	2.08
F	Intangibles (excluding goodwill)	#2.65	2.75	2.34
F	Interim reporting	2.63	2.68	2.08
A	Requirements for professional certification (CPA)	2.61	2.55	2.16
F	Pensions	2.60	2.51	2.16
A	Operational auditing: objectives	#2.57	2.59	1.72
F	Error corrections	2.54	2.61	2.64
M	Cost-volume-profit analysis	2.53	2.59	2.02
M	Internal operational auditing	#2.53	2.56	1.89
M	Variable costing	#2.52	2.72	2.07
T	Tax planning	#2.52	2.37	1.57
F	Convertible debt or equity	#2.52	2.58	2.32
A	Extensions of the attest function: possible areas	2.51	2.53	1.51
A	Audit administration: review	2.49	2.46	1.78
A	Legal responsibilities of auditors: exposure to criminal liability	#2.49	2.49	1.80
A	Management letter	#2.48	2.64	2.00
A	Extensions of the attest function: associated audit risk	2.48	2.53	1.51
M	Overhead control	2.47	2.39	1.81
A	Legal responsibilities of auditors: responses of the auditing profession to classic cases	#2.46	2.45	1.59
M	Cash management	2.45	2.41	1.77
T	Recognition of tax opportunities	#2.44	2.43	1.68
F	Minority interest	#2.44	2.61	2.28
M	Direct costing	#2.43	2.69	2.05
A	Legal responsibilities of auditors: classic cases	#2.40	2.45	1.59
A	Long-form audit report	2.39	2.42	1.82
A	Operational auditing: methodology	2.38	2.42	1.68
F	Treasury stock	2.37	2.39	2.26
F	SEC reporting	2.36	2.37	1.78
A	Audit administration: client relations	#2.36	2.39	1.64
M	Spoilage, waste, defective units and scrap	2.34	2.50	1.97
M	Capital budgeting	#2.34	2.50	1.97
A	Audit administration: planning	2.32	2.49	1.66

EXHIBIT 7-1
(continued)

Area	Topic	Importance	Conceptual Knowledge	Technical Ability
			Means	
M	Flexible budgets	2.31	2.37	1.67
M	Management information systems: design	#2.29	2.26	1.63
M	Budgeted financial statements	2.28	2.34	1.67
M	Joint costs	#2.26	2.46	1.80
M	Short-range planning	#2.26	2.37	1.62
F	Price-level adjusted financial statements	#2.26	2.59	1.77
A	SEC filing requirements	2.26	2.38	1.75
F	Installment sales	2.26	2.45	2.09
F	Segment reporting	2.23	2.30	1.82
T	Tax returns and accompanying schedules	2.23	2.00	1.82
M	Performance evaluation: return on investment	2.22	2.41	1.87
F	Research and development costs	2.20	2.38	1.83
M	Organization theory	2.20	2.16	1.43
A	Audit administration: supervision	2.19	2.24	1.53
T	Non-taxable exchanges	2.18	2.08	1.78
A	Statistical inference in auditing: regression analysis	2.17	2.30	1.80
M	Long-range planning	2.16	2.34	1.51
T	Complex tax provisions: corporations and shareholders	2.15	2.08	1.51
F	Statements from incomplete records	2.14	2.17	2.06
M	Performance evaluation: responsibility accounting	2.11	2.33	1.63
A	Statistical inference in auditing: other statistical methods	2.11	2.27	1.85
A	*Auditing procedures: audit practice case	2.10	2.00	1.92
F	Consignments	2.09	2.38	2.00
M	Performance evaluation: divisional performance	2.08	2.20	1.67
T	Complex tax provisions: individuals	2.08	2.00	1.73
M	Management information systems: implementation	2.08	2.05	1.47
M	Statistical decision theory	2.03	2.14	1.45
T	Complex tax provisions: consolidated corporate returns	2.02	2.05	1.40
T	*State and local taxes	2.00	1.98	1.54
F	Partnership financial statements	1.98	2.22	1.95
M	Performance evaluation: transfer pricing	#1.98	2.17	1.55
T	Tax research methodology	#1.95	1.87	1.40
M	Performance evaluation: common costs	1.95	2.08	1.46
M	Information economics	1.93	1.95	1.24
T	Taxation of deferred compensation	1.93	1.90	1.46
M	Statistical analysis of cost variances	1.93	2.02	1.48
F	Reporting forecasts	1.91	2.22	1.41

EXHIBIT 7-1
(continued)

Area	Topic	Importance	Conceptual Knowledge	Technical Ability
M	Management information systems: administration	1.90	1.89	1.34
M	Behavioral considerations	1.84	1.87	1.07
T	Accumulated earnings tax	1.81	1.88	1.18
F	Foreign currency translation	1.80	2.02	1.58
F	Fund accounting: financial statements	1.80	1.94	1.48
M	*Performance evaluation: non-statistical variance analysis	1.78	2.06	1.44
F	*Fund accounting: governmental units	1.78	1.84	1.39
T	Complex tax provisions: partners and partnerships	1.77	1.72	1.43
F	*Full costing vs. successful effort costing	1.76	2.14	1.49
F	*Fund accounting: types of organizations	1.76	1.85	1.32
M	*Statistical cost estimation	1.76	1.89	1.39
M	*Zero base budgeting	1.75	1.93	1.26
A	*Special considerations in auditing not-for-profit organizations	1.72	1.94	1.18
M	Special considerations in non-manufacturing concerns	1.71	1.88	1.31
T	*Complex tax provisions: subchapter S	1.69	1.63	1.22
T	*Complex tax provisions: foreign tax credit	1.67	1.64	1.14
M	*Simulation	1.65	1.87	1.06
A	*Audit administration: accounting firm organization	1.64	1.63	.96
M	*Corporate planning models	1.62	1.71	1.07
F	*Regulated industries	1.62	1.80	1.11
M	*Performance evaluation: residual income	1.61	1.81	1.13
A	*Historical development of auditing	1.59	1.72	.75
M	*Performance evaluation: non-financial performance measures	1.84	1.59	1.14
M	*Sensitivity analysis	1.57	1.77	1.02
M	*Network methods	1.56	1.74	1.00
F	*Fund accounting: hospitals	1.55	1.73	1.29
T	*Administrative processes in tax matters	1.54	1.58	1.07
T	*Social security taxes	1.54	1.55	1.27
F	*Behavioral considerations in financial reporting	1.53	1.69	.93
T	*Taxation for international operations	1.52	1.53	.97
F	*Fund accounting: colleges and universities	1.48	1.68	1.24
T	*Complex tax provisions: DISC	1.47	1.59	1.00
T	*Theoretical framework of taxation: economic and social concepts	1.47	1.58	.75
M	*Linear programming	1.46	1.75	1.05
F	*International accounting standards	1.45	1.53	.91
M	*Learning curve models	1.44	1.66	1.02

EXHIBIT 7-1
(continued)

Area	Topic	Importance	Conceptual Knowledge	Technical Ability
			Means	
F	*Development stage companies	1.43	1.65	1.06
M	*Social accounting	1.40	1.54	.72
F	*Fiduciary accounting: estates and trusts	1.38	1.81	1.33
T	*Theoretical framework of taxation: alternatives to present framework	1.38	1.53	.75
F	*Fiduciary accounting: bankruptcy	1.37	1.79	1.27
T	*Federal gift tax	1.36	1.45	1.07
T	*Federal estate tax	1.34	1.48	1.07
M	*Planning and control of international operations	1.33	1.44	.86
F	*Fiduciary accounting: receivership	1.32	1.76	1.25
A	*Audit administration: setting and collecting fees	1.32	1.31	.76
T	*Natural resource taxation	1.28	1.27	.87
T	*Judicial processes in tax disputes	1.25	1.34	.88
T	*Complex tax provisions: fiduciaries	1.24	1.23	.93
T	*Personal holding company tax	1.24	1.35	.88
A	*Comparative accounting and auditing standards among nations	1.22	1.35	.72
T	*Judicial doctrines in tax disputes	1.20	1.40	.80
F	*National income accounting	1.19	1.44	.71
T	*Tax practice procedures	1.19	1.21	.95
M	*Requirements for professional certification (CMA)	1.12	1.24	.81
F	*Human resource accounting	1.11	1.31	.71
T	*Preparation of tax communications	1.09	1.14	.80

* ➝ non-area core topics

\# ➝ significant difference (p < .05) between education and practitioner mean importance responses

The auditing area core includes 145 (73.6 percent) of the 197 questionnaire topics. Thus, in addition to the 105 common accounting core topics, an additional 40 topics met the cut-off criterion with regard to auditing educators and auditing practitioners. These 40 topics, rank-ordered by decreasing importance means of auditing respondents, are presented in Exhibit 7-2.

EXHIBIT 7-2

**AUDITING AREA CORE
TOPICS NOT IN COMMON CORE**

Area	Topic	Importance Mean
A	Internal control: relationship of GAAS	3.67
A	Professional rules of conduct	3.26
A	Auditing procedures: working papers	3.01
A	Legal responsibilities of auditors: at common law	2.78
F	Corporate equity	2.76
M	Computer science	2.73
M	Management information systems: impact of external regulatory influences	2.73
F	Earnings-per-share	2.69
F	Business combinations: unconsolidated subsidiaries	2.68
F	Goodwill	2.66
M	Internal financial auditing	2.66
A	Requirements for professional certification (CPA)	2.61
F	Pensions	2.60
A	Operational auditing: objectives	2.57
A	Internal operational auditing	2.53
A	Extension of the attest function: possible areas	2.51
M	Overhead control	2.47
A	Legal responsibilities of auditors: responses of the auditing profession to classic cases	2.46
M	Direct costing	2.43
A	Operational auditing: methodology	2.38
A	Audit administration: client relations	2.36
M	Management information system: design	2.29
A	SEC filing requirements	2.26
F	Segment reporting	2.23
T	Tax returns and accompanying schedule	2.23
T	Complex tax provisions: corporations and shareholders	2.15
F	Consignments	2.09
T	Complex tax provisions: individuals	2.08
M	Statistical decision theory	2.03
T	Complex tax provisions: consolidated corporate returns	2.02
F	Partnership financial statements	1.98
M	Performance evaluation: transfer pricing	1.98
T	Tax research methodology	1.95
M	Performance evaluation: common costs	1.95
M	Management information systems: administration	1.90
M	Behavioral considerations	1.84
T	Accumulated earnings tax	1.81
F	Foreign currency translation	1.80
T	Complex tax provisions: partners and partnerships	1.77
M	Special considerations in non-manufacturing concerns	1.71

Thus, given our cut-off criterion, the implication is that students preparing to enter an auditing career should have some exposure to 145 of the 197 questionnaire topics.

In terms of the questionnaire section in which topics were presented, the auditing core was made up as follows:

Questionnaire Section	Total Number of Topics	Number in Area Core	% in Area Core
Financial	65	51	78.5%
Managerial	51	37	72.5%
Auditing	50	44	88.0%
Taxation	31	13	41.9%
Total	197	145	

Fifty-two of the 197 questionnaire topics were excluded from the auditing area core. These topics are presented in Exhibit 7-3, along with an indication of the group(s) responsible for their exclusion (E for educators, P for practitioners). The topics are listed by questionnaire section in order of decreasing importance means.

EXHIBIT 7-3

TOPICS EXCLUDED FROM AUDITING AREA CORE

Topic	Importance Mean	Excluded by
FINANCIAL:		
Fund accounting: governmental units	1.78	P
Full costing vs. successful efforts costing	1.76	P
Fund accounting: types of organizations	1.76	P
Regulated industries	1.62	E,P
Fund accounting: hospitals	1.55	E,P
Behavioral considerations in financial reporting	1.53	P
Fund accounting: colleges and universities	1.48	E,P
International accounting standards	1.45	E,P
Development stage companies	1.43	E,P
Fiduciary accounting: estates and trusts	1.38	E,P
Fiduciary accounting: bankruptcy	1.37	E,P
Fiduciary accounting: receiverships	1.32	E,P
National income accounting	1.19	E,P
Human resources accounting	1.11	E,P

EXHIBIT 7-3
(continued)

Topic	Importance Mean	Excluded by
MANAGERIAL:		
Performance evaluation: non-statistical variance analysis	1.78	P
Statistical cost estimation	1.76	P
Zero base budgeting	1.75	P
Simulation	1.65	P
Corporate planning models	1.62	P
Performance evaluation: residual income	1.61	P
Performance evaluation: non-financial performance measures	1.59	P
Sensitivity analysis	1.57	P
Network methods	1.56	E,P
Linear programming	1.46	E,P
Learning curve models	1.44	E,P
Social accounting	1.40	P
Planning and control of international operations	1.33	E,P
Requirements for professional certification (CMA)	1.12	E,P
AUDITING:		
Auditing procedures: audit practice case	2.10	E
Special considerations in auditing not-for-profit organizations	1.72	P
Audit administration: accounting firm organization	1.64	E,P
Historical development of auditing	1.59	E,P
Audit administration: setting and collecting fees	1.32	E,P
Comparative accounting and auditing standards among nations	1.22	E,P
TAXATION:		
State and local taxes	2.00	E
Complex tax provisions: subchapter S	2.69	E,P
Complex tax provisions: foreign tax credit	1.67	E,P
Administrative processes in tax matters	1.54	E,P
Social security taxes	1.54	P
Taxation for international operations	1.52	E,P
Complex tax provisions: DISC	1.47	E,P
Theoretical framework of taxation: economic and social concepts	1.47	P
Theoretical framework of taxation: alternatives to present framework	1.38	P
Federal gift tax	1.36	E,P
Federal estate tax	1.34	E,P
Natural resource taxation	1.28	E,P
Judicial processes in tax disputes	1.25	E,P
Complex tax provisions: fiduciaries	1.24	E,P
Personal holding company tax	1.24	E,P
Judicial doctrines in tax disputes	1.20	E,P
Tax practice procedures	1.19	E,P
Preparation of tax communications	1.09	E,P

Looking at the financial accounting topics excluded from the auditing area core, we see that auditing practitioners scaled all 14 of these topics sufficiently low to exclude them, while auditing educators scaled 10 of the 14 sufficiently low. Likewise, auditing practitioners scaled all 14 of the managerial topics excluded sufficiently low to exclude them, five of the six excluded auditing topics and 17 of the 18 excluded taxation topics. Except in the managerial accounting section, educators and practitioners seem to be in substantial agreement with respect to the low-ranking topics. In the managerial accounting area, however, educators attach more importance to the excluded topics, many of which are quantitative topics, than do practitioners.

Analysis of Auditing Area Core

IMPORTANCE ANALYSIS

Financial Accounting Topics

As is apparent by scanning Exhibit 7-1, auditing respondents considered the following financial accounting topics to be most important (listed in order of decreasing importance means):

Income statement
Balance sheet
U.S. financial accounting and reporting standards
Statement of changes in financial position
Revenue and expense recognition
Transaction analysis
Double-entry system
Accruals and deferrals
Inventories
Theoretical framework: current structure
Regulatory influences
Materiality

There are no particular surprises in this list, since it is quite similar to the comparable list based upon all respondents combined (see Chapter 3). It does appear that auditing respondents consider the topics *inventories* and *materiality* to be slightly more important relative to other financial accounting topics than do all respondents combined. On the other hand, auditing respondents scaled the topics *deferred taxes* and *information needs of financial statements users* lower relative to other financial accounting topics than did all respondents combined. With the possible exceptions of *regulatory influences* and *materiality,* these most important financial accounting topics appear to receive a substantial amount of attention in most existing curricula.

At the other end of the spectrum are the 14 financial accounting topics excluded from the auditing area core (see Exhibit 7-3). Most accounting graduates appear to receive some exposure to the various *fund accounting* and *fiduciary ac-*

counting topics, even though auditing respondents attach only minimal importance to such topics. The other excluded topics do not currently receive any appreciable attention in accounting curricula.

Most of the 39 financial accounting topics falling in between the most-important and the excluded topics are in the upper and middle portion of Exhibit 7-1, indicating the substantial importance attached to financial accounting topics as a group by auditing respondents. Auditing respondents seem to attach more importance to the topics *financial statement analysis, accounting for income taxes, contingencies, information needs of financial statement users, interim reporting, SEC reporting, segment reporting, research and development costs,* and *reporting forecasts* than that currently reflected in accounting curricula. The importance attached to the remaining financial accounting topics by auditing respondents does not appear to depart significantly from existing educational practices.

Managerial Accounting Topics

Auditing respondents considered the following managerial accounting topics to be most important in preparing an individual to enter a career in auditing (listed in order of decreasing importance means):

> Management information systems: internal control aspects
> Standard costs
> Accounting information requirements for management decisions
> Computer science
> Full costing
> Management information systems: impact of external regulatory influences
> Job order costing
> Tax considerations in managerial decisions
> Process costing
> Internal financial auditing

Only the first of these topics is in the very upper portion of the rank-ordering (nine out of 197). Managerial accounting topics, as a group, were scaled lower with respect to importance, by auditing respondents, than were financial accounting and auditing topics.

Included in this list of most-important managerial accounting topics are some topics which are typically well-covered in a basic managerial accounting course, *i.e., standard costs, full costing, job order costing* and *process costing.* Likewise, accounting graduates usually have a reasonably good background in computer science. However, unless students judiciously select elective courses, they may receive inadequate background in preparation for an auditing career in the two *management information systems* topics listed, *accounting information requirements for management decisions, tax considerations in managerial decisions* and *internal financial auditing.*

Fourteen managerial accounting topics were excluded from the auditing area core (see Exhibit 7-3). Seven of these 14 topics are quantitative techniques. The topics excluded do not appear currently to receive significant coverage in accounting curricula, unless a student chooses to take one or more advanced electives in the managerial accounting area.

Looking at the managerial accounting topics in between those identified as most important and those excluded from the auditing area core, we see some apparent inconsistencies between the importance responses of auditors and current emphasis in accounting curricula. The topic *internal operational auditing* is considered much more important by auditing respondents than that reflected in currently popular textbooks. Also, unless a student takes a systems course, it is likely that background preparation in the systems topics of *design, implementation* and *administration* will be inadequate in the views of auditing respondents. In general, however, importance responses of auditors seem to be pretty much in accord with existing emphasis in accounting curricula.

Auditing Topics

Auditing respondents considered the following auditing topics to be most important in preparing an individual to begin an auditing career (listed in order of decreasing importance means):

Internal control: principles
Generally accepted auditing standards (GAAS)
Internal control: relationship of GAAS
Internal control: evaluation
Internal control: modifications in audit program based on evaluation
Audit evidence: types
Internal control: audit exposure due to weaknesses
Internal control: in an EDP environment
Audit evidence: relative strength of types
Statistical inference in auditing: statistical sampling

Naturally, these topics were also among the most important considering all topics. In general, the auditing topics dominated the upper part of the rank ordering.

It is interesting to note that auditing respondents considered the same topic, *internal control: principles,* to be the most important auditing topic as did all respondents combined (see Chapter 3). Likewise, the internal control topics dominated the most important auditing topics lists of both auditing respondents and all respondents combined.

Six auditing topics were excluded from the auditing area core, perhaps the most noteworthy being *auditing procedures: audit practice case.* The value of taking students through an audit practice case has been the subject of continuing debate for many years. Given our cut-off criterion, auditing educators do not attach enough importance to the topic to warrant including it in the auditing area core. The other five excluded topics do not appear to receive significant attention in existing curricula.

In addition to the 10 auditing topics included in the most-important list, several other auditing topics were scaled relatively high with respect to importance. In general, these topics appear to receive substantial emphasis, as desired by auditing respondents, in existing curricula. However, the topics *influence of professional and regulatory bodies upon auditing, users' expectations regarding the auditor's role, legal responsibilities of auditors: under securities acts* and *legal responsibilities of auditors: at common law* may receive less emphasis currently than that indicated as desirable by auditing respondents. Other auditing topics which appear to be scaled relatively high compared to the existing emphasis are *operational auditing: objectives, extensions of the attest function: possible areas, audit administration: review, extensions of the attest function: associated audit risk* and *operational auditing: methodology.*

Taxation Topics

Taxation topics considered most important by auditing respondents were as follows (listed in order of decreasing importance means):

Fundamentals of Federal income tax determination
Capital gains and losses
Tax planning
Recognition of tax opportunities

Only the first topic was anywhere near the top in the rank-ordering on importance means (Exhibit 7-1). Taxation topics, in general, were located in the middle and bottom portion of the rank-ordering based on the responses of auditors. The four topics listed above were also considered by all respondents to be the most important taxation topics (see Chapter 3).

As indicated in Exhibit 7-3, 18 taxation topics were excluded from the auditing area core. It is not likely that an accounting student would receive significant exposure to any of these topics unless the student elected to take one or more advanced courses in taxation.

The other nine taxation topics (excluding the 18 not qualifying for the auditing area core and the four identified as most important) are in the auditing area core but at a relatively low level of importance. This appears to be consistent with existing curricula for accounting graduates not emphasizing taxation.

Educators vs. Practitioners

The 197 questionnaire topics are rank-ordered by the mean importance responses of auditing educators and auditing practitioners in Appendices 7A and 7B, respectively. Topics for which there was a significant difference between educator and practitioner mean importance responses were identified in Exhibit 7-1 by the "#" preceding the importance mean.

Significant differences (at the .05 level) between educator and practitioner mean importance responses existed for 39 (26.9 percent) of the 145 auditing area core topics. Composing the 39 topics were 13 (25.5 percent) of the 51 financial accounting topics in the area core, eight (21.6 percent) of the 37 managerial accounting topics in the area core, 14 (31.8 percent) of the 44 auditing topics in the area core and four (30.1 percent) of the 13 taxation topics in the area core. Thus, a larger proportion of significant differences occurred for auditing topics than for any other area.

The overall mean importance response of auditing educators (over all 197 topics) was 2.47, while that for auditing practitioners was 2.33. Thus, one would expect the educator importance mean to exceed the practitioner importance mean for most topics, including most of those for which significant differences exist. Such was indeed the case, as the practitioner mean exceeded the educator mean for only the following seven of the 39 topics for which significant differences existed:

Materiality
Legal responsibilities of auditors: classic cases
Auditing procedures: working papers
Management letter
Audit administration: client relations
Operational auditing: methodology
Recognition of tax opportunities

CONCEPTUAL KNOWLEDGE AND TECHNICAL ABILITY ANALYSIS
The conceptual knowledge and technical ability mean responses for all auditing respondents were included in Exhibit 7-1. Almost invariably auditing respondents placed more emphasis upon conceptual knowledge than upon technical ability. The overall conceptual knowledge mean response for auditors was 2.41, while their overall technical ability mean response was only 1.87. The only two topics for which the technical ability mean exceeded the conceptual knowledge mean for auditing respondents were *double-entry system* and *error corrections*.

Educators vs. Practitioners
On an overall basis, auditing educators and auditing practitioners placed virtually the same emphasis upon conceptual knowledge. The overall mean conceptual knowledge response for auditing educators was 2.38 and the overall mean for auditing practitioners was 2.41. Educator mean conceptual knowledge responses exceeded practitioner mean conceptual knowledge responses for 90 (45.7 percent) of the 197 questionnaire topics.

With respect to technical ability, auditing educators tended to scale topics more highly than did auditing practitioners. The overall auditing educator mean on technical ability was 1.96, while the overall auditing practitioner mean was 1.85. However, the practitioner mean did exceed the educator mean on technical ability for 76, a significant minority, of the 197 questionnaire topics. Included in these 76 topics were 33 auditing topics, which implies that, even though on an overall basis educators place more emphasis on technical ability than do practitioners, practitioners place more emphasis upon technical ability with respect to auditing topics than do educators.

EXHIBIT 8-1
(continued)

Area	Topic	Importance	Conceptual Knowledge	Technical Ability
			Means	
A	Statistical inference in auditing: statistical sampling	#3.05	3.13	2.50
F	Corporate equity	3.05	3.12	2.63
A	Legal responsibilities of auditors: at common law	#3.03	3.05	2.29
T	Capital gains and losses	3.03	2.76	2.68
M	Management information systems: internal control aspects	3.02	2.90	2.35
F	Earnings-per-share	3.02	3.05	2.73
F	Accounting for income taxes	3.02	2.93	2.58
F	Present value and future worth concepts	#3.00	3.05	2.61
F	Long-term liabilities	3.00	3.00	2.83
A	Auditing procedures: review of operations	3.00	3.13	2.63
F	Theoretical framework: alternatives to current structure	#2.98	3.12	2.23
M	Cost-volume-profit analysis	#2.98	2.95	2.60
A	Legal responsibilities of auditors: under the securities acts	#2.98	2.97	2.21
T	Tax planning	2.97	2.95	2.46
F	Cash	2.95	2.78	2.90
F	Short-term liabilities	2.95	2.90	2.78
M	Flexible budgets	2.95	2.95	2.50
F	Investments in securities	2.93	2.93	2.71
F	Deferred taxes	2.93	2.95	2.63
M	Performance evaluation: return on investment	#2.93	2.90	2.40
A	Auditing procedure: tests of transactions	#2.93	3.00	2.63
A	Statistical inference in auditing: judgmental sampling	#2.92	3.03	2.43
M	Short-range planning	2.90	2.93	2.35
M	Budgeted financial statements	2.90	2.79	2.46
A	Auditing procedures: compliance tests	#2.90	3.00	2.66
M	Capital budgeting	#2.88	2.98	2.50
A	User's expectations regarding the auditor's role	#2.87	2.97	1.78
A	Auditing procedures: tests of account balances	#2.87	2.97	2.65
M	Tax considerations in managerial decisions	2.85	2.65	2.38
A	Internal control: description based on narrative	2.84	2.83	2.61
M	Computer science	#2.83	2.59	2.13
A	Internal control: description based on flowchart	2.82	2.75	2.47
F	Business combinations: consolidation procedures	#2.81	2.88	2.63
M	Full costing	2.80	2.80	2.43

EXHIBIT 8-1
(continued)

Area	Topic	Importance	Means Conceptual Knowledge	Means Technical Ability
A	Internal control: description based on questionnaire	2.79	2.75	2.44
F	Leases	2.79	2.88	2.46
M	Cash management	2.78	2.60	2.33
F	Goodwill	2.76	2.95	2.40
M	Long-range planning	2.76	2.90	2.15
A	Auditing procedures: working papers	#2.75	2.68	2.53
T	Recognition of tax opportunities	2.73	2.61	2.19
A	Requirements for professional certification (CPA)	2.73	2.59	2.17
F	Contingencies	2.71	2.85	2.25
F	Price-level adjusted financial statements	2.71	2.95	2.23
M	Performance evaluation: responsibility accounting	2.69	2.63	2.13
F	Intangibles (excluding goodwill)	#2.69	2.80	2.34
M	Management information systems: impact of external regulatory influences	2.68	2.50	2.13
M	Variable costing	#2.68	2.78	2.38
F	Convertible debt or equity	2.67	2.73	2.29
A	Management letter	#2.67	2.74	2.08
M	Process costing	2.63	2.65	2.33
M	Overhead control	2.63	2.53	2.28
T	Non-taxable exchanges	2.63	2.53	2.27
M	Direct costing	#2.63	2.80	2.30
A	Legal responsibilities of auditors: exposure to criminal liability	#2.63	2.67	1.97
A	Audit administration: planning	#2.63	2.66	2.05
A	Statistical inference in auditing: regression analysis	2.62	2.72	2.11
F	Business combinations: purchase vs. pooling of interests	2.62	2.78	2.29
T	Tax research methodology	#2.61	2.64	2.27
T	Tax returns and accompanying schedules	2.58	2.22	2.36
A	Legal responsibilities of auditors: classic cases	2.58	2.65	2.00
A	Audit administration: review	#2.58	2.61	2.00
A	Statistical inference in auditing: other statistical methods	#2.57	2.58	2.11
T	Complex tax provisions: individuals	#2.57	2.47	2.31
F	Error corrections	2.55	2.38	2.74
M	Job order costing	2.54	2.55	2.33
A	Long-form audit report	#2.53	2.49	2.22
A	Audit administration: client relations	#2.53	2.32	1.78
F	Pensions	2.52	2.75	2.20
F	Segment reporting	2.51	2.62	2.18

EXHIBIT 8-1
(continued)

Area	Topic	Importance	Conceptual Knowledge	Technical Ability
			Means	
F	Reporting forecasts	2.51	2.87	2.21
F	Minority interests	2.50	2.66	2.15
F	Treasury stock	2.50	2.68	2.29
M	Performance evaluation: divisional performance	#2.50	2.61	2.21
A	Extensions of the attest function: associated audit risk	#2.49	2.57	1.63
F	Interim reporting	#2.48	2.65	2.23
M	Organization theory	2.46	2.59	1.81
F	Business combinations: unconsolidated subsidiaries	2.45	2.68	2.33
A	Extensions of the attest function: possible areas	#2.41	2.51	1.50
M	Joint costs	2.39	2.51	1.86
A	Operational auditing: objectives	2.39	2.61	1.62
M	Performance evaluation: non-statistical variance analysis	#2.39	2.34	1.97
A	Audit administration: supervision	#2.38	2.39	1.86
M	Management information systems: design	2.37	2.56	2.08
M	Performance evaluation: common costs	#2.35	2.31	1.94
T	Complex tax provisions: corporations and shareholders	#2.35	2.51	2.06
A	Legal responsibilities of auditors: responses of the auditing profession to classic cases	#2.33	2.68	1.85
M	Statistical cost estimation	#2.33	2.43	2.00
M	Statistical decision theory	#2.32	2.53	2.00
T	Complex tax provisions: partners and partnerships	#2.32	2.43	2.14
T	Theoretical framework of taxation: economic and social concepts	#2.32	2.57	1.19
F	Research and development costs	2.31	2.49	1.85
M	Information economics	2.31	2.68	1.74
T	Taxation of deferred compensation	2.30	2.20	1.91
T	Federal estate tax	#2.29	2.33	1.83
A	SEC filing requirements	2.28	2.18	1.79
T	Complex tax provisions: subchapter S	#2.28	2.29	1.97
M	Management information systems: implementation	2.28	2.29	1.78
T	Federal gift tax	#2.26	2.31	1.81
F	SEC reporting	2.26	2.35	1.83
F	Partnership financial statements	2.26	2.43	2.25
M	Spoilage, waste, defective units and scraps	2.26	2.32	2.03
F	Statements from incomplete records	#2.25	2.38	2.44
M	Statistical analysis of cost variances	#2.24	2.33	1.81

EXHIBIT 8-1
(continued)

Area	Topic	Importance	Conceptual Knowledge	Technical Ability
			Means	
F	Installment sales	2.24	2.43	2.18
M	Performance evaluation: transfer pricing	#2.24	2.27	1.89
A	Operational auditing: methodology	2.24	2.33	1.54
A	Auditing procedures: audit practice case	#2.23	2.24	2.13
M	Performance evaluation: non-financial performance measures	#2.19	2.29	1.58
T	Administrative processes in tax matters	2.18	2.29	1.51
M	Simulation	#2.17	2.18	1.65
F	Fund accounting: financial statements	#2.17	2.35	1.93
T	Theoretical framework of taxation: alternative to present framework	2.14	2.44	1.24
F	Full costing vs. successful effort costing	2.11	2.31	1.78
T	Accumulated earnings tax	2.11	2.21	1.54
M	Linear programming	#2.08	2.23	1.66
M	Corporate planning models	2.08	2.17	1.44
M	*Management information systems: administration	2.05	2.08	1.70
F	Fund accounting: types of organizations	#2.05	2.25	1.83
M	Sensitivity analysis	#2.03	2.15	1.69
M	Behavioral considerations	#2.00	2.21	1.42
M	Internal operational auditing	2.00	2.13	1.71
T	State and local taxes	2.00	1.81	1.64
F	Consignments	1.98	2.10	1.90
F	Fund accounting: governmental units	#1.98	2.15	1.68
M	Zero base budgeting	1.97	2.26	1.76
A	Audit administration: accounting firm organization	1.95	2.03	1.42
M	Internal financial auditing	1.95	2.00	1.59
T	*Complex tax provisions: consolidated corporate returns	1.95	2.23	1.69
M	*Performance evaluation: residual income	1.88	2.03	1.68
A	Historical development of auditing	#1.87	2.22	1.14
M	*Social accounting	1.87	2.25	1.23
A	Special considerations in auditing not-for-profit organizations	#1.87	1.92	1.33
T	*Tax practice procedures	1.86	1.88	1.56
F	*Regulated industries	1.86	2.05	1.54
F	*Audit administration: setting and collecting fees	1.83	1.76	1.42
M	Network methods	1.82	2.00	1.30
F	Fiduciary accounting: estates and trusts	#1.80	2.13	1.67
F	*Foreign currency translation	1.79	2.15	1.55
T	*Complex tax provisions: fiduciaries	1.78	1.89	1.47
T	Social security taxes	1.76	1.57	1.50
F	Fund accounting: hospitals	#1.76	1.90	1.62

EXHIBIT 8-1
(continued)

Area	Topic	Importance	Means Conceptual Knowledge	Technical Ability
F	Human resources accounting	1.70	1.95	1.13
F	Fund accounting: colleges and universities	#1.68	1.79	1.50
M	*Special considerations in non-manufacturing concerns	1.68	1.65	1.19
T	*Judicial doctrines in tax disputes	1.68	1.75	1.19
T	*Preparation of tax communications	1.68	1.69	1.40
M	*Learning curve models	1.67	1.89	1.34
F	Fiduciary accounting: bankruptcy	1.62	2.03	1.45
T	*Complex tax provisions: foreign tax credit	1.61	1.77	1.11
F	*National income accounting	1.61	1.87	1.18
T	*Judicial processes in tax disputes	1.59	1.67	1.22
T	*Personal holding company tax	1.58	1.83	1.19
F	*Fiduciary accounting: receivership	1.55	1.90	1.33
T	*Complex tax provisions: DISC	1.53	1.63	1.03
F	*Development stage companies	1.53	1.92	1.33
T	*Taxation for international operations	1.51	1.68	1.11
M	*Planning and control of international operations	1.46	1.42	1.12
T	*Natural resource taxation	1.43	1.71	1.17
F	*International accounting standards	1.40	1.77	1.24
M	*Requirements for professional certification (CMA)	1.36	1.33	1.36
A	*Comparative accounting and auditing standards among nations	1.00	1.19	.72

* → non-area core topic
\# → significant difference (at the .05 level) between
educator and practitioner importance mean response

Included in the generalist area core are 171 (86.8 percent) of the 197 question-naire topics. Thus, this area core includes 66 topics which are not in the common accounting core. These 66 topics are presented in Exhibit 8-2 (rank-ordered by de-creasing mean importance responses of all generalist respondents).

EXHIBIT 8-2
(continued)
GENERALIST AREA CORE TOPICS
NOT IN COMMON CORE

Area	Topic	Importance Mean
A	Internal control: relationship of GAAS	3.48
A	Professional rules of conduct	3.23
F	Corporate equity	3.05
A	Legal responsibilities of auditors: at common law	3.03
F	Earnings-per-share	3.02
M	Computer science	2.83
F	Goodwill	2.76
A	Auditing procedures: working papers	2.75
A	Requirements for professional certification (CPA)	2.73
M	Management information systems: impact of external regulatory influences	2.68
M	Overhead control	2.63
M	Direct costing	2.63
T	Tax research methodology	2.61
T	Tax returns and accompanying schedules	2.58
T	Complex tax provisions: individuals	2.57
A	Audit administration: client relations	2.53
F	Pensions	2.52
F	Segment reporting	2.51
F	Business combinations: unconsolidated subsidiaries	2.45
A	Extensions of the attest function: possible areas	2.41
A	Operational auditing: objectives	2.39
M	Performance evaluation: non-statistical variance analysis	2.39
M	Management information systems: design	2.37
M	Performance evaluation: common costs	2.35
T	Complex tax provisions: corporations and shareholders	2.35
A	Legal responsibilities of auditors: responses of auditing profession to classic cases	2.33
M	Statistical cost estimation	2.33
M	Statistical decision theory	2.32
T	Complex tax provisions: partners and partnerships	2.32
T	Theoretical framework of taxation: economic and social concepts	2.32
T	Federal estate tax	2.29
A	SEC filing requirements	2.28
T	Complex tax provisions: subchapter S	2.28
T	Federal gift tax	2.26
F	Partnership financial statements	2.26
M	Performance evaluation: transfer pricing	2.24
A	Operational auditing: methodology	2.24
A	Auditing procedures: audit practice case	2.23
M	Performance evaluation: non-financial performance measures	2.19

EXHIBIT 8-2
(continued)

Area	Topic	Importance Mean
T	Administrative processes in tax matters	2.18
M	Simulation	2.17
T	Theoretical framework of taxation: alternatives to present framework	2.14
F	Full costing vs. successful effort costing	2.11
T	Accumulated earnings tax	2.11
M	Linear programming	2.08
M	Corporate planning model	2.08
F	Fund accounting: types of organizations	2.05
M	Sensitivity analysis	2.03
M	Behavioral considerations	2.00
M	Internal operational auditing	2.00
T	State and local taxes	2.00
F	Consignments	1.98
F	Fund accounting: governmental units	1.98
M	Zero base budgeting	1.97
A	Audit administration: accounting firm organization	1.95
M	Internal financial auditing	1.95
A	Historical development of auditing	1.87
A	Special considerations in auditing not-for-profit organizations	1.87
M	Network methods	1.82
F	Fiduciary accounting: estates and trusts	1.80
T	Social security taxes	1.76
F	Fund accounting: hospitals	1.76
F	Human resource accounting	1.70
F	Fund accounting: colleges and universities	1.68
F	Fiduciary accounting: bankruptcy	1.62

As indicated by Exhibit 8-2, the 66 additional topics meeting our cut-off criterion for inclusion in the generalist area core do not come predominantly from any single questionnaire section. In fact, they seem to be fairly evenly disbursed throughout the four topical areas of the questionnaire. This result is to be expected, since the generalist respondents would presumably consider some coverage of a broad spectrum of accounting topics to be desirable.

The following tabulation indicates the composition of the generalist area core according to the section of the questionnaire in which the topics were presented:

Questionnaire Section	Total Number of Topics	Number in Area Core	% in Area Core
Financial	65	59	90.8%
Managerial	51	44	86.3%
Auditing	50	48	96.0%
Taxation	31	20	64.5%
Total	197	171	

Thus, the auditing section of questionnaire topics had the largest proportion of its topics in the core, followed closely by financial and managerial and, lastly, taxation.

The 26 topics excluded from the generalist area core are presented in Exhibit 8-3. These topics are presented by questionnaire section in order of decreasing mean importance responses of educators and practitioners combined. The group(s) responsible for the exclusion from the area core (E for educators, P for practitioners) is also indicated.

EXHIBIT 8-3

TOPICS EXCLUDED FROM GENERALIST AREA CORE

Topic	Importance Mean	Excluded by
FINANCIAL:		
Regulated industries	1.86	E
Foreign currency translation	1.79	P
National income accounting	1.61	E,P
Fiduciary accounting: receivership	1.55	E,P
Development stage companies	1.53	E,P
International accounting standards	1.40	E,P
MANAGERIAL:		
Management information systems: administration	2.05	E
Performance evaluation: residual income	1.88	P
Social accounting	1.87	P
Special considerations in nonmanufacturing concerns	1.68	P
Learning curve models	1.67	P
Planning and control of interational operations	1.46	E,P
Requirements for professional certification (CMA)	1.36	E,P
AUDITING:		
Audit administration: setting and collecting fees	1.83	E
Comparative accounting and auditing standards among nations	1.00	E,P
TAXATION:		
Complex tax provisions: consolidated corporate returns	1.95	E
Tax practice procedures	1.86	E
Complex tax provisions: fiduciaries	1.78	E
Judicial doctrines in tax disputes	1.68	E
Preparation of tax communications	1.68	E
Complex tax provisions: foreign tax credit	1.61	E
Judicial processes in tax disputes	1.59	E
Personal holding company tax	1.58	E,P
Complex tax provisions: DISC	1.53	E,P
Taxation for international operations	1.51	E,P
Natural resource taxation	1.43	E,P

Only one topic in each of the financial, managerial and auditing questionnaire section was excluded from the generalist area core due solely to the responses of generalist educators. The other 12 topics excluded from the area core from these questionnaire sections were excluded due to the responses of both generalist educators and practitioners (seven) or due solely to the responses of generalist practitioners (five). On the contrary, seven of the 11 taxation topics excluded from the generalist area core were excluded due solely to the responses of generalist educators, while the other four excluded taxation topics were excluded due to both educator and practitioner responses. Thus, practitioners played a role in 12 of the 15 exclusions from the financial, managerial and auditing questionnaire sections, educators played a role in 10 of these 15 exclusions, and educator responses were sufficiently low to account for all 11 of the taxation topics area core exclusions. Both educators and practitioners scaled 11 of the 26 excluded topics sufficiently low to eliminate them from the generalist area core.

Analysis of Generalist Area Core

IMPORTANCE ANALYSIS

Financial Accounting Topics

As indicated by Exhibit 8-1, financial accounting topics dominate the top of the rank-ordering of topics by importance means. Those financial accounting topics deemed most important by generalist respondents were as follows (listed in order of decreasing importance means):

Income statement
Balance sheet
Revenue and expense recognition
Statement of changes in financial position
Theoretical framework: current structure
Information needs of financial statement users
Accruals and deferrals
Financial statement analysis
Inventories
Transaction analysis
Regulatory influences
U.S. financial accounting and reporting standards
Double-entry system

This list of most-important financial accounting topics in the generalist area core is very similar to comparable lists prepared for all respondents combined and for the other area cores. Two topics, *financial statement analysis* and *inventories,* are considered more important, relative to other financial accounting topics, by generalist respondents than by all respondents combined. On the other hand, the topic *deferred taxes* is deemed relatively less important by generalists than by all respondents combined.

In comparing this list of most-important financial accounting topics with current emphasis in accounting curricula, determined primarily by existing popular textbook coverage, some differences are apparent. It appears that generalist respondents would like to see more emphasis upon the topics *information needs of financial statement users, financial statement analysis* and *regulatory influences* than that which currently exists.

At the other end of the spectrum are those six financial accounting topics excluded from the generalist area core (see Exhibit 8-3). Coverage of these topics appears to be very limited in most existing curricula. Thus, these results do not appear to suggest any major changes in the status quo.

In between the 13 most important financial accounting topics and the six exclusions from the area core are the other 46 financial accounting topics. A perusal of Exhibit 8-1 provides one with a general feeling for the distribution of these remaining topics within the rank-ordering by importance means. There appear to be some differences between desired emphasis on certain of these topics and current emphasis as reflected by existing textbooks. For example, the topic *theoretical framework: alternatives to current structure* ranks fairly high in Exhibit 8-1, yet appears to receive only very limited attention in existing curricula. Likewise, the topics *segment reporting, reporting forecasts* and *interim reporting,* which have recently assumed increasing importance to practitioners, are roughly in the middle of the rank-ordering but they apparently receive only limited coverage in existing curricula. *SEC reporting* is comfortably within the generalist area core, but it also appears to be a very lightly-covered topic, except in those few, but increasing, number of colleges and universities which have adopted a module, or couse, dealing with SEC reporting issues.

Managerial Accounting Topics

In general, the managerial accounting topics were not scaled as highly with respect to importance by generalists as were the financial accounting topics. However, following are the managerial accounting topics scaled most highly by generalist respondents (listed in order of decreasing importance means):

Accounting information requirements for management decisions
Standard costs
Management information systems: internal control aspects
Cost-volume-profit analysis
Flexible budgets
Performance evaluation: return on investment
Short-range planning
Budgeted financial statements
Capital budgeting
Tax considerations in managerial decisions
Computer science
Full costing
Cash management
Long-range planning

Included in the above list are the four managerial accounting topics deemed most important by all respondents combined (see Exhibit 3-1 in Chapter 3):

Tax considerations in managerial decisions
Accounting information requirements for management decisions
Standard costs
Management information systems: internal control aspects

These four topics and most of the others in the above list seem to receive substantial attention in most existing curricula. Thus, the degree of importance attached to these topics by generalist questionnaire respondents is pretty much consistent with the status quo, in a relative sense. Possibly exceptions might be the planning topics (*short-range planning* and *long-range planning*) and the topics *budgeted financial statements* and *capital budgeting*. It may be the case that, unless a student takes one or more advanced managerial accounting courses, these topics receive less attention than that indicated as desirable by generalist questionnaire respondents. Also, the topic *accounting information requirements for management decisions,* the highest-ranking managerial accounting topic, does not appear currently to be emphasized to the extent deemed desirable by generalist questionnaire respondents.

The seven managerial accounting topics excluded from the generalist area core were listed in Exhibit 8-3. None of these topics appear to receive more than a very limited amount of attention in existing curricula. Thus, exclusion of such topics from the generalist area core seems to be consistent with present educational practices.

The remainder of the managerial accounting topics seemed to fall primarily in the middle and lower part of the rank-ordering of all topics based on mean importance responses of generalist respondents (see Exhibit 8-1). Thus, to prepare for a career as a generalist, all but seven of the managerial accounting topics should receive some attention in accounting curricula, but these topics are not generally considered as important as the financial accounting and auditing topics by generalist respondents.

Auditing Topics

As noted earlier in this chapter, the proportion of auditing topics included in the generalist area core (96.0 percent) was greater than the proportion from any of the other three questionnaire sections. Many of these auditing topics were not only in the area core, but they, along with several of the financial accounting topics, dominated the top of the rank-ordering of topics in Exhibit 8-1.

The auditing topics deemed most important by generalist questionnaire respondents were as follows (listed in order of decreasing mean importance responses):

Internal control: principles
Generally accepted auditing standards (GAAS)
Internal control: relationship of GAAS
Internal control: evaluation
Standard short-form audit report
Audit evidence: relative strength of types
Internal control: audit exposure due to weaknesses
Audit evidence: types
Professional rules of conduct
Internal control: modifications in audit program based on evaluation
Internal control: in an EDP environment
Modifications of the standard short-form audit report
Influence of professional and regulatory bodies on auditing

All of the above topics are considered quite important in preparing an individual for a career as a generalist. It is noteworthy that six of the 13 topics in this list relate to internal control, a subject area obviously considered quite important by generalist respondents. As indicated in Chapter 3, internal control topics were also considered very important by all respondents combined. The high degree of importance attached to internal control by questionnaire respondents seems to indicate the need for an increased emphasis on this area in accounting education.

Most of the remaining auditing topics appear in the upper and middle portion of Exhibit 8-1, indicating the relatively high importance attached to auditing topics as a group by generalist respondents. As indicated earlier, only two of the 50 auditing topics did not meet the cut-off criterion for inclusion in the area core. Besides the two topics excluded, only three other auditing topics, *audit administration: accounting firm organization, historical development of auditing,* and *special considerations in auditing not-for-profit organizations,* were even close to the cut-off criterion. All the other auditing topics were comfortably within the generalist area core.

Taxation Topics

Taxation topics appear to be considered, as a group, the least important topics in the generalist area core, both in terms of the proportion of such topics included in the area core (64.5 percent) and in terms of the relative rank-ordering of the topics. Taxation topics are virtually nonexistent in the upper portion of the rank-orderings.

Generalist respondents scaled the following taxation topics most highly (listed in order of decreasing mean importance responses):

Fundamentals of Federal income tax determination
Capital gains and losses
Tax planning
Recognition of tax opportunities

These same four topics were among the top-ranking taxation topics based upon all respondents combined.

The remaining 27 taxation topics are either included in the area core in the middle and lower portion of the rank-ordering (16 topics) or excluded from the area core (11 topics). For the most part, these topics appear to receive either no attention or limited attention in existing accounting curricula unless a student takes one or more advanced courses in taxation. However, generalist respondents do indicate the desirability of some coverage of the majority of the taxation topics.

In summarizing the means of generalist respondents on taxation topics, it appears that the two highest-ranking taxation topics are presently covered fairly thoroughly. However, the next two highest-ranking taxation topics, *tax planning* and *recognition of tax opportunities,* probably do not receive the degree of emphasis deemed desirable by generalist respondents in most existing curricula. Also, unless a student takes more than one taxation course, it is not likely that the student will be introduced to all of the other 16 taxation topics included in the generalist area core.

Educators vs. Practitioners

The 197 questionnaire topics are rank-ordered by the mean importance response of generalist educators and generalist practitioners in Appendices 8A and 8B, respectively. On an overall basis, generalist practitioners tended to scale topics more highly with respect to importance than did generalist educators. The overall importance mean for generalist educators was 2.46 while the overall importance mean for generalist practitioners was 2.55. This result is just the opposite of our findings for other areas and thus for our overall sample.

In Exhibit 8-1, the symbol "#" precedes the generalist area core topics for which significant differences (at the .05 level) existed between generalist educator and generalist practitioner mean importance responses. Significant differences occurred for 74 (43.3 percent) of the 171 generalist area core topics, including 16 (27.1 percent) of the 59 financial accounting topics in the area core, 17 (38.6 percent) of the 44 managerial accounting topics in the area core, 33 (68.8 percent) of the 48 auditing topics in the area core and eight (40.0 percent) of the 20 taxation topics in the area core.

As one would expect, since the overall generalist practitioners mean on the importance scale exceeded the overall generalist educator mean response, the practitioner mean exceeded the educator mean for most of the topics on which significant differences existed. However, the educator mean did exceed the practitioner mean on 30 of the 74 topics for which significant differences occurred.

CONCEPTUAL KNOWLEDGE AND TECHNICAL ABILITY ANALYSIS

The conceptual knowledge and technical ability mean responses for all generalist respondents are included in Exhibit 8-1, whereas generalist educator and generalist practitioner mean responses on those scales are presented in Appendices 8A and 8B, respectively.

In general, conceptual knowledge was more heavily emphasized by generalist respondents than was technical ability. The overall mean conceptual knowledge response for generalist respondents was 2.57, whereas the overall technical ability response was 2.12.

The mean technical ability response of generalists exceeded the mean conceptual knowledge response for only six of the 171 generalist area core topics, as follows:

| | Mean | |
	Conceptual Knowledge	Technical Ability
Accruals and deferrals	3.25	3.34
Double-entry system	3.20	3.39
Cash	2.78	2.90
Tax returns and accompany schedules	2.22	2.36
Error corrections	2.38	2.74
Statements from incomplete records	2.38	2.44

Educators vs. Practitioners

In comparing the responses of generalist educators with those of generalist practitioners on the conceptual knowledge scale, we see that practitioners tended to scale topics slightly higher than did educators. The overall generalist practitioner mean response on conceptual knowledge was 2.60, whereas the comparable mean for generalist educators was 2.52. While the practitioner mean did exceed the educator mean on conceptual knowledge for the majority of topics, the educator mean exceeded the practitioners mean on 82 (41.6 percent) of the 197 questionnaire topics, a substantial minority.

However, on the technical ability scale, educators (overall mean response of 2.24) tended to scale topics more highly than did practitioners (overall mean response of 2.05). Both of these means are substantially lower than the corresponding conceptual knowledge means. The educator technical ability mean response exceeded the practitioner technical ability mean response for most of the questionnaire topics. However, the practitioner technical ability mean was higher than the educator technical ability mean on 68 (34.5 percent) of the 197 questionnaire topics. Included in the 68 topics were 28 auditing topics and 20 taxation topics, indicating that although educators in general placed more emphasis on technical ability than did practitioners, the practitioner respondents did place relatively more emphasis on technical ability for the auditing and taxation topics.

9

Summary, Conclusions and Recommendations

The objectives of this concluding chapter are to highlight some major findings resulting from the research effort, to suggest possible implications of the research findings, and to indicate how this research effort may be utilized as a stepping stone for additional substantive research and writing in the area of accounting education.

We set out with a general objective of providing useful information for the evaluation and development of accounting curricula. Based upon the consensus recommendation of the previously described 1974 symposium, a major specific objective of this research was to identify a body of common knowledge. This collection of subject matter which every accounting major should be required to take and be expected to understand was presented and discussed in Chapter 3. Referred to as the common core, it consisted of 105 of the 197 questionnaire topics.

We found significant differences (at the .05 level) between the mean importance responses of educators and practitioners for the majority (107 out of 197) of the questionnaire topics. This is an important finding because it emphasizes the fact that individuals charged with curricula decisions must somehow decide how much weight to attach to these diverse views. Should educator views dominate? Should practitioners views dominate? Should educator views dominate with respect to certain topics and practitioner views with respect to other topics? Should educator and practitioner views be weighted equally? The data is included in the research findings. The decision regarding appropriate weights is beyond the scope of the study.

Educators generally tended to scale topics more highly with respect to importance than did practitioners. Thus, for most (78.5 percent) topics on which significant differences existed, the educator mean exceeded the practitioner mean.

Referring to Exhibit 3-1, financial accounting and auditing topics tended to dominate the upper part of the rank-ordering on importance means. However, one must be wary of misinterpreting this result, since slightly more than 45 percent of our respondents were in either financial accounting or auditing. Thus, the views from these two areas were most influential in the rank-orderings in Exhibit 3-1. To discover the relative importance attached to topics by each area of specialization, one must go to Chapters 4 through 8.

On an overall basis, respondents placed more emphasis upon conceptual knowledge (overall mean of 2.33) than upon technical ability (overall mean of 1.86). The implication from our respondents, therefore, is that accounting education, looked at from an overall standpoint, should be more conceptual than technical in its orientation. This is not necessarily an either/or decision. That is, one does not have to give up technical education in order to strengthen conceptual education, except to the extent that time becomes a constraining factor. How do these findings compare with existing educational practices? Again, this is a question beyond the scope of this study.

Educators tended to scale topics higher with respect to both conceptual knowledge and technical ability than did practitioners. However, in certain topical areas, such as *internal control* and *management information systems*, practitioner responses were generally higher with respect to both conceptual knowledge and technical ability. These findings raised the interesting and unavoidable question of how such differences in opinion should influence curricula decisions. This question likewise is beyond the scope of this study.

In Chapters 4 through 8, area cores of accounting subject matter were identified and discussed. These area cores included the 105 common core topics plus those additional topics which met our cut-off criterion described in Chapter 2 for educators and practitioners within the area of specialization. The number of topics in the area cores ranged from 145 in the auditing area core to 171 in the generalist area core. Thus, in addition to coverage of the 105 common core topics, accounting graduates should be exposed to from 40 to 66 additional accounting topics depending upon their choice of specialty (or generalist, as the case may be).

We have assumed in our research approach that the accounting discipline has become a discipline of specialties and yet significant commonalities exist. An obvious question that arises is to what extent should the formal university portion of an individual's education prepare one for this specialization? The data reported herein implies that, in the views of our respondents, a significant amount of specialization should result from the formal education process. While the nature of this chapter prevents a detailed discussion of findings with respect to particular topics by area of specialization, a few summary remarks regarding the various areas of specialization may help the reader to obtain an overview of our results.

All of the managerial accounting topics except *linear programming* were included in the managerial accounting area core. Significant differences (at the .05 level) between educator and practitioner mean importance responses existed for nearly one-fourth (23.1 percent) of the managerial accounting area core topics. The topic *accounting information requirements for management decisions* was the most important topic in this area core. Conceptual knowledge was emphasized more than technical ability on an overall basis by managerial accounting respondents, with educators tending to place more emphasis upon both conceptual knowledge and technical ability than did practitioners. However, managerial accounting practitioners tended to place more emphasis upon technical ability with respect to auditing topics than did managerial accounting educators.

In the taxation area core, which included all 31 taxation topics in the questionnaire, significant differences (at the .05 level) between educator and practitioner importance responses occurred for 38.9 percent of the topics, including 14 taxation topics. For most (92.1 percent) of these topics for which significant differences were found, the educator mean response was higher than the practitioner mean response. Our taxation respondents generally placed more emphasis upon conceptual knowledge than upon technical ability, even though the mean technical ability response exceeded the mean conceptual knowledge response for more than one-third (35.5 percent) of the taxation topics. Taxation respondents placed a high degree of importance on not only many of the taxation topics, as expected, but also on the various *internal control* topics.

Financial accounting respondents placed a very high importance on, among others, the topics *regulatory influences* and *information needs of financial statement users,* two topics which do not appear to currently receive the attention indicated as desirable by our respondents. Financial accounting respondents also considered the *internal control* and *audit evidence* topics to be quite important. Significant differences (at the .05 level) between financial accounting educator and financial accounting practitioner mean importance responses existed for over half (53.6 percent) of the financial accounting area core topics. The practitioner importance mean was higher than the educator importance mean for only four of these topics, as follows:

Foreign currency translation
Interim reporting
Business combinations: consolidation procedures
Complex tax provisions: consolidated corporate returns

Financial accounting respondents also generally placed more emphasis upon conceptual knowledge than upon technical ability.

The topic *audit practice case* was excluded from the auditing area core because of the low importance responses of auditing educators. On the other hand, the *management information systems, internal control* and *audit evidence* topics were considered very important by auditing respondents. Significant differences (at the .05 level) between educator and practitioner mean importance responses were less common (26.9 percent of the area core topics) for auditing respondents than for financial accounting respondents. Auditing respondents likewise almost invariably placed more emphasis upon conceptual knowledge than upon technical ability. However, in contrast to most other areas, practitioners emphasized conceptual knowledge slightly more than did educators in the auditing area. Also, even though educators emphasized technical ability more than did practitioners generally, practitioners placed more emphasis upon technical ability for auditing topics than did educators.

Generalist respondents seemed to attach greater importance to the topics *financial statement analysis, information needs of financial statement users,* and *regulatory influences* than that currently reflected in accounting curricula. These respondents also consider the *internal control* and *audit evidence* topics to be quite important. Virtually all (96 percent) of the auditing topics were included in the generalist area core. On nearly half (43.3 percent) of the generalist area core topics, significant differences (at the .05 level) existed between the mean importance response of educators and practitioners. Included in this group of topics were 33 of the 48 auditing topics in the generalist area core. In contrast to other areas, in the majority of instances where significant differences were found, the practitioner importance mean exceeded the educator importance mean. However, consistent with the other areas, generalist respondents indicated that a greater emphasis should be placed upon conceptual knowledge that upon technical ability. In comparing educators and practitioners on these two scales, we found that practitioners placed a greater emphasis upon conceptual knowledge than did educators, but educators tended to scale topics more highly on the technical ability than did practitioners.

To what extent are the area core topics beyond the common core "common" to two or more areas? While we have not performed this analysis, a cursory review of the additional topics in each area core indicates that significant commonalities exist. However, the importance may differ by area as may the emphasis upon conceptual knowledge and/or technical ability. Such differences may, indeed do, exist for common core topics also.

How can the common core and area core material best be packaged to accomplish the objectives implied by our data? Again, this question is beyond the scope of our study, but our data should provide valuable raw material for these efforts. Textbook writers should certainly peruse our findings to determine the possible implications regarding the extent and type of coverage of the various accounting topics.

Accounting curriculum committees within universities and colleges should find this study to be an invaluable source of data. While differing objectives among colleges and universities make the identification of an "ideal" curriculum an impossibility, individual institutions of higher education ought to be able to utilize this data effectively given their particular educational objectives. For example, a particular institution may decide that its only objective is to produce generalists. Given this objective, the material in Chapter 8 takes on prime importance and the remainder of the study is of only secondary interest. Likewise, if a particular institution is interested in developing a taxation specialization within its accounting curriculum that is "marketable" to practitioners, Chapter 5 should prove invaluable.

What are the implications of this study regarding the time requirements for an accounting degree? This question again takes us beyond the scope of our study, but the data provided by the study should provide useful information for discussions regarding this issue. It may be that specialization in some areas should take longer than specialization in other areas.

What has the passage of time since this data was gathered (1975) done to the usefulness of the data? There seems to be no reason that a similar study performed at this time would produce significantly different results from an overall standpoint. Those analyzing the data for the purpose of evaluating accounting curricula must be aware of environmental changes that have taken place since 1975 (for example, FASB pronouncements and SEC requirements) which might have an impact upon the perceived importance and/or educational objectives for selected topics. In fact, recent developments seem to reinforce and strengthen the implications of our study regarding the importance of *internal control* topics, as evidenced by the Foreign Corrupt Practices Act requirements regarding internal control and the sponsoring of a series of studies in the field of internal control by the Financial Executives Research Foundation

How would the results have differed had the respondents been randomly selected? While we can only speculate at this time on the answer to this question, it would certainly seem to be worthwhile to gather and analyze data which would tell us how accounting educators and practitioners in general view these topics.

It would also be helpful to conduct research using more detailed topics within certain areas of specialization. For example, an institution interested in pursuing a taxation specialization may find it helpful to subdivide some of the more general taxation topics, such as *tax planning* and *recognition of tax opportunities,* and solicit input on this more detailed topical list regarding importance and emphasis on various educational objectives.

This study can perhaps be best described as an exploratory study. It merely represents the tip of the iceberg regarding accounting education research. So little has been done and so much remains undone. This study provides what we believe is a valuable data bank for those responsible for the education of future accountants. As this final chapter indicates, in addition to providing a significant source of data for curricula decisions, this study has stimulated many researchable questions. It is hoped that the study will encourage and promote continuing discussion and evaluation of accounting education. It is further hoped that in the future this research effort may be looked back upon as a significant step in a continuing effort to improve the quality of accounting education.

BIBLIOGRAPHY

ACCOUNTING EDUCATION

AAA Committee on the Accounting Curriculum for Junior and Community Colleges. "Report of the Committee on the Accounting Curriculum for Junior and Community Colleges." *The Accounting Review,* suppl. to vol. 45 (1970): 10-26.

AAA Committee on Accounting History. "Committee on Accounting History." *The Accounting Review,* suppl. to vol. 45 (1970): 52-64.

AAA Committee on Advanced Accounting Instruction — 1963. "Report of Committee on Advanced Accounting Instruction."

AAA Committee on Applications of Learning and Communications Theories to Accounting Instruction. "Report of the Committee on Application of Learning and Communications Theories to Accounting Instruction." *The Accounting Review,* suppl. to vol. 47 (1972): 267-92.

AAA Committee on Auditing. "Report of the Committee on Auditing: 1972-73." *The Accounting Review,* suppl. to vol. 49 (1974): 157-75.

AAA Committee on Auditing Education. "Report of the Committee on Auditing Education." *The Accounting Review,* suppl. to vol. 48 (1973): 1-16.

AAA Committee on Auditing Instruction — 1963. "Committee on Auditing Instruction — Final Report."

AAA Committee on Basic Auditing Concepts. *A Statement of Basic Auditing Concepts (ASOBAC), Studies in Accounting Research #6.* Sarasota, Fl.: American Accounting Association, 1973.

AAA Committee on Basic Auditing Concepts, 1969-71. "Report of the Committee on Basic Auditing Concepts." *The Accounting Review,* suppl. to vol. 47 (1972): 15-74.

AAA Committee on Behavioral Science Content of the Accounting Curriculum. "Report of the Committee on Behavioral Science Content of the Accounting Curriculum." *The Accounting Review,* suppl. to vol. 46 (1971): 246-85.

AAA Committee on Concepts of Accounting Applicable to the Public Sector, 1970-71. "Report of the Committee on Concepts of Accounting Applicable to the Public Sector, 1970-71." *The Accounting Review,* suppl. to vol. 47 (1972): 77-108.

AAA Committee on Continuing Education — 1961. "Report of Committee on Continuing Education."

AAA Committee on Cost Accounting Instruction — 1962. "Report of Committee on Cost Accounting Instruction."

AAA Committee on Courses and Curricula — 1962. "Report of the AAA Committee on Courses and Curricula — 1962."

AAA Committee on Courses and Curricula — Professional Degree Education in Accounting — 1960. "Report of the Committee on Courses and Curricula — Professional Degree Education in Accounting."

AAA Committee on Courses in Financial Accounting. "Report of the Committee on Courses in Financial Accounting." *The Accounting Review,* suppl. to vol. 47 (1972): 295-315.

AAA Committee on Courses in Managerial Accounting. "Report of the Committee on Courses in Managerial Accounting." *The Accounting Review,* suppl. to vol. 47 (1972): 1-13.

AAA Committee on CPA Examinations — 1963. "Final Report of the Committee on CPA Examinations."

AAA Committee on CPA Examinations — 1964. "Report of the 1964 Committee on CPA Examinations."

AAA Committee on CPA Examinations. "Report of the Committee on the CPA Examination." *The Accounting Review,* suppl. to vol. 47 (1972): 215-35.

AAA Committee on the CPA Examination. "Report of the Committee on the CPA Examination." *The Accounting Review,* suppl. to vol. 48 (1973): 19-35.

AAA Committee on Educational Planning — 1964. "Report of the Committee on Educational Planning — 1964."

AAA Committee on Federal Income Taxes. "Committee on Federal Income Taxes." *The Accounting Review,* suppl. to vol. 49 (1974): 177-201.

AAA Committee on Federal Taxation. "Report of the Committee on Federal Taxation." *The Accounting Review,* suppl. to vol. 47 (1972): 259-65.

AAA Committee on Foreign Accounting — 1963. "Report of the Committee on Foreign Accounting."

AAA Committee on Income Tax Instruction. "Report of the Committee on Income Tax Instruction." *The Accounting Review,* 37 (July 1962): 538-40.

AAA Committee on Income Tax Instruction. "A Statement of Tax Concepts to be Used as a Basis for Teaching Income Taxation." *The Accounting Review,* suppl. to vol. 44 (1969): 1-18.

AAA Committee on Income Tax Instruction. "Subject Matter Outline to Accompany the Statement of 'Concepts of Federal Income Taxation.' " *The Accounting Review,* suppl. to vol. 44 (1969): 19-41.

AAA Committee on Information Systems. "Accounting and Information Systems." *The Accounting Review,* suppl. to vol. 46 (1971): 286-350.

AAA Committee on Information Systems. "Report of the Committee on Information Systems." *The Accounting Review,* suppl. to vol. 47 (1972): 187-213.

AAA Committee on International Accounting — 1964. "Report of the Committee on International Accounting."

AAA Committee on International Accounting. "Report of the Committee on International Accounting." *The Accounting Review,* suppl. to vol. 48 (1973): 121-67.

AAA Committee on International Accounting. "Report of the Committee on International Accounting." *The Accounting Review,* suppl. to vol. 49 (1974): 251-69.

AAA Committee on Introductory Accounting Courses — 1961. "Committee on Introductory Accounting Courses — Final Report."

AAA Committee on Junior (Community) College Curriculum in Accounting. "Report of the Committee on Junior (Community) College Curriculum in Accounting." *The Accounting Review,* suppl. to vol. 47 (1972): 165-85.

AAA Committee on Managerial Accounting. "Committee Report — Committee on Managerial Accounting." *The Accounting Review,* suppl. to vol. 45 (1970): 1-8.

AAA Committee on Managerial Accounting. "Report of the 1969-70, 1970-71 Committee on Managerial Accounting." *The Accounting Review,* suppl. to vol. 47 (1972): 317-35.

AAA Committee on the Masters' Program in Accounting. "Report of the Committee on Masters' Programs in Accounting." *The Accounting Review,* suppl. to vol. 45 (1970): 44-51.

AAA Committee on the Measurement Methods Content of the Accounting Curriculum. "Report of Committee on the Measurement Methods Content of the Accounting Curriculum." *The Accounting Review,* suppl. to vol. 46 (1971): 212-45.

AAA Committee on Measures of Effectiveness for Social Programs. "Report of the Committee on Measures of Effectiveness for Social Programs." *The Accounting Review,* suppl. to vol. 47 (1972): 337-96.

AAA Committee on Multi-Media Instruction in Accounting. "Committee on Multi-Media Instruction in Accounting." *The Accounting Review,* suppl. to vol. 47 (1972): 111-62.

AAA Committee on Not-For-Profit Organizations, 1972-73. "Report of the Committee on Not-For-Profit Organizations, 1972-73." *The Accounting Review,* suppl. to vol. 49 (1974): 225-49.

AAA Committee on Post-Degree Continuing Education in Accounting — 1960. "Report of Committee on Post-Degree Continuing Education in Accounting."

AAA Committee on Professional Education in Accounting. "Report of Committee on Professional Education in Accounting." *The Accounting Review,* 34 (April 1959): 195-99.

AAA Committee on Professional Schools of Accounting. "Report of the Committee on Professional Programs of Accounting." *The Accounting Review,* suppl. to vol. 43 (1968): 23-49.

AAA Committee on the Role of the Computer in Accounting Education. "Report of the 1968-69 Committee on the Role of the Computer in Accounting Education." *The Accounting Review,* suppl. to vol. 45 (1970): 28-43.

AAA Committee on Study of Accreditation — 1962. "Final Report of Committee on Accreditation."

AAA Committee on the Relationship of Behavioral Science and Accounting. "Report of the Committee on the Relationship of Behavioral Science and Accounting." *The Accounting Review,* suppl. to vol. 49 (1974), 127-39.

AAA Committee on the Scope of the Four Year Accounting Major. "Trends in Undergraduate Accounting Education." *The Accounting Review* 35 (April 1960): 203-5.

AAA Committee on Standards of Accounting Instruction. "Undergraduate Curriculum Study, Report of the Task Committee on Standards of Accounting Instruction." *The Accounting Review* 31 (January 1956): 36-42.

AAA Committee on the Study of the Ford and Carnegie Foundation Reports. "Report of the Committee on the Study of the Ford and Carnegie Foundation Reports." *The Accounting Review* 36 (April 1961): 191-96.

AAA Committee on Teaching Methods — New Developments Committee — 1961. "Final Committee Report."

AAA Committee to Compile a Revised Statement of Educational Policy. "A Restatement of Matters Relating to Educational Policy: A Report of the 1964-67 American Accounting Association Committee to Compile a Revised Statement of Educational Policy." *The Accounting Review,* suppl. to vol. 43 (1968): 51-124.

AAA Committee to Examine the 1969 Report of the AICPA Committee on Education and Experience Requirements for CPAs. "Report of the Committee to Examine the 1969 Report of the AICPA Committee on Education and Experience Requirements for CPAs." *The Accounting Review,* suppl. to vol. 47 (1962): 237-57.

Addington, Conley R. "Undergraduate Course in Income Taxation for Accounting Majors." *The Accounting Review* 32 (January 1957): 93-94.

Andersen, Anker V. "Defense of Accounting Education." *The Accounting Review* 37 (October 1962): 768-69.

Anderson, Hershel M. and Griffin, Fred B. "The Accounting Curriculum and Postgraduate Achievement." *The Accounting Review* 38 (October 1963): 813-18.

Anderson, John A. "Integrated Instruction in Computers and Accounting." *The Accounting Review* 42 (July 1967): 583-88.

Aslanian, Paul J. and Duff, John T. "Why Accounting Teachers are so Academic." *The Journal of Accountancy* 136 (October 1973): 47-53.

The Australasian Association of University Teachers in Accounting. *Proceedings, Third International Conference on Accounting Education.* 1972.

Backer, Morton and Fertig, Paul E. "Statistical Sampling and the Accounting Curriculum." *The Accounting Review* 33 (July 1958): 415-18.

Ball, J.T. "Changing Concepts in the Education and Training of Accountants." *The Journal of Accountancy* (July 1967), 83-85.

Bastable, C.W. "Why Can't Johnny Account?" *Journal of Accountancy* (January 1977), 63-69.

Bedford, Norton M. "Education for Accounting as a Learned Profession." *The Journal of Accountancy* 112 (December 1961): 33-41.

_____. "The Laws of Learning and Accounting Instruction." *The Accounting Review* 38 (April 1963): 406-8.

Bevis, Donald J. "Professional Education for Public Accounting." *The Accounting Review* 33 (July 1958): 445-49.

Birkett, W.P. and Walker, R.G. "Aims of an Accounting Education." Working paper, University of Sydney, 1975.

Boyd, Orton W. "That Federal Tax Course." *The Accounting Review* 31 (January 1956): 131-35.

Boyd, F. Virgil. "New Look in Accounting Education — The Managerial Approach to Tax Accounting." *The Accounting Review* 35 (October 1960): 726-28.

Boyd, Virgil and Taylor, Dale. "Magic Words — 'Managerial Accounting.' " *The Accounting Review* 36 (January 1961): 105-11.

Buckley, John W. "The Myth of the Compleat Accountant." *Federal Accountant* 21 (September 1972): 40-52.

_____. "Programmed and Non-Programmed Instruction: Integration Criteria in Curriculum Design." *The Accounting Review* 44 (April 1969): 389-97.

_____. "A Perspective on Professional Accounting Education." *The Journal of Accountancy* 130 (August 1970): 41-47.

Buckley, John W. and McDonough, John J. "Forces of Change in Accounting Education and its Meaning for the Profession." *AIS Working Paper No. 72-10*. Los Angeles: Accounting-Information Systems Research Program, Graduate School of Management, University of California — Los Angeles, December 1971.

Buckley, John W. and McDonough, John J. "Three Critical Issues in Accounting Education." *AIS Working Paper No. 71-8*. Los Angeles: University of California — Los Angeles, February 1971.

Burnet, Mary. "Enriching the Intermediate Accounting Course." *Collegiate News and Views* 23 (December 1969): 25-27.

Burns, Thomas L., ed. *Accounting Trends*. New York: McGraw-Hill, annual editions since 1967.

Burton, John C. "An Educator Views the Public Accounting Profession." *The Journal of Accountancy* 132 (September 1971): 47-53.

Campfield, William L. "Broad-Gauge Course in Governmental Accounting." *The Accounting Review* 33 (October 1958): 669-75.

_____. "Toward Making Accounting Education Adaptive and Normative." *The Accounting Review* 45 (October 1970): 683-89.

Canning, R.J. "Training for an Accounting Career." *The Accounting Review* 33 (July 1958): 359-67.

Carlson, Marvin L. "An Application of Concepts in the Theory Course." *The Accounting Review* 42 (July 1967): 596-98.

Carmichael, D.R. and Willingham, John J. "New Directions in Auditing Education." *The Accounting Review* 44 (July 1969): 611-15.

Chastain, Clark E. *Teaching Undergraduate Tax Accounting in the 1970s*. Ann Arbor: University of Michigan, 1972.

Christiansen, Irving K. "Bringing Reality into the Accounting Program." *The Accounting Review* 36 (April 1961): 293-96.

Cobb, E. Kennedy. "Current Status of Managerial Accounting as a Course of Study." *The Accounting Review* 35 (January 1960): 125-29.

Committee on Education and Experience Requirements for CPAs of the AICPA. *Report of the Committee on Education and Experience Requirements for CPAs.* New York: AICPA, 1969.

Committee on Relations with the General Accounting Office of AICPA. *Auditing Standards Established by the GAO — Their Meaning and Significance for CPAs.* New York: AICPA, 1973.

Cox, Robert G. "Place of Tax and Fiscal Policy Issues in the Federal Income Tax Course." *The Accounting Review* 32 (January 1957): 95-97.

Cyert, Richard M. and Wheeler, John T. "A Proposal for an Integrated Course in Statistics and Accounting." *The Accounting Review* 35 (January 1960): 51-59.

Davidson, Sidney. "The CPA and the Educator." *The Journal of Accountancy* 128 (September 1969): 93-94.

Deakin, Edward B. III, Granof, Michael H. and Smith, Charles H. "Educational Objectives for an Accounting Program." *The Accounting Review* 49 (July 1974): 584-89.

Dickerson, W.E. "Tax Planning and Tax Research in the Tax Accounting Courses." *The Accounting Review* 32 (January 1957): 98-100.

Dilley, Merrill B. and Dilley, David R. "College Accounting Courses — 1964." *The Accounting Review* 39 (October 1964): 1050-53.

Dominiak, Geraldine F. "Wanted: Advice from Accountants Not in Public Practice." *Federal Accountant* 19 (June 1970): 49-56.

Dunn, Clarence L. "Helping Accounting Students to Learn How to Analyze a Business Transaction." *The Accounting Review* 31 (July 1956): 501-3.

Edwards, James Don, et al., eds. *Accounting Education: Problems and Prospects.* Sarasota, Fla.: American Accounting Association, 1974.

Emblen, Donald. "When Should Techniques be Presented." *The Accounting Review* 38 (January 1963): 159-60.

Federal Government Accountants Association. *Educational Guidelines.* Arlington, Va.: Federal Government Accountants Association, 1971.

Ferrara, William L., et al., eds. *Researching the Accounting Curriculum: Strategies for Change.* Sarasota, Fla.: American Accounting Association, 1975.

Fertig, Paul E. "Organization of an Accounting Program." *The Accounting Review* 35 (April 1960): 190-96.

Firmin, Peter A. "Educating Tomorrow's Accountant — Today." *The Accounting Review* 32 (October 1957): 569-75.

Frumer, Samuel. "Incorporating Managerial Controls into Introductory Cost Accounting." *The Accounting Review* 37 (July 1962): 551-54.

Gerber, Quentin N. "Accounting Education Below CPA Standards — An International Approach." *The Accounting Review* 37 (April 1962): 346-49.

Goetz, Billy E. "Professional Obsolescence." *The Accounting Review* 42 (January 1967): 53-61.

Hart, Donald J. "An Outsider Looks at the Accounting Curriculum." *The Journal of Accountancy* (March 1969), 87-89.

Henke, Emerson. "Teaching Accounting by Principle and Convention." *The Accounting Review,* 33 (April 1958): 302-5.

Holstrum, Gary L., ed. *Proceedings of the 1973 Management Accounting and Planning Institute, Presentation 74-1.* University of Texas at Austin, September 28, 1973.

Horngren, Charles T. "The Accounting Discipline in 1999." *The Accounting Review* 46 (January 1971): 1-11.

Horngren, Charles T. "Teaching Methods and Participation as a Major Law of Learning." *The Accounting Review* 38 (April 1963): 409-11.

Institute of Internal Auditors. *Statement of Responsibilities of the Internal Auditor.* Orlando, Fla.: Institute of Internal Auditors, 1971.

Jacobson, Lyle E. "Management Accounting: Content and Approach." *The Accounting Review* 35 (January 1960): 64-69.

Keister, Orville R. "The Case for a Certifying Examination in Governmental Accounting." *Federal Accountant* 20 (December 1971): 107-11.

Kemp, Patrick S. "A Current Topics Course in the Accounting Curriculum." *The Accounting Review* 38 (April 1963): 398-400.

Kerrigan, Harry D. "Intermediate Accounting Instruction — Circa 1955." *The Accounting Review* 31 (July 1956): 418-22.

_____. "Major Influences on Accounting Education." *The Accounting Review* 34 (July 1959): 403-14.

_____. "Recent Data on Accounting Majors and Programs." *The Accounting Review* 34 (April 1959): 262-65.

Kohl, Maybelle. "Objectives of Accounting Education in the Liberal Arts College." *The Accounting Review* 36 (October 1961): 631-34.

Langenderfer, Harold Q. and Weinwurm, Ernest H. "Bringing Accounting Curricula Up-to-Date." *The Accounting Review* 31 (July 1956): 423-30.

Lawler, John L. "The Specter of Specialization." *California CPA Quarterly* 36 (March 1969): 9-13.

Mautz, R.K. "Where Do We Go From Here?" *The Accounting Review* 49 (April 1974): 353-60.

McDonough, John J. and Mock, Theodore J. "Accounting Education in a Changing World." *California CPA Quarterly* 38 (September 1970): 9-10, 12, 34.

Meyer, Harvey G. "Some Aspects of Accounting Education." *The Accounting Review* 36 (April 1961): 209-212.

Mitchell, Wiley S. "Relationship of Laws of Learning to Methods of Accounting Instruction." *The Accounting Review* 38 (April 1963): 411-14.

Moonitz, Maurice. "The Beamer Report — A Golden Opportunity for Accounting Education." *The Journal of Accountancy* 136 (August 1973): 64-69.

Moyer, C.A. "Some Common Misconceptions Relating to Accounting Education." *The Accounting Review* 32 (October 1957): 531-35.

Mueller, Gerhard G., ed. *A New Introduction to Accounting: Report of the Study Group on Introductory Accounting.* New York: Price Waterhouse Foundation, 1971.

Neeley, Paden and Robason, G.A. "Governmental Accounting: A Critical Evaluation." *The Accounting Review* 42 (April 1967): 366-69.

Neumann, Frederick L. "Career Education in Accounting in the United States: A Current Appraisal." *The International Journal of Accounting* 9 (Spring 1974): 169-79.

_____. " 'Effect of Circumstances on . . .' Accounting Education." *The Accounting Review* 49 (April 1974): 366-68.

Olson, Wallace E. "The House of Accountancy." *The Journal of Accountancy* 137 (February 1974): 99-102.

Paton, William A. "Accounting's Educational Eclipse." *The Journal of Accountancy* 132 (December 1971): 35-37.

_____. "Some Reflections on Education and Professoring." *The Accounting Review* 42 (January 1967): 7-23.

Patten, Ronald J. "The Trend in Accounting Education." *Managerial Planning* 20 (November/December 1972): 34-37.

Porter, W. Thomas, Jr., ed. *Higher Education and the Accounting Profession: A Summary Report on the Haskins & Sells 75th Anniversary Symposiums.* New York: Haskins & Sells, 1971.

Proceedings of Second International Conference on Accounting Education. Guildhall, London, 1967.

Ray, Delmas D. "Faculty Responsibility with Respect to Correcting Certain Defects in the Accountant's Education." *The Accounting Review* 32 (October 1957): 580-86.

Roller, Julius and Williams, Thomas H. "Professional Schools of Accounting." *The Accounting Review* 42 (April 1967): 349-55.

Roy, Robert H. and MacNeill, James H. *Horizons for a Profession.* New York: AICPA, 1967.

Rueschoff, N.G. "The Undergraduate International Accounting Course." *The Accounting Review* 47 (October 1972): 833-36.

Seidler, Lee. "International Accounting — The Ultimate Theory Course." *The Accounting Review* 42 (October 1967): 775-81.

Seiler, Robert E. and Label, Wayne A. "Impact of Curricular Changes Upon Professional Staff Training Efforts." *The Accounting Review* 49 (October 1974): 854-59.

Seitz, James E. "Accreditation and Specialization: Yesterday, Today, and Tomorrow." *California CPA Quarterly* 41 (September 1973): 21-23, 50.

Shenkir, William G. "Media and Accounting Education." *The Accounting Review* 45 (April 1970): 347-50.

_____., ed. *The Future of Accounting Education.* New York: AICPA, 1974.

Shenkir, William G. and Wheelen, Thomas L. "Three Dimensional Staff Development." *The Journal of Accountancy* 132 (July 1971): 83-84.

Shenkir, William G., Wheelen, Thomas L. and Strawser, Robert H. "The Making of an Accountant." *The CPA Journal* (March 1973), 218-21.

Singer, Frank A. "Management Accounting." *The Accounting Review* 36 (January 1961): 112-18.

_____. "A System Approach to Teaching the Accounting Process." *The Accounting Review* 45 (April 1970): 351-64.

Smith, C. Aubrey. "The Internship in Accounting Education." *The Accounting Review* 39 (October 1964): 1024-27.

Smith, Jay M., Taylor, Dale and Western, Harold. "Experiment in Modularized Learning for Intermediate Accounting." *The Accounting Review* 49 (April 1974): 385-90.

Smyth, E. Bryan. "Accounting Education in the United States." *The Australian Accountant* (November 1965), 576-77, 581.

Smyth, J.E. "Case for National Income Accounting in the Accounting Curriculum." *The Accounting Review* 34 (July 1959): 376-80.

Solomon, Stanley H. "Objectives of Undergraduate Collegiate Accounting Education: Perceptions of Educators and Practitioners." Ph.D. dissertation, New York University, 1972.

Staubus, George J. "The Responsibility of Accounting Teachers." *The Accounting Review* 50 (January 1975): 160-70.

Sterling, Robert R. "Accounting Research, Education and Practice." *The Journal of Accountancy* 136 (September 1973): 44-52.

Stevens, Robert G. "Motivation Program to Increase the Effectiveness of Accounting Courses." *The Accounting Review* 35 (October 1956): 666-71.

Stone, Williard E. "Can Accounting Meet the Challenge of Liberalized Business Education?" *The Accounting Review* 35 (July 1960): 515-20.

_____. "Developments in Accounting Instruction." *The Accounting Review* 36 (July 1961): 474-77.

Swick, Ralph D. "Objectives of Accounting Education." *The Accounting Review* 36 (October 1961): 626-30.

OTHER

Ahrens, M.R. "Curriculum Improvement through Action Research." *High School Journal* 39 (1956): 364-69.

Ammons, Margaret. "An Empirical Study of Process and Product in Curriculum Development." *Journal of Educational Research* (May-June 1964), 451-57.

Astin, Alexander W. "Classroom Environment in Different Fields of Study." *Journal of Educational Psychology* 56 (1965): 275-82.

Ausubel, D.P. *Educational Psychology: A Cognitive View.* New York: Holt, Rinehart and Winston, 1968.

Bachman, C.W. and Secord, P.F. *A Social Psychological View of Education.* New York: Harcourt, Brace and World, 1968.

Backstrom, C.M. and Hursh, G. *Survey Research.* Evanston, Ill.: Northwestern University Press, 1963.

Banathy, Bela H. *Developing a Systems View of Education: The Systems-Model Approach.* Belmont, Calif.: Fearon Publishers, 1973.

Barzun, Jacques. *House of Intellect.* New York: Harper and Row, 1959.

Blauch, L.E., ed. *Education for the Professions.* Washington, D.C.: U.S. Office of Education, 1955.

Bloom, Benjamin S., Hastings, J. Thomas, Madaus, George F., et al. *Handbook on Formative and Summative Evaluation of Student Learning.* New York: McGraw-Hill, 1971.

Bloom, Benjamin S., Krathwohl, D.R. and Masia, B.B. *Taxonomy of Educational Objectives, The Classification of Educational Goals: Cognitive and Affective Domains.* New York: David McKay Co., 1969.

Borg, Walter R. *Educational Research.* New York: David McKay Co., 1963.

Borton, Terry. "What's Left When School's Forgotten?" *Saturday Review,* April 18, 1970, pp. 69-71, 79-80.

Brown, G.I. *Human Teaching for Human Learning: An Introduction to Confluent Education.* New York: Viking Press, 1971.

Bruner, Jerome S. *The Process of Education.* Cambridge, Mass.: Harvard University Press, 1960.

Buckley, John W. *In Search of Identity — An Inquiry into Identify Issues in Accounting.* Los Angeles: California Certified Public Accountants Foundation for Education and Research, 1972.

Buckley, John W. And Buckley, Marlene H. *The Accounting Profession.* Los Angeles: Melville Publishing Co., 1974.

Carey, John L. *The Rise of the Accounting Profession: To Responsibility and Authority, 1937-1969.* New York: American Institute of Certified Public Accountants, 1970.

_____. *The Rise of the Accounting Profession: From Technician to Professional, 1896-1936.* New York: American Institute of Certified Public Accountants, 1969.

Carr-Saunders, A.M. and Wilson, P.A. *The Professions.* Oxford, England: Clarendon Press, 1933.

Citizens Commission on Graduate Medical Education. Report of the Commission. *The Graduate Education of Physicians.* Chicago: American Medical Association, 1966.

Clark, John J. and Opulente, Blaise J., eds. *Professional Education for Business.* Jamaica, N.Y.: St. John's University Press, 1964.

Conant, James B. *The Education of American Teachers.* New York: McGraw-Hill, 1963.

Cook, Walter W., Hovet, Kenneth O., and Kearney, Nolan C. "Curriculum Research." *Review of Educational Research* 26 (1956): 224-240.

Corey, Stephen M. "Editorial: Curriculum Research." *Educational Leadership* 11 (1954): 463-65.

Craig, Robert C. *The Psychology of Learning in the Classroom*. New York: Macmillan Co., 1966.

Craven, Olga, Todd, Alden L., and Ziegler, Jesse H., eds. *Theological Education as Professional Education*. Vandalia, Ohio: The Association of Theological Schools in the U.S. and Canada, 1969.

Cronbach, L.J. and Suppes, P., eds. *Research for Tomorrow's Schools: Disciplined Inquiry for Education*. New York: Macmillan Co., 1969.

Cross, Kathryn P. "When Will Research Improve Education?" *The Research Reporter* 2 (1967): 1-4.

De Cecco, J.P. *The Psychology of Learning and Instruction: Educational Psychology*. Englewood Cliffs, N.J.: Prentice-Hall, 1968.

Deese, James E. and Hulse, Stewart H. *The Psychology of Learning*. 3rd ed. New York: McGraw-Hill, 1967.

Developing and Writing Behavior Objectives. Tucson, Ariz.: Educational Innovators Press, 1968.

Developing and Writing Performance Objectives. Tucson, Ariz.: Educational Innovators Press, 1971.

Dillman, Caroline Matheny and Rahmlow, Harold F. *Writing Instructional Objectives*. Belmont, Calif.: Fearon Publishers, 1972.

Dixon, John R. "The Lost Mission in Engineering." *Journal of Engineering Education* 53 (March 1963): 434-38.

Doherty, R.E. *The Development of Professional Education*. Pittsburg, Pa.: Carnegie Press, 1950.

Dubin, R. and Taveggia, T.C. *The Teaching-Learning Paradox: A Comparative Analysis of College Teaching Methods*. Eugene, Ore.: Center for the Advanced Study of Educational Administration, University of Oregon, 1968.

Ebel, Robert L. "Behavioral Objectives: A Close Look." *Phi Delta Kappan* 52 (1970): 171-73.

_____. *Essentials of Educational Measurement*. Englewood Cliffs, N.J.: Prentice-Hall, 1972.

Eisner, Elliot W. "Educational Objectives: Help or Hindrance." *School Review* (Autumn 1967), 250-60.

Eiss, Albert F. and Harbule, Mary Blatt. *Behavioral Objectives in the Affective Domain*. Washington, D.C.: National Science Supervisors Association, A Section of the National Science Teachers Association, 1969.

Engelhart, Max D. *Methods of Educational Research*. Chicago: Rand McNally & Co., 1972.

Fattu, N.A. "The Role of Research in Education — Present and Future." *Review of Educational Research* 30 (1960): 409-21.

Gage, N.L., ed. *Handbook of Research on Teaching*. Chicago: Rand-McNally, 1963.

Gagne, Robert M. *The Conditions of Learning*. 2nd ed. New York: Holt, Rinehart & Winston, 1970.

Gardner, John. *No Easy Victories.* New York: Harper & Row, 1968.

_____. *Self-Renewal: The Individual and the Innovative Society.* New York: Harper & Row, 1963.

Gilchrist, Robert S. and Roberts, Bernice R. *Curriculum Development: A Humanized Systems Approach.* Belmont, Calif.: Fearon Publishers, 1974.

Goode, W.J. "Community within a Community: The Professions." *American Sociological Review* 22 (1957): 194-200.

_____. "Encroachment Charlatanism, and the Emerging Profession: Psychology, Sociology, and Medicine." *American Sociological Review* 25 (1960): 902-14.

Goode, W.J. "The Librarian: From Occupation to Profession?" *The Library Quarterly* 31 (1961): 306-20.

Gordon, Robert Aaron and Howell, James Edwin. *Higher Education for Business.* New York: Columbia University Press, 1959.

Grieder, C. "Is it Possible to Word Educational Goals?" *Nation's Schools* 68 (1961).

Gronlund, Norman E. *Measurement and Evaluation in Teaching.* 2nd ed. New York: Macmillan Co., 1971.

_____. *Stating Behavioral Objectives for Classroom Instruction.* New York: Macmillan Co., 1970.

Gustafson, J.M. "The Clergy in the United States." *Daedalus* 92 (Fall 1963): 724.

Harman, H.H. *Modern Factor Analysis.* 2nd ed. Chicago: University of Chicago Press, 1967.

Hayman, John L., Jr. *Research in Education.* Columbus, Ohio: Charles E. Merrill, 1968.

Hilgard, Ernest R., ed. "Postscript: Twenty Years of Learning Theory in Relation to Education." *Theories of Learning and Instruction.* The Sixty-third Yearbook of the National Society for the Study of Education, Part I. Chicago: National Society for the Study of Education, 1964.

Hilgard, Ernest R. and Bower, Gordon H. *Theories of Learning.* 3rd ed. New York: Appleton-Century-Crofts, 1966.

Hodenfield, G.K. and Stinnet, T.M. *The Education of Teachers.* Englewood Cliffs, N.J.: Prentice-Hall, 1961.

Horowitz, M.J. *Educating Tomorrow's Doctors.* New York: Appleton-Century-Crofts, 1964.

Hutchins, E.B. "The AAMC Longitudinal Study: Implications for Medical Education." *Journal of Medical Education* 39 (1964): 265.

Koerner, James D. *The Miseducation of American Teachers.* Boston: Houghton Mifflin, 1963.

Krathwohl, David R. "Stating Objectives Appropriately for Program, for Curriculum, and for Instructional Material Development." *Journal of Teacher Education* (March 1965), 83-92.

Ladinsky, Jack. "Careers of Lawyers, Law Practice and Legal Institutions." *American Sociological Review* 28 (1963): 47-54.

Lee, P.V. *Medical Schools and the Changing Times: Nine Case Reports on Experimentation in Medical Education.* Evanston, Ill.: Association of American Medical Colleges, 1962.

Lieberman, Myron. *Education as a Profession.* Englewood Cliffs, N.J.: Prentice-Hall, 1956.

Lindquist, E.F. *Statistical Analysis in Educational Research.* Boston: Houghton Mifflin, 1940.

Lindvall, Carl. M., ed. *Defining Educational Objectives.* Pittsburg: University of Pittsburgh Press, 1964.

Lynn, Kenneth, ed. *Professions in America.* Boston: Houghton Mifflin, 1965.

Mager, Robert F. *Developing Attitude Toward Learning.* Belmont Calif.: Fearon Publishers, 1968.

_____. *Goal Analysis.* Belmont, Calif.: Fearon Publishers, 1972.

_____. *Preparing Instructional Objectives.* Belmont, Calif.: Fearon Publishers, 1962.

Mann, et al. *The College Classroom: Conflict, Change, and Learning.* New York: John Wiley & Sons, 1970.

Mauldin, W.P. and Marks, E.S. "Problems of Response in Enumerative Surveys." *American Sociological Review* 15 (1950): 649-57.

McGlothen, William J. *Patterns of Professional Education.* New York: G.P. Putnam's Sons, 1960.

Mednick, Sarnoff A. *Learning.* Englewood Cliffs, N.J.: Prentice Hall, 1964.

Mehrens, William A. and Lehmann, Irvin J. *Measurement and Evaluation in Education and Psychology.* New York: Holt, Rinehart & Winston, 1973.

Melton, A.W., ed. *Categories of Human Learning.* New York: Academic Press, 1964.

Merton, Robert K., Bloom, Samuel and Rogoff, Natalie. "Studies in the Sociology of Medical Education." *Journal of Medical Education* 31 (1956): 552-65.

Merton, Robert K., Reader, G.G. and Kendall, P.L. *The Student-Physician: Introductory Studies in the Sociology of Medical Education.* Cambridge: Harvard University Press, 1957.

Miller, G.E., ed. *Teaching and Learning in Medical School.* Cambridge: Harvard University Press, 1961.

Moonitz, Maurice, ed. *Public Accounting: 1980.* Palo Alto, Calif.: California Certified Public Accountants Foundation for Education and Research, 1971.

Morrison, A. and McIntyre, D., eds. *Social Psychology of Teaching.* Baltimore: Penguin Books, 1972.

Nelson, H.G. "Impact and Validity of the Ford and Carnegie Reports on Business Education." *The Accounting Review* (April 1961): 179-85.

Niebuhr, H.R., Williams, D.D. and Gustafson, J.M. *The Advancement of Theological Education.* New York: Harper & Row, 1957.

Norwood, William F. "The Mainstream of American Medical Education, 1765-1965." *Annals of the New York Academy of Science* 128 (1965): 463-72.

Ojemann, Ralph H. "Should Educational Objectives be Stated in Behavioral Terms? Part I." *Elementary School Journal* (February 1968), 223-31.

_____. "Should Educational Objectives be Stated in Behavioral Terms? Part II." *Elementary School Journal* (February 1969), 229-35.

_____. "Should Educational Objectives be Stated in Behavioral Terms? Part III." *Elementary School Journal* (February 1970), 271-78.

Olsen, Rees G. "On Not Forgetting What We've Learned About Learning." *Music Educators Journal* 55 (1968): 57-59.

Oppenheim, A.N. *Questionnaire Design and Attitude Measurement.* New York: Basic Books, 1966.

Parten, Mildred. *Surveys, Polls, and Samples: Practical Procedures.* New York: Cooper Square Publishers, 1966.

Peddiwell, J.A. *The Saber-Tooth Curriculum.* New York: McGraw-Hill, 1939.

Pierson, Frank C., et al. *The Education of American Businessmen.* New York: McGraw-Hill, 1959.

Pipe, Peter. *Objectives — Tool for Change.* Belmont, Calif.: Fearon Publishers, 1975.

Popham, W. James. *The Uses of Instructional Objectives: A Personal Perspective.* Belmont, Calif.: Fearon Publishers, 1973.

_____. *Criterion-Referenced Instruction.* Belmont, Calif.: Fearon Publishers, 1973.

Popper, Hans. "New Objectives in Medical Education." *Annals of the New York Academy of Science* 128 (1965): 473-79.

Postman, Neil and Weingartner, Charles. *Teaching as a Subversive Activity.* New York: Delacorte Press, 1969.

Potter, Dale R., et al. *Questionnaires for Research: An Annotated Bibliography on Design, Construction, and Use.* USDA Forest Service Research Paper PNW-140. Portland, Ore.: USDA Forest Service, 1972.

Runkel, Philip, Harrison, Roger and Runkel, Margaret, eds. *The Changing College Classroom.* San Francisco: Jossey-Bass, 1969.

Sanazaro, P.J. "An Agenda for Research in Medical Education." *Journal of the American Medical Association* 197 (1966): 979-84.

Sax, Gilbert. *Empirical Foundations of Educational Research.* Englewood Cliffs, N.J.: Prentice Hall, 1968.

Scriven, Michael. "The Philosophy of Science in Educational Research." *Review of Educational Research* 30 (1960): 422-29.

Selltiz, Claire, et al. *Research Methods in Social Research.* New York: Holt, Rinehart and Winston, 1959.

Sheth, Jagdish N. and Roscoe, A. Marvin, Jr. "Impact of Questionnaire Length, Follow-Up Methods, and Geographical Location on Response Rate to a Mail Survey." *Journal of Applied Psychology* 60 (1975): 252-54.

Shulman, L.S. "Reconstruction of Educational Research." *Review of Educational Research* 40 (1970): 371-96.

Sieker, H.O. "A New Curriculum for Medical Education." *Clinical Research* 13 (1965): 3.

Silberman, Charles. *Crisis in the Classroom*. New York: Random House. Random House, 1969.

Spence, K.W. "The Relation of Learning Theory to the Technology of Education." *Harvard Educational Review* 29 (1959): 84-95.

Sterret, J.E. "The Profession of Accountancy." *Annals of the American Academy of Political and Social Science* (July-December 1906), 16-27.

Stowe, L.M. "Planning for the Several Products of a Medical School." *Journal of the American Medical Association* 194 (1965): 1299.

"Symposium on Medical Education: The Have and Have-Not Medical Schools." *Journal of the American Medical Association* 185 (1963): 367-85.

Tatsuoka, Maurice M. *Multivariate Analysis: Techniques for Educational and Psychological Research*. New York: John Wiley & Sons, 1971.

Thelen, Herbert A. "Some Classroom Quiddities for People-Oriented Teachers." *Journal of Applied Behavioral Science* 1 (1965): 270-85.

Toffler, Alvin. *Future Shock*. New York: Random House, 1970.

Torgerson, W.S. *Theory and Methods of Scaling*. New York: John Wiley & Sons, 1958.

Travers, Robert M.W., ed. *Second Handbook of Research on Teaching*. Chicago: Rand McNally & Co., 1973.

Trow, M. "Methodological Problems in the Evaluation of Innovation." *The Evaluation of Instruction: Issues and Problems*. Edited by M.C. Wittrock and D.E. Wiley. New York: Holt, Rinehart & Winston, 1970.

Tyler, Ralph W. "Achievement Testing and Curriculum Construction." *Trends in Student Personnel Work*. Edited by E.G. Williamson. Minneapolis: University of Minnesota Press, 1949.

_____. "The Relation Between Recall and Higher Mental Processes." *Education as Cultivation of the Higher Mental Processes*. Edited by C.H. Judd. New York: Macmillan, 1936.

Venn, Grant. *Man, Education and Work*. Washington, D.C.: American Council on Education, 1964.

Vollmer, Howard M. and Mills, Donald L., eds. *Professionalization*. Englewood Cliffs, N.J.: Prentice-Hall, 1966.

Watson, Goodwin. "What Do We Know About Learning?" *NEA Journal* 52 (March 1963): 20-22.

Weinberg, Carl. *Education is A Shuck*. New York: William Morrow, 1974.

Whitehead, Alfred North. *The Aims of Education*. Mentor Edition, published by The New American Library of World Literature, 1949. New York: Macmillan Co., 1929.

Wilensky, Harold L. "The Professionalization of Everyone?" *The American Journal of Sociology* (September 1964), 137-58.

Winer, B.J. *Statistical Principles in Experimental Design*. 2nd ed. New York: McGraw-Hill, 1971.

The American Accounting Association, with the financial support of the Price Waterhouse Foundation, is conducting a research project designed to enhance the quality of accounting education. We would appreciate your assistance in this important endeavor by completing and returning the enclosed questionnaire. This is *not* a random sample survey. We are convinced that you can assist us in obtaining important information on the issues with which we are concerned.

The main purpose of the research project is to make well-grounded recommendations with respect to the objectives and composition of formal accounting education. The basis for our recommendations will be primarily the views of a limited number of individuals, such as yourself, with recognized expertise in accounting education or practice. It is anticipated that the research will result in one or more publications in the Education Series of the American Accounting Association and that it may have a significant impact upon the future direction of accounting education.

Specific instructions for the completion of the questionnaire are included therein. It should require about sixty minutes to complete the questionnaire. Individual responses will be maintained strictly confidential. The questionnaire is coded solely for the benefit of the researchers in their follow-up efforts.

Please complete and return the questionnaire to Professor Richard Flaherty, project director for the American Accounting Association, at your earliest convenience in the envelope provided for you.

Thank you for your cooperation.

Sincerely,

Wilton T. Anderson
President

Encs.

Demographic Information

AN OPINION SURVEY
OF
ACCOUNTING CURRICULA

Conducted
under the auspices of the
AMERICAN ACCOUNTING ASSOCIATION

Richard E. Flaherty, Ph.D., CPA
Project Director, American Accounting Association
361 Commerce West
University of Illinois
Urbana, Illinois 61801

This questionnaire contains a personal data section (Part I), a section for assessing the importance of and educational objectives for certain accounting topics (Part II), and a section for soliciting your views regarding other aspects of accounting curricula (Part III). **Please respond to all items in the questionnaire.**

PART I

EDUCATION:

Degrees Earned	Name of Institution	Major Area of Concentration	Year Degree Granted
[ ] Bachelors	_____	_____	_____
[ ] Masters	_____	_____	_____
[ ] Doctorate	_____	_____	_____
[ ] Law	_____	_____	_____

AGE: [ ] Under 30   [ ] 30-39   [ ] 40-49   [ ] 50-59   [ ] 60 or over

PROFESSIONAL CERTIFICATION:
   [ ] CPA   [ ] CMA   [ ] CIA   [ ] Other (specify) _____

EXPERIENCE:

Experience	Number of Years
[ ] Education	_____
[ ] Dean, Department Head (Chairman) or Area Coordinator	_____
[ ] Public Accounting	_____
[ ] Corporate Accounting	_____
[ ] Not-for-profit Accounting	_____
[ ] Other (specify) _____	_____

PRIMARY AREA OF ACCOUNTING EXPERTISE   *(Please check only one response. Your response to this question indicates the viewpoint from which you should respond to the remainder of the questionnaire.)*

   [ ] Managerial accounting
   [ ] Information systems
   [ ] Taxation
   [ ] Financial accounting and reporting
   [ ] Auditing
   [ ] Not-for-profit accounting
   [ ] Generalist

TYPE OF FIRM WITH WHICH AFFILIATED:
   [ ] National
   [ ] Regional
   [ ] Local

PART II

PLEASE READ THIS PAGE CAREFULLY BEFORE RESPONDING TO PART II.

We are interested in your views on the following two issues:

(1) the degree of importance of selected accounting topics in the accounting curriculum and

(2) the degree to which two specified educational objectives should be achieved.

Your responses should reflect the following frame of reference:

(1) your perception of desired *entry-level accounting education* for an accounting graduate beginning a career in your area of accounting expertise. Your area of accounting expertise (as indicated in Part I) is _____;

(2) your perception of the *future environment* in which accounting graduates in your area of accounting expertise will operate; and

(3) an awareness that time and other resources are scarce commodities in a formal educational program.

Scales are provided on the following pages for your responses to these issues. The scales are defined and described on the fold-out sheet. ***Please read the fold-out sheet carefully before responding to Part II.***

(FOLD-OUT SHEET)

SCALE DESCRIPTIONS

IMPORTANCE. Your responses on this scale indicate your feelings about the importance of the topic in a curriculum designed to prepare an individual for a career in your area of accounting expertise. You are to indicate the importance you attach to each topic by circling the appropriate number according to the following scale:

	0 1 2 3 4	
Not Important		Extremely Important

EDUCATIONAL OBJECTIVES. The responses on these scales indicate your feelings about the degree to which each of the two educational objectives should be achieved. The two educational objectives are described as "conceptual knowledge" and "technical ability."

Conceptual knowledge refers to mental processes ranging from simple recall or awareness to creative thinking or evaluation. Indicate the degree of conceptual knowledge that should be achieved for each topic by circling the appropriate number according to the following scale:

	0 1 2 3 4	
No Conceptual Knowledge		Very High Conceptual Knowledge

Technical ability refers to skill in applying existing knowledge to the solution of problems ranging from classification and definition to the application of complex theories in novel problem situations. Indicate the degree of technical ability that should be achieved for each topic by circling the appropriate number according to the following scale:

	0 1 2 3 4	
No Technical Ability		Very High Technical Ability

If you do not understand the meaning of a topic, please do not respond to the applicable scales.

If an educational objective appears to be inapplicable for a particular topic, your response should be "0."

TOPIC	IMPORTANCE	Conceptual Knowledge	Technical Ability
FINANCIAL:			
Regulatory influences (e.g., Financial Accounting Standards Board and governmental agencies)	0 1 2 3 4	0 1 2 3 4	0 1 2 3 4
U.S. financial accounting and reporting standards	0 1 2 3 4	0 1 2 3 4	0 1 2 3 4
International accounting standards	0 1 2 3 4	0 1 2 3 4	0 1 2 3 4
Foreign currency translation	0 1 2 3 4	0 1 2 3 4	0 1 2 3 4
Information needs of financial statement users	0 1 2 3 4	0 1 2 3 4	0 1 2 3 4
Theoretical framework:			
Current structure	0 1 2 3 4	0 1 2 3 4	0 1 2 3 4
Alternatives to current structure (e.g., current value accounting)	0 1 2 3 4	0 1 2 3 4	0 1 2 3 4
Behavioral considerations in financial reporting	0 1 2 3 4	0 1 2 3 4	0 1 2 3 4
Double-entry system	0 1 2 3 4	0 1 2 3 4	0 1 2 3 4
Accruals and deferrals	0 1 2 3 4	0 1 2 3 4	0 1 2 3 4
Transaction analysis	0 1 2 3 4	0 1 2 3 4	0 1 2 3 4
SEC reporting	0 1 2 3 4	0 1 2 3 4	0 1 2 3 4
Balance sheet (general concepts, classifications, preparation, etc.)	0 1 2 3 4	0 1 2 3 4	0 1 2 3 4
Income statement (general concepts, classifications, preparation, etc.)	0 1 2 3 4	0 1 2 3 4	0 1 2 3 4
Statement of changes in financial position (general concepts, classifications, preparations, etc.)	0 1 2 3 4	0 1 2 3 4	0 1 2 3 4
Financial statement analysis	0 1 2 3 4	0 1 2 3 4	0 1 2 3 4
Present value and future worth concepts	0 1 2 3 4	0 1 2 3 4	0 1 2 3 4
Cash	0 1 2 3 4	0 1 2 3 4	0 1 2 3 4
Receivables	0 1 2 3 4	0 1 2 3 4	0 1 2 3 4
Investments in securities (including both debt and equity)	0 1 2 3 4	0 1 2 3 4	0 1 2 3 4
Inventories	0 1 2 3 4	0 1 2 3 4	0 1 2 3 4
Fixed assets	0 1 2 3 4	0 1 2 3 4	0 1 2 3 4
Depreciation, depletion and amortization	0 1 2 3 4	0 1 2 3 4	0 1 2 3 4
Consignments	0 1 2 3 4	0 1 2 3 4	0 1 2 3 4
Installment sales	0 1 2 3 4	0 1 2 3 4	0 1 2 3 4
Intangibles (excluding goodwill)	0 1 2 3 4	0 1 2 3 4	0 1 2 3 4
Goodwill	0 1 2 3 4	0 1 2 3 4	0 1 2 3 4
Error corrections	0 1 2 3 4	0 1 2 3 4	0 1 2 3 4
Statements from incomplete records	0 1 2 3 4	0 1 2 3 4	0 1 2 3 4
Short-term liabilities	0 1 2 3 4	0 1 2 3 4	0 1 2 3 4
Long-term liabilities	0 1 2 3 4	0 1 2 3 4	0 1 2 3 4
Minority interest	0 1 2 3 4	0 1 2 3 4	0 1 2 3 4
Corporate equity	0 1 2 3 4	0 1 2 3 4	0 1 2 3 4
Convertible debt or equity	0 1 2 3 4	0 1 2 3 4	0 1 2 3 4
Treasury stock	0 1 2 3 4	0 1 2 3 4	0 1 2 3 4
Partnership financial statements	0 1 2 3 4	0 1 2 3 4	0 1 2 3 4
Fiduciary accounting:			
Bankruptcy	0 1 2 3 4	0 1 2 3 4	0 1 2 3 4
Receivership	0 1 2 3 4	0 1 2 3 4	0 1 2 3 4
Estates and trusts	0 1 2 3 4	0 1 2 3 4	0 1 2 3 4
Price-level adjusted financial statements	0 1 2 3 4	0 1 2 3 4	0 1 2 3 4
Pensions	0 1 2 3 4	0 1 2 3 4	0 1 2 3 4
Leases	0 1 2 3 4	0 1 2 3 4	0 1 2 3 4
Deferred taxes	0 1 2 3 4	0 1 2 3 4	0 1 2 3 4
Segment reporting	0 1 2 3 4	0 1 2 3 4	0 1 2 3 4
Interim reporting	0 1 2 3 4	0 1 2 3 4	0 1 2 3 4
Contingencies	0 1 2 3 4	0 1 2 3 4	0 1 2 3 4
Materiality	0 1 2 3 4	0 1 2 3 4	0 1 2 3 4
Human resource accounting	0 1 2 3 4	0 1 2 3 4	0 1 2 3 4

TOPIC	IMPORTANCE	Conceptual Knowledge	Technical Ability
		EDUCATIONAL OBJECTIVES	
Development stage companies	0 1 2 3 4	0 1 2 3 4	0 1 2 3 4
Research and development costs	0 1 2 3 4	0 1 2 3 4	0 1 2 3 4
Business combinations:			
Purchase vs. pooling of interest	0 1 2 3 4	0 1 2 3 4	0 1 2 3 4
Consolidation procedures (e.g., intercompany profit elimination, treatment of majority and minority interest, statement preparation)	0 1 2 3 4	0 1 2 3 4	0 1 2 3 4
Unconsolidated subsidiaries	0 1 2 3 4	0 1 2 3 4	0 1 2 3 4
Regulated industries	0 1 2 3 4	0 1 2 3 4	0 1 2 3 4
Earnings-per-share	0 1 2 3 4	0 1 2 3 4	0 1 2 3 4
Reporting forecasts	0 1 2 3 4	0 1 2 3 4	0 1 2 3 4
Accounting for income taxes	0 1 2 3 4	0 1 2 3 4	0 1 2 3 4
Full costing vs. successful effort costing	0 1 2 3 4	0 1 2 3 4	0 1 2 3 4
Fund accounting:			
Types of organizations	0 1 2 3 4	0 1 2 3 4	0 1 2 3 4
Financial statements	0 1 2 3 4	0 1 2 3 4	0 1 2 3 4
Governmental units	0 1 2 3 4	0 1 2 3 4	0 1 2 3 4
Hospitals	0 1 2 3 4	0 1 2 3 4	0 1 2 3 4
Colleges and universities	0 1 2 3 4	0 1 2 3 4	0 1 2 3 4
National income accounting	0 1 2 3 4	0 1 2 3 4	0 1 2 3 4
Revenue and expense recognition	0 1 2 3 4	0 1 2 3 4	0 1 2 3 4
MANAGERIAL:			
Job order costing	0 1 2 3 4	0 1 2 3 4	0 1 2 3 4
Process costing	0 1 2 3 4	0 1 2 3 4	0 1 2 3 4
Full costing (including alternative methods of overhead allocation)	0 1 2 3 4	0 1 2 3 4	0 1 2 3 4
Variable costing	0 1 2 3 4	0 1 2 3 4	0 1 2 3 4
Direct costing	0 1 2 3 4	0 1 2 3 4	0 1 2 3 4
Zero base budgeting	0 1 2 3 4	0 1 2 3 4	0 1 2 3 4
Joint costs	0 1 2 3 4	0 1 2 3 4	0 1 2 3 4
Standard costs	0 1 2 3 4	0 1 2 3 4	0 1 2 3 4
Spoilage, waste, defective units and scrap	0 1 2 3 4	0 1 2 3 4	0 1 2 3 4
Long-range planning	0 1 2 3 4	0 1 2 3 4	0 1 2 3 4
Short-range planning	0 1 2 3 4	0 1 2 3 4	0 1 2 3 4
Flexible budgets	0 1 2 3 4	0 1 2 3 4	0 1 2 3 4
Cash management	0 1 2 3 4	0 1 2 3 4	0 1 2 3 4
Budgeted financial statements	0 1 2 3 4	0 1 2 3 4	0 1 2 3 4
Cost-volume-profit analysis	0 1 2 3 4	0 1 2 3 4	0 1 2 3 4
Tax considerations in managerial decisions	0 1 2 3 4	0 1 2 3 4	0 1 2 3 4
Capital budgeting	0 1 2 3 4	0 1 2 3 4	0 1 2 3 4
Organization theory	0 1 2 3 4	0 1 2 3 4	0 1 2 3 4
Information economics (i.e. cost and benefit of additional information)	0 1 2 3 4	0 1 2 3 4	0 1 2 3 4
Management information systems:			
Internal control aspects	0 1 2 3 4	0 1 2 3 4	0 1 2 3 4
Impact of external regulatory influences (e.g., Cost Accounting Standards Board, Financial Accounting Standards Board, SEC)	0 1 2 3 4	0 1 2 3 4	0 1 2 3 4
Design	0 1 2 3 4	0 1 2 3 4	0 1 2 3 4
Implementation	0 1 2 3 4	0 1 2 3 4	0 1 2 3 4
Administration	0 1 2 3 4	0 1 2 3 4	0 1 2 3 4
Managerial accounting uses of quantitative techniques:			
Simulation	0 1 2 3 4	0 1 2 3 4	0 1 2 3 4
Network methods	0 1 2 3 4	0 1 2 3 4	0 1 2 3 4

TOPIC	IMPORTANCE	EDUCATIONAL OBJECTIVES Conceptual Knowledge	Technical Ability
Linear programming	0 1 2 3 4	0 1 2 3 4	0 1 2 3 4
Sensitivity analysis	0 1 2 3 4	0 1 2 3 4	0 1 2 3 4
Statistical decision theory	0 1 2 3 4	0 1 2 3 4	0 1 2 3 4
Statistical cost estimation	0 1 2 3 4	0 1 2 3 4	0 1 2 3 4
Learning curve models	0 1 2 3 4	0 1 2 3 4	0 1 2 3 4
Statistical analysis of cost variances	0 1 2 3 4	0 1 2 3 4	0 1 2 3 4
Corporate planning models	0 1 2 3 4	0 1 2 3 4	0 1 2 3 4
Computer science	0 1 2 3 4	0 1 2 3 4	0 1 2 3 4
Special considerations in nonmanufacturing concerns	0 1 2 3 4	0 1 2 3 4	0 1 2 3 4
Performance evaluation:			
Return on investment	0 1 2 3 4	0 1 2 3 4	0 1 2 3 4
Divisional performance	0 1 2 3 4	0 1 2 3 4	0 1 2 3 4
Transfer pricing	0 1 2 3 4	0 1 2 3 4	0 1 2 3 4
Common costs	0 1 2 3 4	0 1 2 3 4	0 1 2 3 4
Responsibility accounting	0 1 2 3 4	0 1 2 3 4	0 1 2 3 4
Residual income	0 1 2 3 4	0 1 2 3 4	0 1 2 3 4
Nonfinancial performance measures	0 1 2 3 4	0 1 2 3 4	0 1 2 3 4
Nonstatistical variance analysis	0 1 2 3 4	0 1 2 3 4	0 1 2 3 4
Behavioral considerations	0 1 2 3 4	0 1 2 3 4	0 1 2 3 4
Internal financial auditing	0 1 2 3 4	0 1 2 3 4	0 1 2 3 4
Internal operational auditing	0 1 2 3 4	0 1 2 3 4	0 1 2 3 4
Requirements for professional certification (CMA)	0 1 2 3 4	0 1 2 3 4	0 1 2 3 4
Planning and control of international operations	0 1 2 3 4	0 1 2 3 4	0 1 2 3 4
Social accounting (e.g., costs of meeting societal responsibilities, effect upon management decisions)	0 1 2 3 4	0 1 2 3 4	0 1 2 3 4
Overhead control	0 1 2 3 4	0 1 2 3 4	0 1 2 3 4
Accounting information requirements for management decisions (e.g., pricing, purchasing, production)	0 1 2 3 4	0 1 2 3 4	0 1 2 3 4

AUDITING:

TOPIC	IMPORTANCE	Conceptual Knowledge	Technical Ability
Historical development of auditing	0 1 2 3 4	0 1 2 3 4	0 1 2 3 4
Users' expectations regarding the auditor's role	0 1 2 3 4	0 1 2 3 4	0 1 2 3 4
Influence of professional and regulatory bodies (e.g., AICPA, governmental agencies) upon the auditing function	0 1 2 3 4	0 1 2 3 4	0 1 2 3 4
SEC filing requirements	0 1 2 3 4	0 1 2 3 4	0 1 2 3 4
Requirements for professional certification (CPA)	0 1 2 3 4	0 1 2 3 4	0 1 2 3 4
Generally accepted auditing standards (GAAS)	0 1 2 3 4	0 1 2 3 4	0 1 2 3 4
Professional rules of conduct	0 1 2 3 4	0 1 2 3 4	0 1 2 3 4
Legal responsibilities of the auditor:			
At common law to clients and third party users of financial statements	0 1 2 3 4	0 1 2 3 4	0 1 2 3 4
Under the securities acts to third party users of financial statements	0 1 2 3 4	0 1 2 3 4	0 1 2 3 4
Classic cases	0 1 2 3 4	0 1 2 3 4	0 1 2 3 4
Responses of the auditing profession to classic cases	0 1 2 3 4	0 1 2 3 4	0 1 2 3 4
Exposure to criminal liability	0 1 2 3 4	0 1 2 3 4	0 1 2 3 4
Standard short-form audit report	0 1 2 3 4	0 1 2 3 4	0 1 2 3 4
Modifications of the standard short-form audit report	0 1 2 3 4	0 1 2 3 4	0 1 2 3 4
Long-form audit report	0 1 2 3 4	0 1 2 3 4	0 1 2 3 4
Internal control:			
Relationship of GAAS	0 1 2 3 4	0 1 2 3 4	0 1 2 3 4
Principles	0 1 2 3 4	0 1 2 3 4	0 1 2 3 4

TOPIC	IMPORTANCE	EDUCATIONAL OBJECTIVES: Conceptual Knowledge	EDUCATIONAL OBJECTIVES: Technical Ability
Description based on:			
Narrative	0 1 2 3 4	0 1 2 3 4	0 1 2 3 4
Questionnaire	0 1 2 3 4	0 1 2 3 4	0 1 2 3 4
Flowchart	0 1 2 3 4	0 1 2 3 4	0 1 2 3 4
Evaluation	0 1 2 3 4	0 1 2 3 4	0 1 2 3 4
Audit exposure due to weaknesses	0 1 2 3 4	0 1 2 3 4	0 1 2 3 4
Modifications in audit program based on evaluation	0 1 2 3 4	0 1 2 3 4	0 1 2 3 4
In an EDP environment	0 1 2 3 4	0 1 2 3 4	0 1 2 3 4
Statistical inference in auditing:			
Judgmental sampling	0 1 2 3 4	0 1 2 3 4	0 1 2 3 4
Statistical sampling	0 1 2 3 4	0 1 2 3 4	0 1 2 3 4
Regression analysis	0 1 2 3 4	0 1 2 3 4	0 1 2 3 4
Other statistical methods	0 1 2 3 4	0 1 2 3 4	0 1 2 3 4
Audit evidence:			
Types	0 1 2 3 4	0 1 2 3 4	0 1 2 3 4
Relative strength of types	0 1 2 3 4	0 1 2 3 4	0 1 2 3 4
Post-statement events	0 1 2 3 4	0 1 2 3 4	0 1 2 3 4
Auditing procedures:			
Working papers	0 1 2 3 4	0 1 2 3 4	0 1 2 3 4
Compliance tests	0 1 2 3 4	0 1 2 3 4	0 1 2 3 4
Tests of transactions	0 1 2 3 4	0 1 2 3 4	0 1 2 3 4
Tests of account balances	0 1 2 3 4	0 1 2 3 4	0 1 2 3 4
Review of operations	0 1 2 3 4	0 1 2 3 4	0 1 2 3 4
Audit practice case	0 1 2 3 4	0 1 2 3 4	0 1 2 3 4
Management letter	0 1 2 3 4	0 1 2 3 4	0 1 2 3 4
Audit administration:			
Planning	0 1 2 3 4	0 1 2 3 4	0 1 2 3 4
Supervision	0 1 2 3 4	0 1 2 3 4	0 1 2 3 4
Review (quality control issues)	0 1 2 3 4	0 1 2 3 4	0 1 2 3 4
Client relations	0 1 2 3 4	0 1 2 3 4	0 1 2 3 4
Setting and collecting fees	0 1 2 3 4	0 1 2 3 4	0 1 2 3 4
Accounting firm organization	0 1 2 3 4	0 1 2 3 4	0 1 2 3 4
Operational auditing:			
Objectives	0 1 2 3 4	0 1 2 3 4	0 1 2 3 4
Methodology	0 1 2 3 4	0 1 2 3 4	0 1 2 3 4
Extensions of the attest function:			
Possible areas	0 1 2 3 4	0 1 2 3 4	0 1 2 3 4
Associated audit risk	0 1 2 3 4	0 1 2 3 4	0 1 2 3 4
Comparative accounting and auditing standards among nations	0 1 2 3 4	0 1 2 3 4	0 1 2 3 4
Special considerations in auditing not-for-profit organizations	0 1 2 3 4	0 1 2 3 4	0 1 2 3 4
TAXATION:			
Accumulated Earnings Tax	0 1 2 3 4	0 1 2 3 4	0 1 2 3 4
Administrative processes in tax matters	0 1 2 3 4	0 1 2 3 4	0 1 2 3 4
Fundamentals of Federal income tax determination (i.e., accounting periods and methods, deductions, exclusions, gross income, adjusted gross income and taxable income)	0 1 2 3 4	0 1 2 3 4	0 1 2 3 4
Capital gains and losses	0 1 2 3 4	0 1 2 3 4	0 1 2 3 4
Nontaxable exchanges	0 1 2 3 4	0 1 2 3 4	0 1 2 3 4
Federal Estate Tax	0 1 2 3 4	0 1 2 3 4	0 1 2 3 4
Federal Gift Tax	0 1 2 3 4	0 1 2 3 4	0 1 2 3 4

TOPIC	IMPORTANCE	EDUCATIONAL OBJECTIVES	
		Conceptual Knowledge	Technical Ability
Taxation for international operations	0 1 2 3 4	0 1 2 3 4	0 1 2 3 4
Tax planning	0 1 2 3 4	0 1 2 3 4	0 1 2 3 4
Judicial doctrines in tax disputes	0 1 2 3 4	0 1 2 3 4	0 1 2 3 4
Judicial processes in tax disputes	0 1 2 3 4	0 1 2 3 4	0 1 2 3 4
More complex Federal income tax provisions applicable to:			
Consolidated corporate returns	0 1 2 3 4	0 1 2 3 4	0 1 2 3 4
Domestic international sales corp. (DISC)	0 1 2 3 4	0 1 2 3 4	0 1 2 3 4
Foreign Tax Credit	0 1 2 3 4	0 1 2 3 4	0 1 2 3 4
Corporations and shareholders	0 1 2 3 4	0 1 2 3 4	0 1 2 3 4
Fiduciaries	0 1 2 3 4	0 1 2 3 4	0 1 2 3 4
Individuals	0 1 2 3 4	0 1 2 3 4	0 1 2 3 4
Subchapter S	0 1 2 3 4	0 1 2 3 4	0 1 2 3 4
Partners and partnerships	0 1 2 3 4	0 1 2 3 4	0 1 2 3 4
Natural resource taxation	0 1 2 3 4	0 1 2 3 4	0 1 2 3 4
Personal Holding Company Tax	0 1 2 3 4	0 1 2 3 4	0 1 2 3 4
Preparation of tax communications	0 1 2 3 4	0 1 2 3 **4**	0 1 2 3 4
Recognition of tax opportunities	0 1 2 3 4	0 1 2 3 4	0 1 2 3 4
Social security taxes	0 1 2 3 4	0 1 2 3 4	0 1 2 3 4
Taxation of deferred compensation (pensions, profit sharing, etc.)	0 1 2 3 4	0 1 2 3 4	0 1 2 3 4
State and local taxes	0 1 2 3 4	0 1 2 3 4	0 1 2 3 4
Tax practice procedures	0 1 2 3 4	0 1 2 3 4	0 1 2 3 4
Tax research methodology	0 1 2 3 4	0 1 2 3 4	0 1 2 3 4
Tax returns and accompanying schedules	0 1 2 3 4	0 1 2 3 4	0 1 2 3 4
Theoretical framework of taxation:			
Alternatives to present framework	0 1 2 3 4	0 1 2 3 4	0 1 2 3 4
Economic and social concepts	0 1 2 3 4	0 1 2 3 4	0 1 2 3 4

PLEASE CONTINUE TO PART III

PART III

1. Considering the knowledge and abilities of recent graduates in your area of accounting expertise, should the emphasis in each of the following areas be greater, less, or about the same as that which apparently exists today? (check one response for each topical area)

Greater	Same	Less	
_____	_____	_____	Auditing concepts
_____	_____	_____	Auditing procedures
_____	_____	_____	Financial accounting and reporting concepts
_____	_____	_____	Financial accounting and reporting procedures
_____	_____	_____	Managerial accounting concepts
_____	_____	_____	Managerial accounting procedures
_____	_____	_____	Taxation concepts
_____	_____	_____	Taxation procedures
_____	_____	_____	Information systems concepts
_____	_____	_____	Information systems procedures
_____	_____	_____	Not-for-profit accounting concepts
_____	_____	_____	Not-for-profit accounting procedures
_____	_____	_____	Accounting practice internship
_____	_____	_____	Ethics
_____	_____	_____	Communication skills
_____	_____	_____	Quantitative skills
_____	_____	_____	Other (specify) _____

2. In your opinion, how many years of formal, degree-oriented higher education are necessary to adequately prepare an individual to *begin* an accounting career in your area of accounting expertise?

    ( ) Less than 4 years   ( ) 5 years
    ( ) 4 years   ( ) More than 5 years
    ( ) 4½ years

3. Considering your response to Question 2, indicate the proportion of formal, degree-oriented higher education that should be devoted to each of the following areas by allocating a total of 100 points among the areas.

    _____ Non-business (including economics)

    _____ Business (excluding accounting)

    _____ Accounting

    <u>100</u>

THANK YOU VERY MUCH FOR YOUR ASSISTANCE.

APPENDIX 3A

DEMOGRAPHIC INFORMATION

UNDERGRADUATE DEGREE

Accounting	370
Business	86
Economics	50
Other	54
Unknown (or None)	26
	586

MASTERS DEGREE

Accounting	161
Business	94
Other	19
Unknown (or None)	312
	586

DOCTORATE DEGREE

Accounting	97
Business	21
Economics	11
Other	3
Unknown (or None)	454
	586

AGE

Under 30	16
30 - 39	185
40 - 49	220
50 - 59	129
60 or over	36
	586

PROFESSIONAL CERTIFICATION

CPA	413
CMA	7
CIA	23
Other	52

EXPERIENCE

Education	164
Dean, Department Head (Chairman) or Area Coordinator	77
Public Accounting	408
Corporate Accounting	269
Not-for-Profit Accounting	22
Other	113

CHARACTERISTICS OF EDUCATIONAL INSTITUTION WITH WHICH EDUCATOR RESPONDENTS ARE AFFILIATED

Public vs. Private:

Public	93
Private	35
Unknown	2
	130

Degrees Granted with Accounting Emphasis:

	Yes	No (or Unknown)
Bachelors	114	16
Masters	116	14
Doctorate	100	30

TYPE OF FIRM WITH WHICH PUBLIC ACCOUNTING RESPONDENTS ARE AFFILIATED

National	170
Regional	7
Local	27
Unknown	1
	205

SIZE OF FIRM WITH WHICH INDUSTRY RESPONDENTS ARE AFFILIATED

Sales Dollars (Most Recent Fiscal Year):

Not more than 10 million	5
20-200 million	68
210-400 million	54
410-600 million	44
610-800 million	23
810 million - 1 billion	0
Over 1 billion	30
Unknown	27
	251

Total Assets (Most Recent Fiscal Year):

Not more than 10 million	4
20-200 million	93
210-400 million	37
410-600 million	40
610-800 million	9
810 million - 1 billion	13
Over 1 billion	22
Unknown	33
	251

APPENDIX 3B

RANK ORDERING ON IMPORTANCE MEANS:
ALL EDUCATORS

Area	Topic	Importance	Means Conceptual Knowledge	Technical Ability
F	Income statement	3.66	3.60	3.42
F	Revenue and expense recognition	3.65	3.63	3.27
F	Theoretical framework: current structure	3.62	3.62	3.02
F	Balance sheet	3.59	3.54	3.38
F	Present value and future worth concepts	3.51	3.50	3.12
F	U.S. financial accounting and reporting standards	3.50	3.36	2.99
F	Statement of changes in financial position	3.49	3.46	3.27
F	Transaction analysis	3.48	3.42	3.43
M	Standard costs	3.36	3.30	2.96
F	Accruals and deferrals	3.36	3.41	3.33
F	Regulatory influences (financial)	3.35	3.15	2.47
T	Fundamentals of Federal income tax determination	3.35	3.04	2.84
F	Theoretical framework: alternatives to current structure	3.34	3.40	2.42
F	Information needs of financial statement users	3.33	3.30	2.20
F	Double-entry system	3.31	3.23	3.40
M	Capital budgeting	3.30	3.30	2.87
F	Inventories	3.29	3.29	3.11
M	Cost-volume-profit analysis	3.25	3.25	2.91
A	Internal control: principles	3.24	3.18	2.73
A	Generally accepted auditing standards (GAAS)	3.23	3.24	2.76
M	Flexible budgets	3.21	3.08	2.74
F	Depreciation, depletion and amortization	3.20	3.26	2.98
M	Variable costing	3.19	3.24	2.75
M	Accounting information requirements for management decisions	3.18	3.10	2.62
F	Fixed assets	3.18	3.21	2.97
M	Full costing	3.16	3.19	2.75
T	Capital gains and losses	3.13	2.83	2.65
A	Internal control: evaluation	3.08	2.93	2.42
M	Short-range planning	3.08	3.04	2.49
A	Audit evidence: types	3.08	3.05	2.45
A	*Professional rules of conduct	3.07	3.05	2.58
F	*Corporate equity	3.06	3.13	2.85
F	Investments in securities	3.06	3.07	2.85
A	Audit evidence: relative strength of types	3.06	3.03	2.40
F	Leases	3.06	3.12	2.61
M	Tax considerations in managerial decisions	3.05	2.93	2.51
A	Standard short-form audit report	3.03	2.93	2.61
M	*Direct costing	3.03	3.16	2.66

Area	Topic	Importance	Conceptual Knowledge	Technical Ability
			Means	
F	Receivables	3.02	3.02	2.89
F	Financial statement analysis	3.02	3.11	2.76
A	Influence of professional and regulatory bodies upon auditing	3.02	2.90	2.02
F	Deferred taxes	3.02	3.02	2.56
A	*Internal control: relationship of GAAS	3.01	2.97	2.44
M	Budgeted financial statements	3.01	2.90	2.56
F	Long-term liabilities	3.00	3.05	2.84
M	Process costing	3.00	3.03	2.69
M	Management information systems: internal control aspects	2.99	2.93	2.45
M	Performance evaluation: responsibility accounting	2.99	2.98	2.48
A	Statistical inference in auditing: statistical sampling	2.99	3.03	2.52
F	Materiality	2.98	3.02	2.27
M	Performance evaluation: return on investment	2.98	3.03	2.53
F	Accounting for income taxes	2.97	2.98	2.64
M	Long-range planning	2.97	2.95	2.32
M	Performance evaluation: divisional performance	2.97	3.02	2.56
A	Modifications of the standard short-form audit report	2.96	2.93	2.54
F	Price-level adjusted financial statements	2.94	3.15	2.38
M	Job order costing	2.94	2.98	2.66
F	Business combinations: purchase vs. pooling of interests	2.94	3.10	2.44
T	Tax planning	2.93	2.83	2.15
A	Internal control in an EDP environment	2.93	2.78	2.34
M	Joint costs	2.93	3.06	2.42
F	Business combination: consolidation procedure	2.91	3.11	2.60
F	Cash	2.91	2.77	2.85
A	Audit evidence: post-statement events	2.88	2.87	2.29
M	Cash management	2.88	2.81	2.44
F	*Earnings-per-share	2.87	2.93	2.56
A	Internal control: modifications in audit program based on evaluation	2.87	2.78	2.30
F	*Pensions	2.86	2.93	2.41
M	*Performance evaluation: transfer pricing	2.85	2.97	2.39
A	Auditing procedures: review of operations	2.85	2.86	2.37
F	Intangibles (excluding goodwill)	2.85	3.03	2.56
A	Internal control: audit exposure due to weaknesses	2.84	2.74	2.22
M	*Performance evaluation: common costs	2.83	2.89	2.34
A	*Legal responsibilities of auditors: at common law	2.83	2.81	2.02

APPENDIX 3B

(continued)

Area	Topic	Importance	Conceptual Knowledge	Technical Ability
			Means	
A	Legal responsibilities of auditors: under the securities act	2.83	2.79	1.99
F	Short-term liabilities	2.83	2.89	2.73
A	Statistical inference in auditing: judgmental sampling	2.82	2.89	2.32
A	Auditing procedures: tests of account balances	2.82	2.72	2.35
A	Auditing procedures: tests of transaction	2.81	2.72	2.35
F	*Segment reporting	2.80	2.87	2.38
A	User's expectations regarding the auditor's role	2.79	2.78	1.56
F	*Goodwill	2.79	2.98	2.49
T	Non-taxable exchanges	2.77	2.58	2.30
A	Auditing procedures: compliance tests	2.77	2.73	2.30
M	*Overhead control	2.75	2.69	2.24
F	Convertible debt or equity	2.74	2.87	2.52
M	*Management information systems: impact of external regulatory influences	2.74	2.64	2.13
F	*Business combinations: unconsolidated subsidiaries	2.69	2.88	2.31
F	Research and development costs	2.69	2.82	2.21
A	*Operational auditing: objectives	2.68	2.68	1.83
M	*Computer science	2.68	2.59	2.17
M	*Performance evaluation: non-statistical analysis	2.67	2.73	2.25
F	Error corrections	2.66	2.69	2.70
M	*Behavioral considerations (managerial)	2.64	2.73	1.88
F	Interim reporting	2.63	2.77	2.22
F	Contingencies	2.63	2.02	2.20
A	Internal control: description based on flowchart	2.61	2.52	2.25
F	*Behavioral considerations in financial reporting	2.60	2.71	1.70
M	Information economics	2.59	2.81	1.91
A	Legal responsibilities of auditors: exposure to criminal liability	2.58	2.54	1.79
M	*Performance evaluation: non-financial performance measures	2.56	2.66	1.98
M	Organization theory	2.56	2.64	1.86
M	*Statistical decision theory	2.53	2.62	2.10
T	Recognition of tax opportunities	2.52	2.47	1.82
A	*Auditing procedures: working papers	2.50	2.50	2.09
M	*Statistical cost estimation	2.50	2.60	2.17
F	Minority interest	2.48	2.74	2.29
M	*Management information systems: design	2.48	2.58	2.02

APPENDIX 3B
(continued)

Area	Topic	Importance	Conceptual Knowledge	Technical Ability
			Means	
T	*Theoretical framework of taxation: economic and social concepts	2.48	2.64	1.33
M	*Performance evaluation: residual income	2.47	2.58	2.07
F	Treasury stock	2.47	2.73	2.42
A	Statistical influence in auditing: regression analysis	2.47	2.60	2.00
A	*Requirements for professional certification (CPA)	2.46	2.26	1.86
M	*Sensitivity analysis	2.45	2.53	1.99
M	*Corporate planning models	2.44	2.54	1.98
M	*Linear programming	2.44	2.63	2.00
A	Legal responsibilities of auditors: classic cases	2.42	2.50	1.73
A	Internal control: description based on questionnaire	2.42	2.39	2.08
M	Statistical analysis of cost variances	2.42	2.53	1.98
A	Long-form audit report	2.41	2.44	1.86
F	SEC reporting	2.40	2.38	1.78
M	*Simulation	2.40	2.59	1.90
T	*Tax research methodology	2.39	2.37	2.11
A	Internal control: description based on narrative	2.38	2.45	2.08
A	*Operational auditing: methodology	2.38	2.45	1.81
A	*Extensions of the attest function: possible areas	2.38	2.47	1.48
A	*Legal responsibilities of auditors: responses of auditing profession to classic cases	2.37	2.38	1.65
A	Statistical inference in auditing: other statistical methods	2.37	2.46	1.94
T	*Theoretical framework of taxation: alternatives to present framework	2.37	2.59	1.38
M	Spoilage, waste, defective units and scrap	2.37	2.47	2.15
F	Reporting forecasts	2.35	2.64	1.98
A	Extensions of the attest function: associated audit risk	2.35	2.39	1.43
A	Management letter	2.32	2.30	1.77
A	*SEC filing requirements	2.30	2.26	1.74
M	*Internal operational auditing	2.29	2.46	1.87
F	Statements from incomplete records	2.28	2.44	2.41
T	*Tax returns and accompanying schedules	2.27	2.01	2.09
M	*Internal financial auditing	2.26	2.42	1.84
M	Management information systems: implementation	2.26	2.30	1.83
F	Fund accounting: financial statements	2.23	2.39	1.87

APPENDIX 3B
(continued)

Area	Topic	Importance	Means Conceptual Knowledge	Technical Ability
F	*Full costing vs. successful effort costing	2.19	2.49	1.82
M	*Special considerations in non-manufacturing concerns	2.19	2.20	1.76
A	Audit administration: review	2.19	2.20	1.69
T	Taxation of deferred compensation	2.17	2.19	1.70
F	*Partnership financial statements	2.16	2.31	2.02
T	*Complex tax provisions: individuals	2.16	2.16	1.93
A	Audit administration: planning	2.14	2.21	1.72
F	*Fund accounting: types of organizations	2.13	2.25	1.67
M	*Zero base budgeting	2.13	2.41	1.76
M	*Social accounting	2.12	2.30	1.49
F	*Fund accounting: governmental units	2.11	2.24	1.74
M	*Network methods	2.11	2.31	1.68
F	Installment sales	2.10	2.39	2.07
M	*Learning curve models	2.09	2.37	1.68
T	*Complex tax provisions: corporations and shareholders	2.07	2.11	1.69
F	*Foreign currency translation	2.07	2.35	1.72
T	*Administrative processes in tax matters	1.98	1.93	1.38
F	*Regulated industries	1.98	2.17	1.52
M	*Management information systems: administration	1.97	2.04	1.59
A	*Special considerations in auditing not-for-profit organizations	1.96	2.03	1.44
T	*Social security taxes	1.96	1.91	1.63
T	*Federal estate tax	1.95	1.97	1.50
A	*Audit administration: client relations	1.93	1.91	1.46
T	*Complex tax provisions: Subchapter S	1.92	1.90	1.60
T	*Accumulated earnings tax	1.92	1.98	1.44
A	Audit administration: supervision	1.91	2.01	1.52
T	*Complex tax provisions: partners and partnerships	1.91	1.98	1.63
T	*Federal gift tax	1.90	1.90	1.45
F	*National income accounting	1.85	2.10	1.27
T	*State and local taxes	1.85	1.80	1.52
T	*Judicial doctrines in tax disputes	1.83	1.86	1.16
M	*Planning and control of international operations	1.81	1.89	1.39
T	*Complex tax provisions: consolidated corporate returns	1.77	1.87	1.41
F	*Fund accounting: hospitals	1.76	1.92	1.50
F	*Development stage companies	1.74	2.07	1.40
A	*Historical development of auditing	1.71	1.90	1.01
A	*Auditing procedures: audit practice case	1.70	1.66	1.64
F	*Consignments	1.68	2.02	1.72

APPENDIX 3B
(continued)

Area	Topic	Importance	Conceptual Knowledge	Technical Ability
			Means	
T	*Taxation for international operations	1.68	1.81	1.17
A	*Audit administration: accounting firm organization	1.66	1.61	1.17
F	*Fund accounting: colleges and universities	1.65	1.82	1.39
T	*Judicial processes in tax disputes	1.64	1.71	1.16
F	*International accounting standards	1.62	1.86	1.25
T	*Natural resource taxation	1.60	1.78	1.25
T	*Complex tax provisions: foreign tax credit	1.56	1.67	1.21
F	*Human resource accounting	1.52	1.92	1.13
F	*Fiduciary accounting: estates and trusts	1.49	1.77	1.31
M	*Requirements for professional certification (CMA)	1.48	1.51	1.23
T	*Tax practice procedures	1.47	1.41	1.22
T	*Personal holding company tax	1.47	1.61	1.22
T	*Complex tax provisions: fiduciaries	1.45	1.55	1.23
T	*Preparation of tax communications	1.44	1.51	1.35
A	*Comparative accounting and auditing standards among nations	1.43	1.54	.93
A	*Audit administration: setting and collecting fees	1.41	1.48	1.11
F	*Fiduciary accounting: bankruptcy	1.41	1.78	1.19
T	*Complex tax provisions: DISC	1.41	1.59	1.06
F	*Fiduciary accounting: receivership	1.38	1.69	1.14

* ➝ non-core topics

APPENDIX 3C

RANK ORDERING ON IMPORTANCE MEANS:
ALL PRACTITIONERS

Area	Topic	Importance	Conceptual Knowledge	Technical Ability
			Means	
A	Internal control: principles	3.18	3.07	2.02
F	Balance sheet	3.17	3.11	2.68
A	Internal control: evaluation	3.13	2.97	2.17
A	Internal control: audit exposure due to weaknesses	3.10	2.91	2.00
A	Internal control: in an EDP environment	3.04	2.81	1.97
F	Double-entry system	3.01	2.99	2.74
F	Revenue and expense recognition	3.00	3.03	2.55
F	Income statement	2.98	2.97	2.56
A	Audit evidence: types	2.96	2.81	2.52
F	U.S. financial accounting and reporting standards	2.96	2.89	2.35
T	Fundamentals of Federal income tax determination	2.95	2.69	2.51
F	Deferred taxes	2.94	2.94	2.39
A	Internal control: modifications in audit program based on evaluation	2.91	2.70	1.66
F	Theoretical framework: current structure	2.90	2.85	2.31
T	Recognition of tax opportunities	2.88	2.65	1.51
F	Accruals and deferrals	2.86	2.90	2.47
A	Internal control: description based on narrative	2.83	2.72	1.96
F	Transaction analysis	2.81	2.82	2.40
F	Information needs of financial statement users	2.79	2.74	2.10
F	Financial statement analysis	2.78	2.76	2.32
A	Audit evidence: relative strength of types	2.78	2.64	1.86
F	Statement of changes in financial position	2.76	2.77	2.36
A	Modifications of the standard short-form audit report	2.73	2.47	1.89
A	Audit evidence: post-statement events	2.72	2.60	2.60
A	Internal control: description based on questionnaire	2.71	2.60	2.20
F	Business combinations: consolidation procedures	2.71	2.74	2.24
T	Tax planning	2.70	2.40	1.96
F	Regulatory influences (financial)	2.70	2.65	2.07
M	Tax considerations in managerial decisions	2.70	2.68	2.18
F	Materiality	2.70	2.73	2.15
T	Capital gains and losses	2.69	2.38	2.23
A	Legal requirements of auditors: under the securities acts	2.69	2.40	1.67
A	Standard short-form audit report	2.67	2.38	1.77

APPENDIX 3C
(continued)

Area	Topic	Importance	Conceptual Knowledge	Technical Ability
			Means	
T	*Complex tax provisions: corporations and shareholders	2.67	2.46	2.03
F	Error corrections	2.67	2.72	2.40
M	Management information systems: internal control aspects	2.66	2.60	2.11
M	Accounting information requirements for management decisions	2.65	2.66	2.04
T	Non-taxable exchanges	2.65	2.33	1.97
F	SEC reporting	2.63	2.63	2.10
F	Inventories	2.63	2.69	2.27
F	Contingencies	2.62	2.62	2.05
F	Accounting for income taxes	2.62	2.67	2.23
F	Theoretical framework: alternatives to current structure	2.61	2.69	2.02
A	Statistical inference in auditing: judgmental sampling	2.60	2.37	1.92
F	Leases	2.60	2.58	2.10
M	Standard costs	2.58	2.66	2.13
A	Generally accepted auditing standards (GAAS)	2.57	2.57	2.18
A	Statistical influence in auditing: statistical sampling	2.57	2.45	2.52
A	Legal responsibilities of auditors: classic cases	2.55	2.34	1.65
M	Process costing	2.54	2.66	2.13
M	Budgeted financial statements	2.51	2.57	2.11
F	Business combinations: purchase vs. pooling of interests	2.49	2.63	2.00
M	Long-range planning	2.48	2.54	2.09
A	Auditing procedures: tests of account balances	2.48	2.28	2.25
A	Auditing procedures: tests of transactions	2.48	2.28	2.25
M	Cash management	2.48	2.52	2.05
F	Short-term liabilities	2.48	2.55	2.12
F	Interim reporting	2.47	2.46	1.93
F	Long-term liabilities	2.47	2.53	2.11
M	Short-range planning	2.47	2.50	2.03
T	*State and local taxes	2.46	2.23	1.77
A	Internal control: description based on flowchart	2.46	2.23	2.31
A	*Internal control: relationship of GAAS	2.45	2.19	2.20
M	Full costing	2.45	2.56	2.08
M	Job order costing	2.45	2.58	2.13
A	Management letter	2.45	2.34	1.91
A	Auditing procedures: review of operations	2.44	2.36	2.16
F	Minority interest	2.44	2.55	2.05

APPENDIX 3C
(continued)

Area	Topic	Importance	Conceptual Knowledge	Technical Ability
			Means	
F	Present value and future worth concepts	2.44	2.55	2.00
M	Variable costing	2.44	2.54	2.05
T	Taxation of deferred compensation	2.43	2.17	1.82
A	Influence of professional and regulatory bodies upon auditing	2.42	2.39	1.70
M	Performance evaluation: return on investment	2.42	2.52	1.92
M	Flexible budgets	2.42	2.51	2.03
F	Intangibles (excluding goodwill)	2.40	2.48	1.94
F	*Earnings-per-share	2.40	2.45	1.98
A	Audit administration: review	2.40	2.27	1.56
F	Fixed assets	2.39	2.46	2.11
T	*Accumulated earnings tax	2.39	2.25	1.35
F	Research and development costs	2.39	2.51	2.03
M	Performance evaluation: divisional performance	2.39	2.46	1.92
F	Depreciation, depletion and amortization	2.38	2.47	2.09
T	*Tax research methodology	2.38	2.12	1.78
A	Auditing procedures: compliance tests	2.37	2.22	2.21
M	Capital budgeting	2.37	2.44	1.90
F	*Behavioral considerations in financial reporting	2.37	2.40	1.78
A	Long-form audit report	2.36	2.00	1.68
M	Management information systems: implementation	2.36	2.38	1.86
M	Performance evaluation: responsibility accounting	2.36	2.41	1.87
F	Statements from incomplete records	2.36	2.44	2.04
A	*Auditing procedures: working papers	2.36	2.19	1.90
F	*Corporate equity	2.35	2.46	1.99
A	Extensions of the attest function: associated audit risk	2.35	1.99	1.36
A	*Audit administration: client relations	2.31	2.12	1.53
A	Statistical inference in auditing: regression analysis	2.31	2.25	2.39
M	Cost-volume-profit analysis	2.31	2.34	1.98
F	*Business combinations: unconsolidated subsidiaries	2.30	2.37	1.87
M	*Management information systems: administration	2.30	2.29	1.80
A	Audit administration: planning	2.30	2.23	1.49
F	Cash	2.29	2.40	2.08
T	*Judicial doctrines in tax disputes	2.29	2.13	1.10
F	Investments in securities	2.29	2.42	1.94
A	*Professional rules of conduct	2.28	2.35	1.73
A	User's expectations regarding the auditor's role	2.27	2.34	1.50

APPENDIX 3C
(continued)

Area	Topic	Importance	Conceptual Knowledge	Technical Ability
			Means	
F	Convertible debt or equity	2.27	2.40	1.91
F	Receivables	2.26	2.38	2.00
A	Statistical inference in auditing: other statistical methods	2.25	2.16	1.42
F	Fund accounting: financial statements	2.25	2.30	1.81
M	*Learning curve models	2.25	2.31	1.78
M	Joint costs	2.25	2.36	1.88
M	Statistical analysis of cost variances	2.24	2.30	1.81
M	Spoilage, waste, defective units and scrap	2.24	2.32	1.84
A	Legal responsibilities of auditors: exposure to criminal liability	2.23	2.01	1.63
T	*Administrative processes in tax matters	2.22	2.00	1.32
F	Installment sales	2.21	2.32	1.87
A	*Requirements for professional certification (CPA)	2.20	2.25	1.92
F	*Foreign currency translation	2.20	2.31	1.81
M	Information economics	2.20	2.25	1.74
F	*Development stage companies	2.19	2.32	1.86
T	*Theoretical framework of taxation: economic and social concepts	2.19	2.02	.86
T	*Complex tax provisions: foreign tax credit	2.19	1.95	1.48
F	Treasury stock	2.19	2.25	1.86
T	*Complex tax provisions: DISC	2.19	2.03	1.22
T	*Tax practice procedures	2.18	1.94	1.63
M	Organization theory	2.16	2.21	1.65
F	Reporting forecasts	2.16	2.27	1.77
T	*Taxation for international operations	2.15	1.92	1.36
T	*Tax returns and accompanying schedules	2.15	1.85	2.30
M	*Management information systems: impact of external regulatory influences	2.14	2.17	1.64
A	Audit administration: supervision	2.13	1.99	1.40
F	*Fund accounting: types of organizations	2.13	2.21	1.72
M	*Direct costing	2.13	2.33	1.82
T	*Social security taxes	2.12	1.90	1.44
F	*Goodwill	2.11	2.17	1.75
A	*Legal responsibilities of auditors: at common law	2.10	2.20	1.45
F	*International accounting standards	2.10	2.16	1.60
M	*Performance evaluation: non-statistical variance analysis	2.09	2.17	1.73
A	*Auditing procedures: audit practice case	2.09	1.92	1.82
F	*Pensions	2.08	2.18	1.60
M	*Corporate planning models	2.07	2.15	1.63
F	Price-level adjusted financial statements	2.07	2.31	1.62

APPENDIX 3C
(continued)

Area	Topic	Importance	Conceptual Knowledge	Technical Ability
			Means	
T	*Complex tax provisions: consolidated corporate returns	2.06	1.84	1.71
F	*Consignments	2.04	2.15	1.70
T	*Judicial processes in tax disputes	2.01	1.84	1.06
M	*Performance evaluation: non-financial performance measures	1.99	2.08	1.59
A	*Special consideration in auditing not-for-profit organizations	1.96	1.82	.90
M	*Overhead control	1.96	2.04	1.64
F	*Full costing vs. successful effort costing	1.96	2.09	1.60
F	*Partnership financial statements	1.96	2.14	1.57
M	*Computer science	1.96	2.06	1.51
A	*Operational auditing: objectives	1.95	1.75	1.56
M	*Management information systems: design	1.95	2.03	1.52
A	*SEC filing requirements	1.94	1.98	1.52
M	*Internal financial auditing	1.93	2.06	1.64
F	*National income accounting	1.92	2.01	1.56
M	*Zero base budgeting	1.91	2.07	1.60
T	*Complex tax provisons: individuals	1.91	1.67	1.95
A	*Legal responsibilities of auditors: responses of the auditing profession	1.89	1.73	1.38
A	*Operational auditing: methodology	1.87	1.67	1.51
A	*Extensions of the attest function: possible areas	1.87	1.66	1.34
A	*Audit administration: setting and collecting fees	1.87	1.66	.97
F	*Segment reporting	1.87	2.01	1.45
M	*Internal operational auditing	1.86	2.01	1.50
T	*Complex tax provisions: fiduciaries	1.86	1.67	1.68
F	*Fund accounting: governmental units	1.85	1.97	1.57
M	*Simulation	1.85	1.94	1.34
M	*Performance evaluation: transfer pricing	1.85	1.96	1.45
T	*Theoretical framework of taxation: alternatives to present framework	1.84	1.66	1.15
A	*Comparative accounting and auditing standards among nations	1.81	1.61	.66
F	*Fiduciary accounting: bankruptcy	1.80	2.05	1.47
M	*Performance evaluation: residual income	1.80	1.89	1.45
M	*Statistical decision theory	1.79	1.96	1.39
F	*Fiduciary accounting: receivership	1.79	2.01	1.44
T	*Complex tax provisions: partners and partnerships	1.78	1.57	2.01
F	*Regulated industries	1.78	1.88	1.32
M	*Network methods	1.78	1.88	1.30
M	*Performance evaluation: common costs	1.78	1.84	1.37

APPENDIX 3C
(continued)

Area	Topic	Importance	Conceptual Knowledge	Technical Ability
			Means	
T	*Complex tax provisions: subchapter S	1.77	1.59	1.68
M	*Statistical cost estimation	1.76	1.89	1.38
F	*Fund accounting: colleges and universities	1.76	1.89	1.51
A	*Audit administration: accounting firm organization	1.73	1.60	.99
F	*Fund accounting: hospitals	1.73	1.89	1.49
F	*Human resource accounting	1.72	1.80	1.42
T	*Federal gift tax	1.67	1.46	1.24
M	*Planning and control of international operations	1.64	1.74	1.26
T	*Federal estate tax	1.63	1.43	1.24
T	*Preparation of tax communications	1.56	1.31	1.74
A	*Historical development of auditing	1.54	1.66	1.02
M	*Behavioral considerations (managerial)	1.53	1.68	1.15
F	*Fiduciary accounting: estates and trusts	1.47	1.65	1.22
M	*Special considerations in non-manufacturing concerns	1.47	1.60	1.17
T	*Personal holding company tax	1.45	1.31	1.19
T	*Natural resource taxation	1.45	1.31	1.33
M	*Requirements for professional certification (CMA)	1.44	1.59	1.22
M	*Sensitivity analysis	1.42	1.60	1.10
M	*Linear programming	1.37	1.58	.97
M	*Social accounting	1.30	1.48	.94

* ➔ non-core topic

APPENDIX 4A
RANK ORDERING BY IMPORTANCE MEANS:
MANAGERIAL ACCOUNTING EDUCATORS

| | | | Means | |
| | | | Conceptual | Technical |
Area	Topic	Importance	Knowledge	Ability
F	Present value and future worth concepts	3.68	3.71	3.39
M	Flexible budgets	3.68	3.47	3.07
M	Accounting information requirements for management decisions	3.68	3.63	3.23
M	Capital budgeting	3.65	3.60	3.13
M	Standard costs	3.61	3.57	3.17
M	Cost-volume-profit analysis	3.55	3.52	3.10
M	Performance evaluation: responsibility accounting	3.55	3.48	3.03
F	Income statement	3.52	3.50	3.16
M	Short-range planning	3.45	3.37	2.80
M	Budgeted financial statements	3.45	3.37	2.93
F	Statement of changes in financial position	3.43	3.50	3.13
F	Revenue and expense recognition	3.43	3.47	2.93
M	Variable costing	3.39	3.40	2.87
F	Theoretical framework: current structure	3.35	3.45	2.61
F	Balance sheet	3.35	3.37	3.10
M	Performance evaluation: divisional performance	3.35	3.42	2.87
M	Long-range planning	3.32	3.17	2.60
M	Performance evaluation: transfer pricing	3.32	3.42	2.73
M	Direct costing	3.31	3.39	2.89
M	Cash management	3.29	3.23	2.67
M	Tax considerations in managerial decisions	3.29	3.20	2.50
M	Performance evaluation: return on investment	3.29	3.42	2.70
F	Theoretical framework: alternatives to current structure	3.27	3.27	2.19
F	Transaction analysis	3.23	3.33	3.27
M	Performance evaluation: common costs	3.19	3.23	2.67
M	Behavioral considerations (managerial)	3.19	3.23	2.16
F	U.S. financial accounting and reporting standards	3.16	3.23	2.67
F	Information needs of financial statement users	3.16	3.13	2.20
M	Job order costing	3.16	3.26	2.84
M	Overhead control	3.16	3.17	2.68
M	Process costing	3.13	3.20	2.77
M	Full Costing	3.13	3.33	2.70
T	Fundamentals of Federal income tax determination	3.12	3.04	2.62
F	Price-level adjusted financial statements	3.10	3.28	2.45
F	Segment reporting	3.07	3.00	2.70
M	Management information systems: internal control aspects	3.06	2.97	2.40

APPENDIX 4A
(continued)

			Means	
Area	Topic	Importance	Conceptual Knowledge	Technical Ability
M	Sensitivity analysis	3.06	2.97	2.29
M	Corporate planning models	3.04	3.04	2.32
A	Internal control principles	3.04	3.07	2.36
F	Leases	3.03	3.17	2.48
F	Cash	3.03	2.63	2.73
F	Inventories	3.03	3.03	2.97
F	Regulatory influences (financial)	3.03	3.00	2.10
F	Accruals and deferrals	3.03	3.23	3.03
M	Joint costs	3.03	3.17	2.50
F	Financial statement analysis	3.00	3.17	2.80
M	Performance evaluation: residual income	3.00	3.07	2.33
F	Double-entry system	2.97	3.10	3.10
M	*Linear programming	2.97	3.06	2.07
F	Depreciation, depletion and amortization	2.97	3.03	2.77
M	Management information systems: design	2.94	2.87	2.13
M	Performance evaluation: non-financial performance measures	2.90	2.90	2.27
F	Receivables	2.90	2.83	2.67
M	Computer science	2.90	2.77	2.14
M	Information economics	2.87	2.97	2.17
M	Statistical decision theory	2.87	2.80	2.17
F	Investments in securities	2.87	2.87	2.60
M	Statistical cost estimation	2.87	2.80	2.33
T	Capital gains and losses	2.85	2.62	2.04
M	Organization theory	2.84	2.97	2.07
M	Management information systems: impact of external regulatory influences	2.84	2.73	2.17
M	Performance evaluation: non-statistical variance analysis	2.84	3.00	2.40
F	Fixed assets	2.83	2.90	2.66
M	Simulation	2.81	2.97	2.07
F	Materiality	2.77	2.90	2.10
M	Management information systems: implementation	2.77	2.66	2.10
T	Tax planning	2.73	2.77	1.73
F	*Pensions	2.72	2.79	2.10
F	Deferred taxes	2.72	2.72	2.10
F	Behavioral considerations in financial reporting	2.70	2.73	1.90
F	Long-term liabilities	2.70	2.77	2.46
F	Corporate equity	2.70	2.71	2.46
F	Earnings-per-share	2.70	2.86	2.40
F	Short-term liabilities	2.67	2.73	2.48
F	Interim reporting	2.67	2.72	2.17
F	Accounting for income taxes	2.62	2.61	2.14

APPENDIX 4A
(continued)

Area	Topic	Importance	Conceptual Knowledge	Technical Ability
			Means	
F	Business combinations: purchase vs. pooling of interests	2.60	2.77	2.07
F	Research and development costs	2.58	2.74	2.00
A	Generally accepted auditing standards (GAAS)	2.56	2.64	2.00
A	Internal control evaluation	2.56	2.36	1.84
A	Internal control in an EDP environment	2.56	2.52	1.80
A	Operational auditing: objectives	2.56	2.44	1.56
M	Spoilage, waste, defective units and scrap	2.55	2.70	2.10
M	Network methods	2.52	2.50	1.73
M	Statistical analysis of cost variances	2.52	2.52	1.94
M	Internal operational auditing	2.52	2.53	2.00
F	Business combinations: consolidation procedures	2.50	2.79	2.10
M	Special considerations in non-manufacturing concerns	2.50	2.64	2.00
A	Statistical inference in auditing: statistical sampling	2.50	2.54	1.93
M	Learning curve models	2.48	2.68	1.77
M	Zero base budgeting	2.47	2.55	1.79
F	Intangibles (excluding goodwill)	2.43	2.60	2.07
M	Management information systems: administration	2.43	2.41	1.76
A	Influence of professional and regulatory bodies on auditing	2.43	2.50	1.15
A	Professional rules of conduct	2.43	2.43	1.70
F	Reporting forecasts	2.42	2.59	1.93
T	Recognition of tax opportunities	2.40	2.44	1.48
A	Internal control: relationship of GAAS	2.39	2.46	1.71
F	Convertible debt or equity	2.38	2.46	2.14
A	Legal responsibilities of the auditor: at common law	2.37	2.41	1.19
A	Statistical inference in auditing: judgmental sampling	2.36	2.36	1.75
F	Error correction	2.34	2.48	2.14
F	Goodwill	2.33	2.57	2.00
A	Internal control: audit exposure due to weaknesses	2.33	2.33	1.46
A	Requirements for professional certification (CPA)	2.32	2.15	1.52
A	Standard short-form audit report	2.32	2.25	1.57
A	Operational auditing: methodology	2.31	2.35	1.69
F	Minority interest	2.30	2.59	2.11
T	Non-taxable exchanges	2.28	2.20	1.48
A	User's expectations regarding the auditor's role	2.27	2.28	.96

APPENDIX 4A
(continued)

Area	Topic	Importance	Conceptual Knowledge	Technical Ability
			Means	
A	Statistical inference in auditing: regression analysis	2.25	2.25	1.68
M	Social accounting	2.24	2.31	1.50
A	Auditing procedures: review of operations	2.24	2.13	1.67
A	Auditing procedures: tests of transactions	2.23	2.12	1.62
A	Legal responsibilities of the auditor: under the securities acts	2.22	2.30	1.22
A	Audit evidence: types	2.22	2.35	1.58
A	Internal control: description based on flowchart	2.21	2.13	1.70
F	Business combinations: unconsolidated subsidiaries	2.20	2.41	1.86
M	Internal financial auditing	2.20	2.38	1.83
A	Auditing procedures: tests of account balances	2.19	2.00	1.60
F	Contingencies	2.17	2.24	1.76
A	Internal control: modifications in audit program based on evaluation	2.16	2.24	1.44
A	Audit evidence: relative strength of types	2.15	2.20	1.42
A	SEC filing requirements	2.14	2.14	1.21
A	Long-form audit report	2.14	2.18	1.43
A	Legal responsibilities of the auditor: exposure to criminal liability	2.11	2.07	.89
A	Modifications of the standard short-form audit report	2.11	2.18	1.36
A	Auditing procedures: compliance tests	2.08	2.00	1.50
A	Auditing procedures: working papers	2.08	2.12	1.62
A	Management letter	2.04	1.96	1.36
F	Treasury stock	2.03	2.29	1.82
F	Statements from incomplete records	2.03	2.41	1.97
F	SEC reporting	2.03	1.84	1.32
M	Planning and control of international operations	2.03	2.17	1.37
F	Installment sales	2.00	2.20	1.90
F	Full costing vs. successful effort costing	2.00	2.26	1.70
T	Theoretical framework of taxation: economic and social concepts	2.00	2.40	1.05
F	*Regulated industries	1.97	2.10	1.27
A	Statistical influence in auditing: other statistical methods	1.96	2.00	1.54
A	Audit evidence: post-statement events	1.96	2.04	1.27
A	Internal control: description based on questionnaire	1.96	1.91	1.52
A	Extensions of the attest function: possible areas	1.92	2.04	.92

APPENDIX 4A
(continued)

Area	Topic	Importance	Conceptual Knowledge	Technical Ability
A	Internal control: description based on narrative	1.92	2.00	1.52
F	Partnership financial statements	1.89	2.11	1.50
T	State and local taxes	1.88	1.96	1.42
A	Audit administration: planning	1.85	1.96	1.30
A	Extensions of the attest function: associated audit risk	1.85	1.92	.88
T	Theoretical framework of taxation: alternatives to present framework	1.84	2.28	1.05
M	Requirements for professional certification (CMA)	1.83	2.04	1.54
A	Legal responsibilities of the auditor: classic cases	1.81	1.96	.81
A	*Special considerations in auditing not-for-profit organizations	1.81	1.81	1.27
F	*National income accounting	1.80	2.11	1.14
F	Foreign currency translation	1.77	1.97	1.35
T	Taxation for international operations	1.77	2.12	1.16
T	Social security taxes	1.76	2.00	1.48
F	Fund accounting: financial statements	1.76	2.00	1.39
F	*Fund accounting: governmental units	1.72	1.89	1.39
T	Taxation of deferred compensation	1.72	1.79	1.30
A	*Legal responsibilities of auditors: responses of the auditing profession to classic cases	1.70	1.89	.74
A	Audit administration: review	1.70	1.78	1.11
T	Tax returns and accompanying schedules	1.68	1.75	1.67
F	*Consignments	1.62	2.03	1.69
F	Fund accounting: types of organizations	1.61	1.92	1.31
A	Audit administration: supervision	1.59	1.70	1.15
F	*Fund accounting: hospitals	1.59	1.79	1.32
F	*Development stage companies	1.55	1.79	1.14
F	*Human resource accounting	1.53	1.90	1.07
T	*Administrative processes in tax matters	1.52	1.52	.84
T	*Accumulated earnings tax	1.46	1.63	1.04
F	*International accounting standards	1.45	1.52	.97
A	*Audit administration: client relations	1.44	1.48	.85
A	*Historical development of auditing	1.43	1.48	.65
F	*Fund accounting: colleges and universities	1.41	1.57	1.11
T	*Tax research methodology	1.40	1.44	1.29
T	*Federal estate tax	1.38	1.48	.96
A	*Auditing procedures: audit practice case	1.36	1.25	1.08
T	*Complex tax provisions: consolidated corporate returns	1.36	1.60	.88
T	*Complete tax provisions: subchapter S	1.33	1.50	.87

APPENDIX 4A
(continued)

Area	Topic	Importance	Conceptual Knowledge	Technical Ability
			Means	
A	*Comparative accounting and auditing standards among nations	1.26	1.33	.58
T	*Natural resource taxation	1.24	1.52	.79
A	*Audit administration: setting and collecting fees	1.22	1.37	.70
T	*Complex tax provisions: corporations and shareholders	1.20	1.44	.83
T	*Complex tax provisions: partners and partnerships	1.20	1.44	.88
T	*Complex tax provisions: DISC	1.17	1.50	.70
T	*Federal gift tax	1.15	1.36	.81
A	*Audit administration: accounting firm organization	1.15	1.22	.63
T	*Judicial doctrines in tax disputes	1.14	1.45	.90
F	*Fiduciary accounting: bankruptcy	1.14	1.59	.79
F	*Fiduciary accounting: receivership	1.14	1.55	.76
F	*Fiduciary accounting: estates and trusts	1.14	1.46	.82
T	*Complex tax provisions: foreign tax credit	1.12	1.44	.75
T	*Complex tax provisions: individuals	1.04	1.32	.88
T	*Judicial processes in tax disputes	.95	1.30	.71
T	*Personal holding company tax	.91	1.24	.65
T	*Tax practice procedures	.83	1.08	.73
T	*Complex tax provisions: fiduciaries	.76	1.08	.67
T	*Preparation of tax communications	.73	1.20	.74

* → non-core topics

APPENDIX 4B
RANK ORDERING BY IMPORTANCE MEANS:
MANAGERIAL ACCOUNTING PRACTITIONERS

| | | | Means | |
| | | | Conceptual | Technical |
Area	Topic	Importance	Knowledge	Ability
A	Internal control principles	3.18	2.93	1.89
F	Balance sheet	3.08	3.02	2.25
A	Internal control evaluation	3.03	2.78	2.15
M	Accounting information requirements for management decisions	3.00	2.98	2.43
A	Audit evidence: types	2.95	2.45	2.24
M	Performance evaluation: responsibility accounting	2.93	2.88	2.45
F	Double-entry system	2.90	2.90	2.68
F	Income statement	2.90	2.87	2.41
M	Process costing	2.90	2.93	2.38
A	Internal control: audit exposure due to weaknesses	2.90	2.65	1.92
A	Internal control: description based on narrative	2.87	2.74	2.05
M	Long-range planning	2.85	2.95	2.35
M	Performance evaluation: return on investment	2.83	2.90	2.36
F	Accruals and deferrals	2.83	2.76	2.32
A	Internal control: description based on questionnaire	2.82	2.59	2.24
F	Revenue and expense recognition	2.82	2.92	2.34
M	Performance evaluation: divisional performance	2.81	3.00	2.41
F	Regulatory influences (financial)	2.80	2.68	1.93
F	Statement of changes in financial position	2.80	2.83	2.18
F	Financial statement analysis	2.80	2.83	2.18
M	Full costing	2.79	2.85	2.15
M	Standard costs	2.77	2.74	2.15
M	Tax considerations in managerial decisions	2.76	2.76	2.17
M	Flexible budgets	2.75	2.80	2.08
M	Variable costing	2.74	2.79	2.21
M	Management information systems: internal control aspects	2.73	2.67	2.18
M	Budgeted financial statements	2.72	2.77	2.21
M	Cost-volume-profit analysis	2.70	2.70	2.25
A	Audit evidence: relative strength of types	2.68	2.42	1.34
F	Theoretical framework: current structure	2.68	2.63	2.03
M	Short-range planning	2.68	2.69	2.18
M	Job order costing	2.67	2.47	2.35
A	Audit evidence: post-statement events	2.66	2.47	2.35
A	Internal control in an EDP environment	2.65	2.48	1.78
F	Information needs of financial statement users	2.63	2.54	1.85

APPENDIX 4B
(continued)

Area	Topic	Importance	Conceptual Knowledge	Technical Ability
F	Business combinations: consolidation procedures	2.63	2.63	1.93
M	Cash management	2.63	2.73	1.93
T	Recognition of tax opportunities	2.62	2.51	1.25
F	U.S. financial accounting and reporting standards	2.61	2.61	2.00
M	Management information systems: implementation	2.60	2.70	1.95
T	State and local taxes	2.59	2.45	1.62
F	Research and development costs	2.58	2.63	1.95
M	Overhead control	2.56	2.60	2.28
M	Capital budgeting	2.55	2.68	2.10
F	Transaction analysis	2.54	2.50	2.19
F	Behavioral considerations in financial reporting	2.54	2.55	2.03
M	Information economics	2.54	2.59	2.03
T	Taxation of deferred compensation	2.54	2.15	1.59
F	SEC reporting	2.54	2.56	2.00
F	Earnings-per-share	2.54	2.65	1.95
F	Theoretical framework: alternatives to current structure	2.53	2.55	1.92
M	Management information systems: administration	2.51	2.59	1.77
F	Deferred taxes	2.51	2.50	1.74
M	Statistical analysis of cost variances	2.50	2.54	2.02
T	Tax planning	2.49	2.05	1.45
A	Internal control: modification in audit program based on evaluation	2.46	2.28	1.53
M	Management information systems: impact of external regulatory influences	2.45	2.46	1.82
M	Learning curve models	2.45	2.55	1.85
M	Direct costing	2.45	2.50	2.03
M	Performance evaluation: non-financial performance measures	2.44	2.44	2.05
F	Inventories	2.41	2.56	2.14
M	Performance evaluation: non-statistical variance analysis	2.41	2.49	2.08
F	Business combinations: purchase vs. pooling of interest	2.40	2.51	1.67
M	Organization theory	2.40	2.50	1.85
M	Corporate planning models	2.40	2.38	1.87
T	Capital gains and losses	2.38	2.18	1.85
F	Present value and future worth concepts	2.38	2.59	2.08
A	Modifications of the standard short-form audit report	2.37	2.05	1.50

APPENDIX 4B
(continued)

Area	Topic	Importance	Means Conceptual Knowledge	Means Technical Ability
A	Management letter	2.35	2.13	2.15
F	Short-term liabilities	2.34	2.41	1.92
M	Spoilage, waste, defective units and scrap	2.33	2.44	1.74
A	Standard short-form audit report	2.33	2.03	1.39
A	Internal control: relationship of GAAS	2.33	1.94	2.00
T	*Complex tax provisions: corporation and shareholders	2.33	2.21	2.17
F	Interim reporting	2.32	2.35	1.59
M	Internal operational auditing	2.31	2.39	1.82
A	Influence of professional and regulatory bodies on auditing	2.30	2.30	1.58
A	Internal control: description based on flowchart	2.30	2.05	2.38
F	Contingencies	2.29	2.17	1.59
A	Generally accepted auditing standards (GAAS)	2.28	2.13	1.62
T	Social security taxes	2.28	2.03	1.39
F	Reporting forecasts	2.28	2.41	1.97
M	Management information systems: design	2.28	2.36	1.76
A	Requirements for professional certification (CPA)	2.28	2.21	1.77
A	Auditing procedures: review of operations	2.28	2.10	1.86
M	Joint costs	2.27	2.35	1.81
F	Leases	2.27	2.25	1.64
M	Performance evaluation: transfer pricing	2.26	2.39	1.85
F	Error corrections	2.25	2.53	1.79
F	Materiality	2.25	2.36	1.56
A	User's expectations regarding the auditor's role	2.25	2.30	1.56
A	Operational auditing: objectives	2.25	2.08	2.11
F	Business combinations: unconsolidated subsidiaries	2.23	2.30	1.68
F	Accounting for income taxes	2.23	2.30	1.77
A	Auditing procedures: tests of account balances	2.23	2.00	1.67
F	Long-term liabilites	2.22	2.41	1.85
A	Statistical inference in auditing: judgmental sampling	2.21	2.03	1.50
A	Statistical inference in auditing: statistical sampling	2.21	1.97	2.32
M	Performance evaluation: common costs	2.20	2.18	1.78
F	Depreciation depletion and amortization	2.18	2.32	1.87
T	*Accumulated earnings tax	2.17	1.83	.94
F	Cash	2.16	2.22	1.89
A	Professional rules of conduct	2.15	2.32	1.61
T	Fundamentals of Federal income tax determination	2.15	1.95	2.10

APPENDIX 4B
(continued)

Area	Topic	Importance	Conceptual Knowledge	Technical Ability
			Means	
A	Auditing procedures: tests of transactions	2.15	1.90	1.71
A	Extensions of the attest function: associated audit risk	2.13	1.79	1.32
T	Non-taxable exchanges	2.13	1.82	1.35
T	Theoretical framework of taxation: economic and social concepts	2.13	1.90	.63
M	Internal financial auditing	2.10	2.32	1.84
F	Foreign currency translation	2.10	2.23	1.63
F	Receivables	2.10	2.18	1.79
A	Long-form audit report	2.08	1.92	1.47
A	Legal responsibilities of auditors: under securities acts	2.08	1.77	1.63
M	Behavioral considerations (managerial)	2.05	2.17	1.73
M	Zero base budgeting	2.05	2.13	1.61
M	Performance evaluation: residual income	2.05	1.92	1.46
A	SEC filing requirements	2.05	2.16	1.43
T	*Tax practice procedures	2.05	1.85	1.23
F	Fixed assets	2.05	2.14	1.82
F	Intangibles (excluding goodwill)	2.05	2.08	1.59
A	Operational auditing: methodology	2.03	1.92	2.11
F	Corporate equity	2.03	2.16	1.56
F	Minority interest	2.02	2.31	1.72
M	Computer science	2.00	2.08	1.60
F	Segment reporting	1.98	2.15	1.41
A	Legal responsibilities of auditors: classic cases	1.98	1.74	1.59
F	Statements from incomplete records	1.97	2.22	1.53
A	*Auditing procedures: audit practice case	1.97	1.82	1.55
T	Taxation for international operations	1.97	1.67	.95
A	Extensions of the attest function: possible areas	1.97	1.92	1.25
F	Price-level adjusted financial statement	1.95	2.18	1.45
F	Convertible debt or equity	1.95	2.19	1.61
A	Statistical inference in auditing: regression analysis	1.95	1.84	2.06
F	Full costing vs. successful effort costing	1.95	2.03	1.43
M	Simulation	1.95	2.08	1.32
F	*International accounting standards	1.93	1.95	1.46
F	Investments in securities	1.93	2.03	1.42
A	Legal responsibilities of auditors: exposure to criminal liability	1.93	1.77	1.49
A	Auditing procedures: compliance tests	1.93	1.85	1.57
A	Audit administration: review	1.93	1.90	1.25
M	Statistical cost estimation	1.92	2.00	1.38

APPENDIX 4B
(continued)

Area	Topic	Importance	Conceptual Knowledge	Technical Ability
			Means	
M	Planning and control of international operations	1.92	2.05	1.41
M	Statistical decision theory	1.90	2.11	1.38
T	*Tax research methodology	1.90	1.62	.78
T	*Complex tax provisions: foreign tax credit	1.87	1.56	1.16
A	Statistical inference in auditing: other statistical methods	1.87	1.78	1.19
F	Fund accounting: financial statements	1.85	1.95	1.36
A	Audit administration: client relations	1.85	1.77	1.15
M	Special considerations in non-manufacturing concerns	1.85	1.94	1.44
F	Goodwill	1.81	1.97	1.40
F	Treasury stock	1.80	2.03	1.47
A	Audit administration: planning	1.80	1.66	1.11
A	Legal responsibilities of auditors: at common law	1.79	1.95	1.14
A	Auditing procedures: working papers	1.79	1.68	1.51
T	*Complex tax provisions: consolidated corporate returns	1.78	1.62	1.00
M	Network methods	1.78	1.92	1.22
T	*Complex tax provisions: DISC	1.77	1.67	1.16
F	*Development stage companies	1.76	1.78	1.30
M	Requirements for professional certification (CMA)	1.76	1.90	1.41
T	Tax returns and accompanying schedules	1.75	1.50	1.68
T	*Judicial doctrines in tax disputes	1.74	1.50	.47
F	*Consignments	1.73	1.84	1.51
F	Installments sales	1.71	1.79	1.44
M	Theoretical framework of taxation: alternatives to present framework	1.70	1.46	.95
A	Audit administration: supervision	1.70	1.55	1.11
A	*Audit administration: setting and collecting fees	1.70	1.53	1.16
F	Partnership financial statements	1.69	1.86	1.19
F	*Pensions	1.66	1.78	1.13
M	Sensitivity analysis	1.66	1.78	1.08
M	Social accounting	1.63	1.79	1.29
T	*Complex tax provisions: individuals	1.62	1.24	1.26
T	*Administrative processes in tax matters	1.60	1.37	.90
A	*Comparative accounting and auditing standards among nations	1.59	1.58	.67
F	Fund accounting: types of organizations	1.58	1.72	1.23
F	*Fiduciary accounting: bankruptcy	1.56	1.59	1.05
F	*Regulated industries	1.55	1.63	1.10
F	*National income accounting	1.54	1.56	1.25

APPENDIX 4B
(continued)

Area	Topic	Importance	Conceptual Knowledge	Technical Ability
A	*Legal responsibilities of auditors: responses of the auditing profession to classic cases	1.54	1.50	1.26
F	*Fiduciary accounting: receivership	1.51	1.56	1.02
F	*Fund accounting: governmental units	1.50	1.65	1.19
A	*Audit administration: accounting firm organization	1.50	1.45	.95
A	*Special considerations in auditing not-for-profit organizations	1.49	1.33	.61
F	*Human resource accounting	1.46	1.55	1.25
T	*Judicial processes in tax dispute	1.43	1.28	.47
F	*Fund accounting: colleges and universities	1.41	1.51	1.03
M	*Linear programming	1.41	1.42	.76
T	*Complex tax provisions: fiduciaries	1.37	1.23	1.25
T	*Complex tax provisions: subchapter S	1.36	1.22	1.29
F	*Fund accounting: hospitals	1.34	1.50	1.03
T	*Natural resources taxation	1.30	1.27	1.31
A	*Historical development of auditing	1.25	1.24	.70
T	*Federal gift tax	1.22	.92	.58
T	*Complex tax provisions: partners and partnerships	1.19	1.03	1.55
T	*Personal holding company tax	1.14	1.00	1.09
F	*Fiduciary accounting: estates and trusts	1.10	1.22	.89
T	*Federal estate tax	1.08	.89	.58
T	*Preparation of tax communications	.97	.76	1.15

* ➞ non-core topics

APPENDIX 5A

RANK ORDERING BY IMPORTANCE MEANS:
TAXATION RESPONDENTS

			Means	
Area	Topic	Importance	Conceptual Knowledge	Technical Ability
F	Double-entry system	3.85	3.92	3.58
T	Fundamentals of Federal income tax determination	3.80	3.64	3.62
T	Tax research methodology	3.80	3.57	3.50
F	Accruals and deferrals	3.77	3.83	3.50
F	Income statement	3.77	3.67	3.58
T	Capital gains and losses	3.73	3.71	3.62
T	Non-taxable exchanges	3.73	3.64	3.62
F	Transaction analysis	3.69	3.83	3.67
T	Recognition of tax opportunities	3.69	3.50	2.60
T	Complex tax provisions: corporations and shareholders	3.67	3.50	2.85
F	Inventories	3.62	3.67	3.17
F	Deferred taxes	3.62	3.58	3.09
F	Revenue and expense recognition	3.62	3.58	3.33
F	Balance sheet	3.62	3.58	3.42
T	Tax planning	3.60	3.50	2.83
F	Depreciation, depletion and amortization	3.54	3.50	3.25
F	Error corrections	3.54	3.58	3.33
M	Tax considerations in management decisions	3.54	3.17	2.83
T	Preparation of tax communications	3.54	2.92	3.09
T	Complex tax provisions: individuals	3.53	3.50	3.46
T	Judicial doctrines in tax disputes	3.50	3.31	2.00
F	Corporate equity	3.50	3.45	3.18
F	Investments in securities	3.46	3.50	3.00
F	Fixed assets	3.46	3.50	3.08
F	Accounting for income taxes	3.46	3.36	3.09
T	Complex tax provisions: subchapter S	3.40	3.21	2.83
A	Professional rules of conduct	3.38	3.58	2.55
T	Judicial processes in tax disputes	3.33	3.14	1.83
T	Theoretical framework of taxation: alternatives to present framework	3.33	3.14	1.73
F	Theoretical framework of financial auditing: current structure	3.31	2.92	2.17
F	Statement of changes in financial position	3.31	3.17	2.92
F	Long-term liabilities	3.31	3.25	2.92
F	Pensions	3.31	3.33	2.45
F	Regulatory influences	3.29	3.17	2.17
T	Theoretical framework of taxation: economic and social concepts	3.27	3.14	1.64
T	Complex tax provisions: partners and partnerships	3.27	3.21	2.91

APPENDIX 5A
(continued)

Area	Topic	Importance	Means Conceptual Knowledge	Technical Ability
F	Financial statement analysis	3.23	3.17	3.00
F	Cash	3.23	3.45	3.00
F	Receivables	3.23	3.45	3.00
T	Administrative processes in tax matters	3.21	3.00	2.25
F	Partnership financial statements	3.15	3.25	2.73
F	Convertible debt or equity	3.08	3.27	3.00
F	Present value and future worth concepts	3.08	3.08	2.50
A	Audit evidence: type	3.08	3.17	2.50
A	Audit evidence: relative strength of types	3.08	3.17	2.50
F	Intangibles (excluding goodwill)	3.08	3.08	2.67
F	Short-term liabilities	3.08	3.00	2.75
F	Business combinations: purchase vs. pooling of interests	3.08	3.25	2.67
F	Business combinations: consolidation procedures	3.08	3.33	2.92
T	Accumulated earnings tax	3.07	2.85	2.00
T	Tax returns and accompanying schedules	3.07	2.79	2.58
T	Taxation of deferred compensation	3.07	3.14	2.18
F	U.S. financial accounting and reporting standards	3.00	2.92	2.42
F	Statements from incomplete records	3.00	3.17	3.08
F	Earnings-per-share	3.00	3.00	2.27
M	Full costing	3.00	3.08	2.45
M	Computer science	3.00	3.08	2.27
A	Generally accepted auditing standards (GAAS)	3.00	3.25	2.45
A	Auditing procedures: tests of account balances	3.00	2.92	2.55
T	Federal gift tax	3.00	2.86	2.31
T	Federal estate tax	2.92	3.00	2.31
F	Materiality	2.92	2.92	1.82
F	Treasury stock	2.92	3.17	2.58
M	Variable costing	2.92	3.00	2.36
A	Audit evidence: post-statement events	2.92	3.08	2.17
T	Tax practice procedures	2.87	2.71	1.92
T	Complex tax provisions: fiduciaries	2.87	2.86	2.31
F	Theoretical framework: alternatives to current structure	2.85	2.92	2.17
F	Installment sales	2.85	2.92	2.75
F	Minority interest	2.85	3.00	2.67
F	Research and development costs	2.85	2.92	2.25
F	Business combinations: unconsolidated subsidiaries	2.85	3.08	2.42
M	Capital budgeting	2.85	2.75	2.45
A	Legal responsibilities of auditors: at common law	2.85	3.08	2.27

APPENDIX 5A
(continued)

Area	Topic	Importance	Means Conceptual Knowledge	Technical Ability
A	Legal responsibilities of auditors: under the securities acts	2.85	3.00	2.27
A	Internal control: relationship of GAAS	2.85	3.08	2.36
A	Auditing procedures: review of operations	2.85	3.00	2.55
A	Internal control: evaluation	2.83	2.82	2.27
F	Leases	2.77	2.83	2.18
M	Standard costs	2.77	2.75	2.27
M	Long-range planning	2.77	2.83	2.09
M	Short-range planning	2.77	2.83	2.00
A	Standard short-form audit report	2.77	3.00	2.36
A	Modifications of the standard short-form audit report	2.77	3.08	2.45
A	Internal control: principles	2.77	3.08	2.27
A	Auditing procedures: tests of transactions	2.77	2.83	2.36
F	Goodwill	2.77	2.92	2.50
F	Information needs of financial statement users	2.75	2.70	2.10
F	Full costing vs. successful effort costing	2.75	2.80	2.10
F	Fund accounting: financial statements	2.75	2.82	2.00
A	Auditing procedures: working papers	2.75	2.82	2.45
T	Personal holding company tax	2.73	2.71	2.38
A	Internal control: description based on questionnaire	2.73	2.60	1.90
M	Process costing	2.69	2.83	2.09
M	*Direct costing	2.69	2.83	2.09
M	Cash management	2.69	2.75	2.36
A	Influence of professional and regulatory bodies on auditing	2.69	2.92	2.00
A	Requirements for professional certification (CPA)	2.69	2.75	2.18
A	Legal responsibilities of auditors: exposure to criminal liability	2.69	2.83	2.27
A	Long-form audit report	2.69	3.00	2.00
A	Internal control: in an EDP environment	2.69	2.75	1.92
A	Auditing procedures: compliance tests	2.69	2.75	2.45
F	*Segment reporting	2.67	2.55	1.90
F	Fund accounting: types of organizations	2.67	2.82	1.82
M	*Management information systems: impact of external regulatory influences	2.67	2.67	2.00
A	Internal control: description based on flowchart	2.64	2.50	2.10
F	Contingencies	2.62	2.58	1.91
M	Joint costs	2.62	2.75	2.27
M	Flexible budgets	2.62	2.58	2.09
M	Budgeted financial statements	2.62	2.73	2.20
M	Cost-volume-profit analysis	2.62	2.50	2.45

APPENDIX 5A
(continued)

Area	Topic	Importance	Conceptual Knowledge	Technical Ability
			Means	
M	*Simulation	2.62	2.82	2.18
A	Internal control: modifications in audit program based on evaluation	2.62	2.75	1.83
A	Statistical inference in auditing: judgmental sampling	2.62	3.00	2.00
A	Extensions of the attest function: associated audit risk	2.62	2.58	1.55
F	Behavioral considerations in financial reporting	2.62	2.50	1.75
T	Complex tax provisions: consolidated corporate returns	2.60	2.50	1.92
T	Complex tax provisions: foreign tax credit	2.60	2.50	2.00
A	Internal control: audit exposure due to weaknesses	2.58	2.73	1.82
M	Accounting information requirements for management decisions	2.58	2.64	1.60
M	*Performance evaluation: common costs	2.58	2.64	2.00
F	SEC reporting	2.54	2.67	2.00
F	Price-level adjusted financial statements	2.54	2.67	2.00
F	Reporting forecasts	2.54	2.75	2.00
M	Job order costing	2.54	2.67	2.00
A	Legal responsibilities of auditors: classic cases	2.54	2.67	2.09
A	Audit administration: client relations	2.54	2.58	1.82
M	Information economics	2.50	2.73	1.83
M	Management information systems: internal control aspects	2.50	2.45	1.83
M	Performance evaluation: return on investment	2.50	2.55	1.90
M	Performance evaluation: divisional performance	2.50	2.55	2.00
M	*Performance evaluation: transfer pricing	2.50	2.64	1.90
F	*Fund accounting: governmental units	2.50	2.45	1.73
A	User's expectations regarding the auditor's role	2.46	2.67	1.45
A	Legal responsibilities of auditors: responses of the auditing profession to classic cases	2.46	2.50	1.91
A	Statistical inference in auditing: statistical sampling	2.46	2.83	2.42
A	*Operational auditing: objectives	2.46	2.33	1.73
A	Extensions of the attest function: possible areas	2.46	2.42	1.55
A	Internal control: description based on narrative	2.45	2.50	1.90
M	Learning curve models	2.42	2.55	1.40

APPENDIX 5A
(continued)

Area	Topic	Importance	Means Conceptual Knowledge	Technical Ability
M	*Performance evaluation: residual income	2.42	2.20	1.78
M	*Internal financial auditing	2.42	2.45	1.80
T	State and local taxes	2.40	2.43	1.75
A	Audit administration: planning	2.38	2.42	2.00
A	Audit administration: supervision	2.38	2.42	2.00
A	*Operational auditing: methodology	2.38	2.42	2.00
M	Organization theory	2.38	2.33	1.64
F	Interim reporting	2.33	2.27	1.30
M	*Statistical cost estimation	2.33	2.36	1.60
M	*Performance evaluation: non-statistical variance analysis	2.33	2.36	1.70
A	Statistical inference in auditing: other statistical methods	2.33	2.73	1.90
T	Taxation for international operations	2.33	2.36	1.58
T	Natural resource taxation	2.33	2.50	1.85
T	Social security taxes	2.33	2.43	1.75
F	*Fiduciary accounting: estates and trusts	2.31	2.42	1.91
M	Spoilage, waste, defective units and scraps	2.31	2.42	2.00
M	Corporate planning models	2.31	2.42	2.00
A	*SEC filing requirements	2.31	2.42	2.18
A	Audit administration: review	2.31	2.33	1.91
M	*Network methods	2.27	2.56	1.89
M	Management information systems: implementation	2.25	2.30	1.82
M	*Linear programming	2.25	2.36	1.80
M	*Sensitivity analysis	2.25	2.27	1.50
M	*Statistical decision theory	2.25	2.27	1.50
M	*Social accounting	2.25	2.36	1.50
A	Statistical inference in auditing: regression analysis	2.23	2.67	1.91
M	*Special considerations in non-manufacturing concerns	2.18	2.00	1.44
M	*Performance evaluation: residual income	2.18	2.20	1.78
M	*Internal operational auditing	2.18	2.20	1.67
M	*Behavioral considerations (managerial)	2.17	2.36	1.70
M	Management information systems: administration	2.17	2.30	1.82
M	*Overhead control	2.17	2.27	1.40
F	Regulated industries	2.15	2.42	1.58
F	National income accounting	2.15	2.25	1.75
A	Management letter	2.15	2.08	1.64
T	Complex tax provisions: DISC	2.13	2.29	1.67
F	*Fund accounting: hospitals	2.08	2.09	1.64
M	*Performance evaluation: non-financial performance measures	2.08	2.09	1.60

APPENDIX 5A
(continued)

Area	Topic	Importance	Conceptual Knowledge	Technical Ability
			Means	
F	Consignments	2.08	2.25	1.92
F	Development stage companies	2.08	2.33	1.58
A	Auditing procedures: audit practice case	2.08	2.00	2.00
A	Audit administration: setting and collecting fees	2.08	2.00	1.82
A	Special considerations in auditing not-for-profit organizations	2.08	2.17	1.27
F	*Fund accounting: colleges and universities	2.00	2.10	1.64
M	*Zero base budgeting	2.00	2.25	1.55
M	*Management information system: design	2.00	2.10	1.82
A	Audit administration: accounting firm organization	2.00	2.25	1.55
M	Statistical analysis of cost variances	1.92	2.00	1.40
F	Foreign currency translation	1.85	2.33	1.67
F	Fiduciary accounting: bankruptcy	1.85	2.08	1.45
F	Fiduciary accounting: receivership	1.77	2.00	1.36
M	*Planning and control of international operations	1.70	1.89	1.63
M	*Requirements for professional certification (CMA)	1.67	1.64	1.10
A	*Historical development of auditing	1.62	1.83	.91
A	Comparative accounting and auditing standards among nations	1.54	1.75	.91
F	*Human resource accounting	1.46	1.50	1.17
F	*International accounting standards	1.33	1.50	1.00

* ⟶ non-core topic

APPENDIX 5B

RANK ORDERING BY IMPORTANCE MEANS:
TAXATION PRACTITIONERS

Area	Topic	Importance	Means Conceptual Knowledge	Means Technical Ability
T	Fundamentals of Federal income tax determination	3.31	2.93	3.37
F	Deferred taxes	3.27	3.17	2.65
T	Recognition of tax opportunities	3.26	2.95	2.06
T	Non-taxable exchanges	3.17	2.79	2.89
T	Tax planning	3.17	2.74	3.09
T	Complex tax provisions: corporations and shareholders	3.10	2.86	2.97
F	Balance sheet	3.10	3.05	2.50
F	Double-entry sheet	3.08	3.03	2.73
T	Tax research methodology	3.00	2.67	2.69
F	Accruals and deferrals	2.98	2.97	2.40
A	Internal control: evaluation	2.96	2.77	1.75
T	Capital gains and losses	2.95	2.56	3.02
A	Internal control: audit exposure due to weaknesses	2.93	2.73	1.65
T	Judicial doctrines in tax disputes	2.92	2.73	2.13
A	Internal control: principles	2.92	2.88	1.61
F	Transaction analysis	2.88	2.88	2.42
T	Administrative processes in tax matters	2.86	2.53	2.47
F	U.S. financial accounting and reporting standards	2.85	2.82	2.15
A	Legal responsibilities of auditors: under securities acts	2.83	2.38	1.62
F	Income statement	2.83	2.82	2.31
A	Legal responsibilities of auditors: classic cases	2.82	2.45	1.78
A	Internal control: in an EDP environment	2.82	2.50	1.53
F	Accounting for income taxes	2.82	2.89	2.43
T	Taxation of deferred compensation	2.82	2.44	2.41
F	Revenue and expense recognition	2.79	2.85	2.39
M	Tax considerations in managerial decisions	2.79	2.81	2.40
A	Audit evidence: types	2.78	2.62	2.38
F	SEC reporting	2.78	2.74	2.07
A	Internal control: description based on narrative	2.78	2.62	1.68
T	Tax practice procedures	2.76	2.40	2.59
A	Modifications of the standard short-form audit report	2.76	2.41	1.63
A	Internal control: modifications in audit program based on evaluation	2.74	2.54	1.19
A	Internal control: description based on questionnaire	2.74	2.60	1.94

APPENDIX 5B
(continued)

Area	Topic	Importance	Conceptual Knowledge	Technical Ability
			Means	
F	Business combinations: consolidation procedures	2.74	2.75	2.13
F	Error corrections	2.70	2.62	2.27
T	Accumulated earnings tax	2.69	2.55	1.96
F	Theoretical framework: current structure	2.68	2.64	2.21
T	State and local taxes	2.68	2.36	2.09
T	Complex tax provisions: foreign tax credit	2.61	2.31	2.38
F	Leases	2.59	2.52	2.08
F	Contingencies	2.59	2.55	1.93
T	Judicial processes in tax disputes	2.58	2.30	2.02
A	Audit evidence: relative strength of types	2.58	2.42	1.79
F	Information needs of financial statement users	2.58	2.50	2.05
F	Business combinations: purchase vs. pooling of interests	2.57	2.70	1.98
F	Financial statement analysis	2.56	2.51	2.05
F	Statements from incomplete records	2.56	2.52	2.13
A	Standard short-form audit report	2.56	2.15	1.55
A	Audit evidence: post-statement events	2.56	2.38	2.56
T	Tax returns and accompanying schedules	2.56	2.19	3.15
T	Complex tax provisions: DISC	2.55	2.33	1.74
F	Development stage companies	2.55	2.60	2.17
F	Materiality	2.54	2.63	1.97
F	Theoretical framework: alternatives to current structure	2.54	2.52	1.93
T	Theoretical framework: economic and social concepts	2.52	2.23	1.35
A	Audit administration: review	2.52	2.26	1.65
A	Long-form audit report	2.49	1.95	1.75
F	Regulatory influences	2.49	2.50	1.93
T	Taxation for international operations	2.47	2.15	2.21
A	Extensions of the attest function: associated audit risk	2.45	1.92	1.30
A	Audit administration: planning	2.44	2.29	1.51
F	Inventories	2.44	2.53	1.99
F	Minority interest	2.44	2.41	1.96
A	Audit administration: client relations	2.43	2.19	1.80
F	Statement of changes in financial position	2.43	2.39	1.92
F	Corporate equity	2.40	2.33	2.01
T	Complex tax provisions: consolidated corporate returns	2.39	2.14	2.68
A	Statistical inference in auditing: judgmental sampling	2.39	2.05	1.35
F	Intangibles (excluding goodwill)	2.38	2.34	1.77
T	Social security taxes	2.38	1.99	1.69
F	Installment sales	2.38	2.36	1.91

APPENDIX 5B
(continued)

Area	Topic	Importance	Means Conceptual Knowledge	Technical Ability
F	Present value and future worth concepts	2.38	2.42	1.94
A	Auditing procedures: tests of account balances	2.38	2.04	1.94
F	Behavioral considerations in financial reporting	2.37	2.35	1.78
F	Fund accounting: financial statements	2.36	2.39	1.95
A	Management letter	2.36	2.18	1.50
M	Standard costs	2.36	2.42	1.89
F	Fixed assets	2.35	2.37	1.97
A	Auditing procedures: working papers	2.35	2.08	1.73
T	Preparation of tax communications	2.34	1.97	2.74
F	*International accounting standards	2.34	2.34	1.72
F	Foreign currency translation	2.33	2.36	1.90
A	Auditing procedures: tests of transactions	2.32	2.03	1.92
M	Short-range planning	2.32	2.35	1.99
A	Statistical inference in auditing: regression analysis	2.32	2.13	2.57
A	Legal responsibilities of auditors: exposure to criminal liability	2.31	1.95	1.73
M	Learning curve models	2.31	2.29	1.92
A	Auditing procedures: review of operations	2.31	2.20	1.86
F	Depreciation, depletion and amortization	2.30	2.35	1.96
F	Interim reporting	2.30	2.19	1.61
M	Long-range planning	2.29	2.32	2.05
A	Statistical inference in auditing: statistical sampling	2.29	2.13	2.41
F	Long-term liabilities	2.28	2.25	1.88
F	Business combinations: unconsolidated subsidiaries	2.27	2.31	1.73
F	Fund accounting: types of organizations	2.27	2.29	1.82
T	Complex tax provisions: individuals	2.26	2.02	2.29
M	Cash management	2.25	2.38	2.02
A	Statistical inference in auditing: other statistical methods	2.25	2.08	1.32
T	Theoretical framework of taxation: alternatives to present framework	2.24	1.94	1.76
F	Convertible debt or equity	2.24	2.23	1.79
F	Short-term liabilities	2.23	2.27	1.88
M	Budgeted financial statements	2.22	2.30	1.88
A	Generally accepted auditing standards (GAAS)	2.22	2.19	1.87
A	Audit administration: supervision	2.21	1.97	1.36
M	Performance evaluation: return on investment	2.21	2.28	1.68
F	Pensions	2.21	2.19	1.56
F	Treasury stock	2.19	2.13	1.80
T	Complex tax provisions: fiduciaries	2.19	1.97	1.74

APPENDIX 5B
(continued)

Area	Topic	Importance	Conceptual Knowledge	Technical Ability
			Means	
A	Audit administration: setting and collecting fees	2.19	1.90	1.36
A	Internal control: description based on flowchart	2.19	1.85	1.94
M	Process costing	2.19	2.31	1.91
A	Auditing procedures: compliance tests	2.18	1.92	1.91
T	Complex tax provisions: partners and partnerships	2.18	1.91	2.40
M	Accounting information requirements for management decisions	2.18	2.25	1.66
M	Spoilage, waste, defective units and scrap	2.18	2.21	1.77
A	Auditing procedures: audit practice case	2.17	1.87	1.79
M	Variable costing	2.16	2.25	1.85
A	Influence of professional and regulatory bodies on auditing	2.15	2.06	1.52
A	Professional rules of conduct	2.15	2.28	1.59
M	Statistical analysis of cost variances	2.14	2.20	1.80
M	Performance evaluation: divisional performance	2.14	2.17	1.63
F	Earnings-per-share	2.13	2.13	1.54
F	Reporting forecasts	2.13	2.19	1.73
M	Full costing	2.12	2.30	1.80
A	Special considerations in auditing not-for-profit organizations	2.12	1.88	.73
M	Job order costing	2.11	2.21	1.95
M	Flexible budgets	2.09	2.23	1.85
F	Investments in securities	2.09	2.20	1.68
T	Complex tax provisions: subchapter S	2.08	1.85	1.87
T	Federal gift tax	2.07	1.74	2.04
M	Capital budgeting	2.06	2.19	1.68
F	Goodwill	2.05	1.98	1.63
M	Joint costs	2.04	2.19	1.72
F	Partnership financial statements	2.04	2.08	1.50
F	Fiduciary accounting: bankruptcy	2.04	2.15	1.62
A	Comparative accounting and auditing standards among nations	2.02	1.66	.58
A	User's expectations regarding the auditor's role	2.02	2.17	1.51
M	Management information systems: implementation	2.02	2.08	1.50
F	Fiduciary accounting: receivership	2.01	2.08	1.56
F	National income accounting	2.00	2.12	1.71
A	Legal responsibilities of auditors: at common law	1.98	2.13	1.38

APPENDIX 5B
(continued)

Area	Topic	Importance	Conceptual Knowledge	Technical Ability
			Means	
A	Audit administration: accounting firm organization	1.97	1.65	1.39
F	Full costing vs. successful effort costing	1.94	2.03	1.61
T	Federal estate tax	1.94	1.75	2.04
F	Cash	1.94	2.11	1.70
F	*Human resource accounting	1.93	1.91	1.52
M	Management information systems: administration	1.92	1.98	1.44
A	Requirements for professional certification (CPA)	1.92	2.02	1.87
M	Management information systems: internal control aspects	1.92	1.92	1.37
M	Performance evaluation: responsibility accounting	1.92	2.00	1.48
A	Legal responsibilities of auditors: responses of the auditing profession to classic cases	1.92	1.57	1.39
T	Personal holding company tax	1.92	1.69	2.05
A	Internal control: relationship of GAAS	1.91	1.63	1.86
F	Consignments	1.90	2.00	1.50
F	Regulated industries	1.90	1.98	1.35
F	Receivables	1.89	2.03	1.61
M	Cost-volume-profit analysis	1.86	1.91	1.63
M	Managerial accounting uses of quantitative techniques: corporate planning models	1.86	2.01	1.61
F	Price-level adjusted financial statements	1.86	1.95	1.38
M	Organization theory	1.84	1.93	1.43
T	Natural resource taxation	1.82	1.61	1.62
A	Extensions of the attest function: possible areas	1.80	1.40	1.32
M	*Direct costing	1.76	1.96	1.52
M	*Performance evaluation: residual income	1.76	1.81	1.40
M	*Performance evaluation: non-statistical variance analysis	1.76	1.81	1.46
F	*Fiduciary accounting: estates and trusts	1.75	1.78	1.43
M	Information economics	1.75	1.83	1.38
M	*Performance evaluation: non-financial performance measures	1.73	1.81	1.41
A	*SEC filing requirements	1.71	1.74	1.32
A	*Operational auditing: objectives	1.71	1.34	1.19
F	*Fund accounting: governmental units	1.71	1.80	1.49
F	*Fund accounting: hospitals	1.71	1.83	1.45
F	*Fund accounting: colleges and universities	1.70	1.79	1.47
A	*Operational auditing: methodology	1.69	1.28	1.07

APPENDIX 5B
(continued)

Area	Topic	Importance	Conceptual Knowledge	Technical Ability
			Means	
M	*Planning and control of international operations	1.65	1.78	1.28
M	*Performance evaluation: transfer pricing	1.65	1.76	1.22
M	*Managerial accounting use of quantitative techniques: network methods	1.65	1.62	1.08
M	*Internal financial auditing	1.64	1.72	1.39
M	*Management information systems: impact of external regulatory influences	1.63	1.75	1.23
F	*Segment reporting	1.61	1.72	1.12
M	*Simulation	1.60	1.58	1.09
M	*Zero base budgeting	1.57	1.74	1.42
M	*Statistical decision theory	1.57	1.66	1.22
A	*Historical development of auditing	1.56	1.65	1.20
M	*Computer science	1.54	1.69	1.23
M	*Performance evaluation: common costs	1.43	1.48	1.01
M	*Overhead control	1.40	1.51	1.14
M	*Statistical cost estimation	1.40	1.50	1.06
M	*Management information systems: design	1.39	1.45	1.01
M	*Internal operational auditing	1.34	1.46	1.09
M	*Special considerations in non-manufacturing concerns	1.33	1.53	1.16
M	*Requirements for professional certification (CMA)	1.31	1.45	1.12
M	*Sensitivity analysis	1.25	1.33	.98
M	*Behavioral considerations	1.20	1.36	.94
M	*Linear programming	1.13	1.28	.78
M	*Social accounting	1.11	1.30	.88

* → non-area core topic

APPENDIX 6A

RANK ORDERING BY IMPORTANCE MEANS:
FINANCIAL ACCOUNTING EDUCATORS

Area	Topic	Importance	Means Conceptual Knowledge	Technical Ability
F	Theoretical framework: current structures	3.87	3.84	3.25
F	U.S. financial accounting and reporting standards	3.77	3.65	3.20
F	Revenue and expense recognition	3.75	3.76	3.42
F	Balance sheet	3.71	3.67	3.51
F	Income statement	3.71	3.69	3.53
F	Present value and future worth concepts	3.69	3.63	3.16
F	Theoretical framework: alternatives to current standards	3.63	3.67	2.59
F	Transaction analysis	3.61	3.52	3.46
F	Regulatory influences	3.58	3.34	2.57
F	Information needs of financial statement users	3.56	3.48	2.24
F	Accruals and deferrals	3.55	3.62	3.50
F	Statement of changes in financial position	3.53	3.54	3.38
A	Generally accepted auditing standards (GAAS)	3.48	3.47	3.02
F	Double-entry system	3.42	3.27	3.41
T	Fundamentals of federal income tax determination	3.40	3.02	2.73
M	Standard costs	3.40	3.39	2.98
F	Inventories	3.39	3.47	3.22
A	Audit evidence: relative strength of types	3.39	3.31	2.82
F	Fixed assets	3.37	3.47	3.20
A	Audit evidence: types	3.37	3.27	2.81
F	Depreciation, depletion and amortization	3.35	3.41	3.16
A	Influence of professional and regulatory bodies on auditing	3.33	3.14	2.30
M	Capital budgeting	3.32	3.33	2.83
A	Professional rules of conduct	3.30	3.24	2.91
A	Standard short-form audit report	3.30	3.29	3.02
F	Business combinations: purchase vs. pooling of interests	3.29	3.53	2.78
M	Cost-volume-profit analysis	3.28	3.30	2.93
M	Full costing	3.26	3.28	2.76
A	Internal control: principles	3.24	3.11	2.82
M	Flexible budgets	3.23	3.09	2.70
F	Deferred taxes	3.23	3.34	2.84
A	Statistical inference in auditing: statistical sampling	3.22	3.23	2.82
A	Modifications of the standard short-form audit report	3.22	3.22	2.89
F	Leases	3.21	3.29	2.80
F	Corporate equity	3.20	3.38	3.10

APPENDIX 6A
(continued)

Area	Topic	Importance	Conceptual Knowledge	Technical Ability
			Means	
T	Capital gains and losses	3.19	2.88	2.66
A	Internal control: evaluation	3.19	3.14	2.71
F	Investments in securities	3.18	3.27	3.02
F	Business combinations: consolidation procedures	3.17	3.41	2.88
M	Variable costing	3.17	3.30	2.67
A	Internal control: relationship of GAAS	3.16	3.07	2.75
F	Materiality	3.15	3.14	2.46
F	Long-term liabilities	3.12	3.25	3.02
F	Accounting for income taxes	3.12	3.29	2.88
A	Audit evidence: post-statement events	3.11	3.16	2.66
F	Business combinations: unconsolidated subsidiaries	3.08	3.24	2.55
A	Legal responsibilities of auditors: under the securities acts	3.07	3.00	2.36
A	User's expectations regarding the auditor's role	3.07	2.95	1.80
M	Performance evaluation: return on investment	3.07	3.11	2.60
M	Process costing	3.06	3.15	2.78
M	Accounting information requirements for management decisions	3.06	2.89	2.48
A	Internal control: modifications in audit program based on evaluation	3.05	2.98	2.64
A	Statistical inference in auditing: judgmental sampling	3.04	3.07	2.73
A	Legal responsibilities of auditors: at common law	3.02	3.05	2.39
A	Auditing procedures: compliance tests	3.02	2.98	2.50
M	Tax considerations in managerial decisions	3.02	2.96	2.52
F	Goodwill	3.02	3.29	2.77
F	Price-level adjusted financial statements	3.02	3.24	2.48
F	Pensions	3.02	3.12	2.59
F	Earnings-per-share	3.02	3.08	2.84
F	Receivables	3.00	3.04	2.92
F	Intangibles (excluding goodwill)	3.00	3.32	2.80
M	Direct costing	3.00	3.25	2.56
A	Internal control in an EDP environment	3.00	2.83	2.60
A	Auditing procedures: review of operations	3.00	3.00	2.52
F	Financial statement analysis	2.98	3.10	2.73
M	Joint costs	2.98	3.17	2.52
M	Management information systems: internal control aspects	2.98	2.96	2.50
A	Auditing procedures: tests of transactions	2.98	2.95	2.57
A	Internal control: audit exposure due to weaknesses	2.98	2.90	2.62

APPENDIX 6A
(continued)

Area	Topic	Importance	Means Conceptual Knowledge	Technical Ability
M	Job order costing	2.96	3.07	2.72
M	Short-range planning	2.96	2.89	2.43
M	Performance evaluation: responsibility accounting	2.96	2.93	2.31
A	Auditing procedures: tests of account balances	2.96	2.93	2.52
T	Tax planning	2.93	2.85	2.20
F	Research and development costs	2.92	3.08	2.52
M	Performance evaluation: divisional performance	2.91	2.96	2.44
T	Non-taxable exchanges	2.90	2.65	2.43
F	Convertible debt or equity	2.90	3.16	2.73
M	Management information systems: impact of external regulatory influences	2.89	2.87	2.26
M	Long-range planning	2.87	2.87	2.24
M	Budgeted financial statements	2.87	2.78	2.46
F	Short-term liabilities	2.84	3.02	2.84
F	Contingencies	2.83	2.92	2.38
A	Operational auditing: objectives	2.82	2.77	1.93
F	Segment reporting	2.79	2.94	2.34
A	Auditing procedures: working papers	2.78	2.84	2.43
A	Legal responsibilities of auditors: exposure to criminal liability	2.77	2.79	2.14
M	Cash management	2.77	2.65	2.39
A	Legal responsibilities of auditors: responses of auditing profession to classic cases	2.76	2.70	2.12
F	Interim reporting	2.75	2.90	2.38
F	Cash	2.75	2.71	2.78
M	Performance evaluation: transfer pricing	2.74	2.91	2.29
M	Performance evaluation: common costs	2.74	2.82	2.20
A	Legal responsibilities of auditors: classic cases	2.74	2.76	2.21
M	Overhead control	2.70	2.64	2.18
F	Error corrections	2.69	2.94	2.82
A	Statistical inference in auditing: regression analysis	2.67	2.80	2.25
F	Treasury stock	2.65	2.94	2.69
F	SEC reporting	2.63	2.63	2.00
A	Management letter	2.61	2.58	2.02
A	Statistical inference in auditing: other statistical methods	2.56	2.66	2.24
M	Information economics	2.54	2.76	1.96
A	Long-form audit report	2.54	2.64	2.13
F	Behavioral considerations in financial reporting	2.54	2.75	1.49

APPENDIX 6A
(continued)

Area	Topic	Importance	Means Conceptual Knowledge	Technical Ability
T	Tax research methodology	2.54	2.62	2.28
M	Performance evaluation: non-statistical variance analysis	2.52	2.54	2.07
A	Internal control: description based on flowchart	2.51	2.59	2.33
M	*Behavioral considerations	2.51	2.61	1.84
A	*Extensions of the attest function: possible areas	2.49	2.55	1.68
M	Computer science	2.49	2.61	2.12
F	Minority interest	2.47	2.86	2.36
T	Theoretical framework of taxation: alternatives to present framework	2.45	2.68	1.53
T	Theoretical framework of taxation: economic and social concepts	2.45	2.60	1.48
T	Recognition of tax opportunities	2.45	2.49	1.92
M	Organization theory	2.45	2.57	1.84
M	Statistical analysis of cost variances	2.45	2.76	2.13
A	Requirements for professional certification (CPA)	2.44	2.30	1.84
M	Performance evaluation: residual income	2.44	2.67	2.05
A	Operational auditing: methodology	2.43	2.49	1.95
F	Foreign currency translation	2.42	2.76	1.98
M	Performance evaluation: non-financial performance measures	2.42	2.58	1.84
A	Extensions of the attest function: associated audit risk	2.42	2.41	1.59
M	*Statistical cost estimation	2.41	2.70	2.28
A	SEC filing requirements	2.40	2.39	1.95
M	*Statistical decision theory	2.39	2.64	2.16
A	Internal control: description based on questionnaire	2.39	2.54	2.26
A	Internal control: description based on narrative	2.38	2.55	2.15
F	Fund accounting: financial statements	2.35	2.54	2.02
T	Tax returns and accompanying schedules	2.33	2.07	2.07
M	Spoilage, waste, defective units and scrap	2.32	2.41	2.17
M	*Linear programming	2.32	2.65	2.09
M	Corporate planning models	2.32	2.53	2.02
F	Fund accounting: types of organizations	2.29	2.42	1.70
T	Complex tax provisions: individuals	2.29	2.26	2.03
M	*Sensitivity analysis	2.28	2.49	2.02
M	Management information systems: design	2.28	2.36	1.86
F	Statements from incomplete records	2.27	2.54	2.55
F	Full costing vs. successful effort costing	2.27	2.64	1.87
F	Reporting forecasts	2.23	2.52	1.94

APPENDIX 6A
(continued)

Area	Topic	Importance	Conceptual Knowledge	Technical Ability
			Means	
A	Audit administration: review	2.22	2.33	1.90
F	Fund accounting: governmental units	2.20	2.40	1.86
M	Internal financial auditing	2.19	2.43	1.80
T	Complex tax provisions: corporations and shareholders	2.17	2.13	1.87
T	Taxation of deferred compensation	2.17	2.18	1.73
F	Partnership financial statements	2.16	2.35	2.11
A	Audit administration: planning	2.15	2.24	1.88
M	*Special considerations in non-manufacturing concerns	2.14	2.29	1.76
F	Development stage companies	2.13	2.55	1.84
M	Simulation	2.13	2.43	1.82
F	Regulated industries	2.08	2.29	1.75
M	Zero base budgeting	2.07	2.54	1.79
T	*Federal estate tax	2.07	2.12	1.63
M	Internal operational auditing	2.07	2.43	1.74
A	Audit administration: client relations	2.07	2.12	1.81
F	Installment sales	2.06	2.52	2.04
T	Administrative processes in tax matters	2.02	1.97	1.46
T	*Federal gift tax	2.02	2.10	1.61
M	*Social accounting	2.00	2.17	1.54
M	Management information systems: implementation	1.98	2.07	1.70
M	Network methods	1.98	2.31	1.76
M	Learning curve models	1.98	2.44	1.84
T	Social security taxes	1.98	1.82	1.67
A	Special considerations in auditing not-for-profit organizations	1.96	2.05	1.42
F	International accounting standards	1.94	2.18	1.46
A	Auditing procedures: audit practice case	1.93	2.00	1.93
M	Planning and control of international operations	1.91	2.05	1.58
A	Audit administration: supervision	1.91	2.07	1.66
A	*Historical development of auditing	1.91	2.18	1.25
F	Fund accounting: hospitals	1.90	2.10	1.60
A	*Audit administration: accounting firm organization	1.89	1.86	1.43
F	National income accounting	1.88	2.14	1.27
T	Accumulated earnings tax	1.88	2.06	1.65
T	Judicial doctrines in tax disputes	1.85	1.82	1.21
T	Complex tax provisions: subchapter S	1.85	1.84	1.68
T	Complex tax provisions: consolidated corporate returns	1.83	1.89	1.58
T	Complex tax provisions: partners and partnerships	1.83	1.92	1.66

APPENDIX 6A
(continued)

Area	Topic	Importance	Means Conceptual Knowledge	Technical Ability
F	Fund accounting: colleges and universities	1.82	2.02	1.50
M	Management information systems: administration	1.81	1.93	1.57
T	State and local taxes	1.76	1.73	1.48
T	*Natural resource taxation	1.75	1.92	1.51
A	*Comparative accounting and auditing standards among nations	1.69	1.80	1.16
T	*Taxation for international operations	1.66	1.76	1.21
T	*Complex tax provisions: foreign tax credit	1.63	1.68	1.39
F	*Consignments	1.63	2.06	1.69
F	*Human resource accounting	1.62	2.21	1.29
T	*Judicial processes in tax disputes	1.61	1.58	1.16
A	*Audit administration: setting and collecting fees	1.50	1.62	1.24
T	*Tax practice procedures	1.50	1.36	1.28
T	*Complex tax provisions: fiduciaries	1.49	1.58	1.34
T	*Preparation of tax communications	1.45	1.46	1.37
T	*Personal holding company tax	1.41	1.50	1.28
F	*Fiduciary accounting: estates and trusts	1.38	1.74	1.30
F	*Fiduciary accounting: bankruptcy	1.37	1.82	1.30
T	*Complex tax provisions: DISC	1.35	1.49	1.22
M	*Requirements for professional certification (CMA)	1.33	1.32	1.10
F	*Fiduciary accounting: receivership	1.31	1.74	1.26

* ⟶ non-area core topics

APPENDIX 6B

RANK ORDERING BY IMPORTANCE MEANS:
FINANCIAL ACCOUNTING PRACTITIONERS

			Means	
Area	**Topic**	**Importance**	**Conceptual Knowledge**	**Technical Ability**
T	Fundamentals of Federal income tax determination	3.42	3.15	2.31
F	U.S. financial accounting and reporting standards	3.36	3.38	2.93
F	Balance sheet	3.36	3.31	3.07
F	Revenue and expense recognition	3.35	3.35	2.92
A	Internal control: principles	3.31	3.16	1.96
F	Business combinations: consolidation procedures	3.27	3.18	2.73
A	Internal control: evaluation	3.23	3.06	2.07
A	Internal control: audit exposure due to weaknesses	3.23	3.01	1.93
F	Contingencies	3.22	3.12	2.67
A	Internal control: in an EDP environment	3.19	2.96	1.84
A	Internal control: modifications in audit program based on evaluation	3.18	2.92	1.68
F	Materiality	3.17	3.02	2.55
F	Theoretical framework: current structure	3.14	3.18	2.66
F	Regulatory influences	3.12	2.98	2.65
F	Deferred taxes	3.12	3.14	2.56
T	Recognition of tax opportunities	3.11	2.80	1.24
A	Audit evidence: types	3.10	2.99	2.60
F	Double-entry system	3.07	3.13	2.86
T	Capital gains and losses	3.04	2.67	2.03
F	Interim reporting	3.03	2.96	2.64
T	Non-taxable exchanges	3.01	2.62	1.78
F	SEC reporting	3.01	2.93	2.59
A	Legal responsibilities of auditors: under the securities acts	3.00	2.78	1.62
M	Management information systems: internal control aspects	2.99	2.84	2.35
F	Earnings-per-share	2.98	2.90	2.51
F	Information needs of financial statement users	2.97	2.92	2.23
F	Business combinations: purchase vs. pooling of interests	2.97	3.00	2.49
F	Income statement	2.94	3.03	2.65
F	Leases	2.94	2.85	2.40
F	Accounting for income taxes	2.94	2.96	2.60
M	Tax considerations in managerial decisions	2.94	2.84	2.39
A	Audit evidence: post-statement events	2.94	2.81	2.82
A	Internal control: description based on narrative	2.92	2.81	1.89

APPENDIX 6B
(continued)

Area	Topic	Importance	Conceptual Knowledge	Technical Ability
			Means	
F	Theoretical framework: alternatives to current structure	2.92	3.08	2.44
A	Audit evidence: relative strength of types	2.88	2.75	1.68
A	Modifications of the standard short-form audit report	2.88	2.63	1.96
T	Tax planning	2.87	2.52	1.81
F	Minority interest	2.86	3.01	2.39
F	Error corrections	2.85	2.95	2.70
F	Statement of changes in financial position	2.84	2.92	2.95
T	Complex tax provisions: corporations and shareholders	2.84	2.54	1.95
F	Financial statement analysis	2.83	2.92	2.46
A	Standard short-form audit report	2.83	2.46	1.74
M	Standard costs	2.80	2.84	2.44
F	Accruals and deferrals	2.80	3.05	2.56
F	Transaction analysis	2.78	2.98	2.44
F	Business combinations: unconsolidated subsidiaries	2.78	2.65	2.20
M	Long-range planning	2.77	2.73	2.30
F	Inventories	2.76	2.95	2.49
A	Legal responsibilities of auditors: classic cases	2.76	2.58	1.51
A	Management letter	2.76	2.57	1.95
F	Long-term liabilities	2.75	2.84	2.31
M	Variable costing	2.74	2.85	2.30
M	Budgeted financial statement	2.74	2.83	2.43
M	Accounting information requirements for management decisions	2.74	2.76	2.11
M	Cash management	2.73	2.71	2.25
M	Process costing	2.72	2.85	2.33
T	*Complex tax provisions: DISC	2.71	2.51	1.14
M	Short-range planning	2.70	2.71	2.28
M	Capital budgeting	2.69	2.60	2.14
A	Generally accepted auditing standards (GAAS)	2.69	2.70	2.18
A	Statistical inference in auditing: statistical sampling	2.68	2.62	2.44
F	Present value and future worth concepts	2.68	2.79	2.13
T	Accumulated earnings tax	2.68	2.56	1.20
A	Internal control: description based on flowchart	2.68	2.51	2.35
F	Foreign currency translation	2.67	2.74	2.34
M	Performance evaluation: divisional performance	2.66	2.68	2.15
A	Statistical inference in auditing: judgmental sampling	2.66	2.41	1.60

APPENDIX 6B
(continued)

Area	Topic	Importance	Conceptual Knowledge	Technical Ability
			Means	
F	Corporate equity	2.65	2.86	2.26
A	Auditing procedures: tests of account balances	2.65	2.46	2.27
F	Behavioral considerations in financial reporting	2.65	2.62	1.94
M	Job order costing	2.64	2.81	2.38
M	Flexible budgets	2.64	2.71	2.28
M	Cost-volume-profit analysis	2.64	2.64	2.33
M	Performance evaluation: return on investment	2.63	2.66	2.05
A	Audit administration: review	2.63	2.49	1.22
F	Short-term liabilities	2.62	2.76	2.22
M	Performance evaluation: responsibility accounting	2.62	2.54	2.06
M	Full costing	2.62	2.77	2.27
F	Intangibles (excluding goodwill)	2.61	2.82	2.25
F	Convertible debt or equity	2.61	2.89	2.27
F	Research and development cost	2.61	2.72	2.27
A	Internal control: description based on questionnaire	2.61	2.59	2.25
A	Influence of professional and regulatory bodies on auditing	2.60	2.56	1.81
A	Auditing procedures: tests of transactions	2.60	2.41	2.27
A	Statistical inference in auditing: other statistical methods	2.57	2.40	1.28
M	Joint costs	2.56	2.56	2.25
A	Auditing procedures: compliance tests	2.55	2.36	2.21
A	Audit administration: planning	2.55	2.41	1.32
M	Performance evaluation: non-statistical variance analysis	2.55	2.62	2.08
T	State and local taxes	2.53	2.30	1.67
A	Statistical inference in auditing: regression analysis	2.53	2.49	2.14
T	Judicial doctrines in tax disputes	2.53	2.33	.77
A	Extensions of the attest function: associated audit risk	2.53	2.19	1.34
F	Investments in securities	2.52	2.80	2.26
A	Internal control: relationship of GAAS	2.52	2.21	2.22
T	Administrative processes in tax matters	2.52	2.18	.89
T	*Taxation for international operations	2.52	2.18	1.40
F	Fixed assets	2.52	2.62	2.29
T	*Complex tax provisions: foreign tax credit	2.51	2.21	1.46
A	Auditing procedures: working papers	2.49	2.33	1.98
A	Auditing procedures: review of operations	2.49	2.42	2.16
M	Spoilage, waste, defective units and scrap	2.49	2.49	2.04
F	Treasury stock	2.48	2.56	2.14

APPENDIX 6B
(continued)

Area	Topic	Importance	Conceptual Knowledge	Technical Ability
			Means	
F	Reporting forecasts	2.48	2.50	2.07
F	Depreciation, depletion and amortization	2.48	2.69	2.25
M	Information economics	2.48	2.44	1.96
F	Statements from incomplete records	2.47	2.59	2.16
M	Management information systems: administration	2.45	2.30	2.00
A	User's expectations regarding the auditor's role	2.45	2.35	1.49
A	Requirements for professional certification (CPA)	2.45	2.39	2.15
F	Fund accounting: financial statements	2.45	2.45	1.95
F	Cash	2.43	2.57	2.22
M	Management information systems: impact of external regulatory influences	2.43	2.44	2.01
M	Management information systems: implementation	2.43	2.44	1.99
A	Long-form audit report	2.42	2.04	1.60
F	International accounting standards	2.42	2.53	2.02
T	Taxation of deferred compensation	2.38	2.22	1.57
M	Organization theory	2.37	2.32	1.78
A	Audit administration: supervision	2.36	2.19	1.16
A	Audit administration: client relations	2.36	2.06	1.08
F	Development stage companies	2.35	2.51	2.07
M	Zero base budgeting	2.34	2.49	2.00
F	Fund accounting: types of organizations	2.34	2.42	2.00
F	*Consignments	2.33	2.38	1.92
F	Receivables	2.32	2.61	2.15
A	Legal responsibilities of auditors: exposure to criminal liability	2.32	2.05	1.45
M	Direct costing	2.31	2.54	2.01
F	Full costing vs. successful effort costing	2.30	2.43	1.91
F	Installment sales	2.30	2.58	2.01
T	Tax research methodology	2.29	2.09	1.51
A	Auditing procedures: audit practice case	2.27	2.14	1.81
M	Learning curve models	2.26	2.37	1.80
F	Pensions	2.26	2.51	1.89
F	National income accounting	2.24	2.27	1.79
A	*Comparative accounting and auditing standards among nations	2.24	1.87	.83
F	Price-level adjusted financial statements	2.24	2.68	1.80
F	Segment reporting	2.22	2.41	1.74
M	Statistical analysis of cost variances	2.22	2.31	1.72
M	Performance evaluation: non-financial performance measures	2.21	2.28	1.78
M	Corporate planning models	2.21	2.21	1.69

APPENDIX 6B
(continued)

Area	Topic	Importance	Means Conceptual Knowledge	Technical Ability
A	Special considerations in auditing not-for-profit organizations	2.19	2.00	.94
F	Goodwill	2.19	2.32	1.96
A	Legal responsibilities of auditors: at common law	2.18	2.13	1.31
T	*Judicial processes in tax disputes	2.16	2.03	.71
A	SEC filing requirements	2.15	2.04	1.66
T	Theoretical framework of taxation: economic and social concepts	2.13	2.03	.69
F	Fund accounting: governmental units	2.13	2.25	1.80
A	Professional rules of conduct	2.11	2.13	1.50
T	Social security taxes	2.09	2.05	1.44
F	Partnership financial statements	2.08	2.43	1.71
T	*Complex tax provisions: fiduciaries	2.07	1.82	1.49
F	Regulated industries	2.06	2.04	1.56
T	Complex tax provisions: consolidated corporate returns	2.05	1.73	1.49
T	Tax returns and accompanying schedules	2.04	1.73	1.84
M	Internal financial auditing	2.04	2.14	1.73
T	*Tax practice procedures	2.03	1.84	1.19
M	Management information systems: design	2.03	2.14	1.54
M	Internal operational auditing	2.00	2.21	1.60
M	Simulation	1.99	2.14	1.57
A	Operational auditing: objectives	1.99	1.72	1.54
M	Performance evaluation: residual income	1.99	2.01	1.65
A	*Audit administration: setting and collecting fees	1.97	1.69	.57
F	*Human resource accounting	1.96	2.00	1.64
F	Fund accounting: colleges and universities	1.96	2.10	1.71
F	*Fiduciary accounting: bankruptcy	1.93	2.31	1.63
M	Planning and control of international operations	1.91	1.87	1.50
M	Overhead control	1.90	1.99	1.54
A	Operational auditing: methodology	1.90	1.65	1.43
F	Fund accounting: hospitals	1.89	2.05	1.65
F	*Fiduciary accounting: receivership	1.88	2.23	1.58
T	Complex tax provisions: individuals	1.88	1.55	1.81
M	Network methods	1.88	2.07	1.48
M	Performance evaluation: transfer pricing	1.88	1.90	1.48
A	Legal responsibilities of auditors: responses to auditing profession to classic cases	1.86	1.69	1.18
T	Complex tax provisions: partners and partnerships	1.83	1.47	2.04
M	Performance evaluation: common costs	1.82	1.89	1.47

APPENDIX 6B
(continued)

Area	Topic	Importance	Conceptual Knowledge	Technical Ability
			Means	
T	Complex tax provisions: subchapter S	1.81	1.53	1.82
T	Theoretical framework of taxation: alternatives to present framework	1.79	1.61	1.02
A	*Extensions of the attest function: possible areas	1.77	1.56	1.31
M	Computer science	1.73	1.87	1.27
M	*Statistical cost estimation	1.71	1.83	1.25
M	*Statistical decision theory	1.64	1.88	1.27
T	*Federal estate tax	1.62	1.25	.75
M	*Requirements for professional certification (CMA)	1.61	1.73	1.45
A	*Audit administration: accounting firm organization	1.60	1.42	.62
A	*Historical development of auditing	1.58	1.74	.99
T	*Federal gift tax	1.57	1.31	.72
M	*Behavioral considerations (managerial)	1.49	1.63	1.08
F	*Fiduciary accounting: estates and trusts	1.46	1.73	1.23
M	*Sensitivity analysis	1.42	1.77	1.19
M	*Local programming	1.41	1.74	1.03
T	*Preparation of tax communications	1.38	1.07	1.60
M	*Social accounting	1.37	1.50	.97
M	*Special considerations in non-manufacturing concerns	1.36	1.42	1.06
T	*Natural resource taxation	1.36	1.17	1.17
T	*Personal holding company tax	1.32	1.12	1.03

* ⟶ non-area core topic

APPENDIX 7A

RANK ORDERING BY IMPORTANCE MEANS:
AUDITING EDUCATORS

Area	Topic	Importance	Means Conceptual Knowledge	Technical Ability
F	U.S. financial accounting and reporting standards	3.77	3.31	3.17
A	Modifications of the standard short-form audit report	3.77	3.31	3.23
A	Internal control: principles	3.69	3.38	3.15
A	Internal control: evaluation	3.69	3.38	2.54
F	Revenue and expense recognition	3.69	3.46	3.23
A	Audit evidence: post-statement events	3.62	3.15	2.77
A	Statistical inference in auditing: statistical sampling	3.62	3.31	3.00
A	Internal control: modifications in audit program based on evaluation	3.62	3.38	2.85
F	Regulatory influences	3.54	3.08	2.77
F	Income statement	3.54	3.46	3.23
F	Statement of changes in financial position (general concepts, classifications, preparations, etc.)	3.54	3.31	3.15
A	Influence of professional and regulatory bodies upon auditing	3.54	3.38	2.38
A	Audit evidence: types	3.54	3.31	3.00
A	Internal control: description based on flowchart	3.54	3.15	2.85
A	Internal control: relationship of GAAS	3.54	3.31	2.69
A	Generally accepted auditing standards (GAAS)	3.54	3.46	3.08
F	Transaction analysis	3.50	3.25	3.42
F	Theoretical framework: current structure	3.46	3.46	3.00
F	Balance sheet	3.46	3.38	3.15
M	Management information systems: internal control aspects	3.46	3.31	2.85
T	Fundamentals of federal income tax determination	3.42	2.83	2.92
F	Information needs of financial statement users	3.38	3.23	2.00
A	Standard short-form audit report	3.38	3.00	3.00
F	Inventories	3.38	3.15	3.15
A	Internal control: audit exposure due to weaknesses	3.31	3.08	2.69
A	Internal control: in an EDP environment	3.31	3.15	2.54
A	Audit evidence: relative strength of types	3.31	3.08	2.85
T	Capital gains and losses	3.25	2.75	2.75
F	Receivables	3.23	3.08	3.08
F	Fixed assets	3.23	3.00	3.00
F	Depreciation, depletion and amortization	3.23	3.15	3.00

APPENDIX 7A
(continued)

Area	Topic	Importance	Conceptual Knowledge	Technical Ability
			Means	
F	Long-term liabilities	3.23	3.00	3.08
F	Corporate equity	3.23	2.85	2.85
A	Legal responsibilities of auditors: under the securities acts	3.23	2.85	2.23
A	Auditing procedures: tests of account balances	3.23	3.15	2.77
F	Accounting for income taxes	3.17	2.83	2.67
F	Short-term liabilities	3.15	3.00	3.00
M	Standard costs	3.15	3.15	2.77
A	Auditing procedures: tests of transactions	3.15	3.00	2.62
F	Accruals and deferrals	3.15	3.23	3.23
F	Leases	3.15	3.00	2.69
A	User's expectations regarding the auditor's role	3.15	3.00	1.62
A	Professional rules of conduct	3.15	3.23	3.00
A	Legal responsibilities of auditors: at common law	3.15	2.77	2.38
A	Auditing procedures: review of operations	3.15	3.31	2.54
F	Goodwill	3.08	2.83	2.58
F	Double-entry system	3.08	2.92	3.38
F	Contingencies	3.08	2.85	2.62
A	Auditing procedures: compliance tests	3.08	3.00	2.54
A	Legal responsibilities of auditors: exposure to criminal liability	3.08	2.77	2.08
F	Theoretical framework: alternatives to current structure	3.00	3.08	2.38
F	Present value and future worth concepts	3.00	3.15	2.92
F	Cash	3.00	2.85	3.23
F	Investments in securities	3.00	2.92	2.92
F	Intangibles (excluding goodwill)	3.00	2.92	2.69
F	Convertible debt or equity	3.00	2.85	2.62
M	Variable costing	3.00	3.00	2.62
F	Error corrections	2.92	2.81	2.92
F	Price-level adjusted financial statements	2.92	3.00	2.15
F	Deferred taxes	2.92	2.62	2.46
F	Materiality	2.92	2.85	1.85
M	Full costing	2.92	2.77	2.62
M	Direct costing	2.92	2.92	2.69
M	Short-range planning	2.92	3.00	2.15
F	Financial statement analysis	2.92	2.92	2.38
M	Joint costs	2.92	2.92	2.15
F	Interim reporting	2.85	2.92	2.23
F	Business combinations: consolidation procedures	2.85	2.77	2.23
F	Earnings-per-share	2.85	2.69	2.08

APPENDIX 7A
(continued)

Area	Topic	Importance	Conceptual Knowledge	Technical Ability
			Means	
M	Job order costing	2.85	2.62	2.38
M	Process costing	2.85	2.62	2.38
M	Cost-volume-profit analysis	2.85	3.00	2.38
M	Accounting information requirements for management decisions	2.85	2.83	2.25
A	Statistical inference in auditing: judgmental sampling	2.85	2.92	2.38
T	Tax planning	2.83	2.42	1.92
A	Internal control: description based on questionnaire	2.77	2.46	2.23
A	Internal control: description based on narrative	2.77	2.69	2.38
M	Internal operational auditing	2.77	2.77	2.08
M	Management information systems: design	2.77	2.85	1.92
M	Capital budgeting	2.77	2.92	2.18
F	Minority interest	2.77	2.69	2.38
M	Internal financial auditing	2.75	2.67	2.00
F	Treasury stock	2.69	2.75	2.75
F	Segment reporting	2.69	2.62	2.08
F	Business combinations: purchase vs. pooling of interest	2.69	2.54	1.92
M	Tax considerations in managerial decisions	2.69	2.85	2.15
A	Audit administration: review	2.69	2.46	1.85
A	Operational auditing: objectives	2.69	2.69	1.69
T	Non-taxable exchanges	2.67	2.33	2.42
M	Long-range planning	2.67	2.83	2.08
F	Pensions	2.62	2.25	2.17
F	Business combinations: unconsolidated subsidiaries	2.62	2.54	2.15
M	Spoilage, waste, defective units and scrap	2.62	2.69	2.23
A	Requirements for professional certification (CPA)	2.62	2.15	1.69
A	Legal responsibilities of auditors: responses of the auditing profession to classic cases	2.62	2.54	1.69
A	Extensions of the attest function: possible areas	2.62	2.62	1.38
M	Performance evaluation: divisional performance	2.58	2.58	2.08
F	Research and development costs	2.54	2.54	1.92
M	Flexible budgets	2.54	2.62	2.17
M	Performance evaluation: transfer pricing	2.54	2.62	2.15
A	Extensions of the attest function: associated audit risk	2.54	2.46	1.31
M	Budgeted financial statements	2.50	2.33	1.64

APPENDIX 7A
(continued)

Area	Topic	Importance	Conceptual Knowledge	Technical Ability
			Means	
T	Tax research methodology	2.50	2.42	1.92
A	SEC filing requirements	2.46	2.38	1.62
F	Statements from incomplete records	2.46	1.85	2.31
M	Overhead control	2.46	2.15	1.77
M	*Performance evaluation: non-statistical variance analysis	2.42	2.58	2.27
T	Tax returns and accompanying schedules	2.42	2.00	2.17
M	Statistical analysis of cost variances	2.38	2.23	1.77
M	Organization theory	2.38	2.15	1.54
M	Statistical decision theory	2.38	2.31	1.92
M	Performance evaluation: common costs	2.38	2.46	1.85
A	Legal responsibilities of auditors: classic cases	2.38	2.54	1.69
F	Reporting forecasts	2.38	2.69	1.85
A	Operational auditing: methodology	2.31	2.46	1.46
A	Audit administration: planning	2.31	2.31	1.62
M	Performance evaluation: responsibility accounting	2.31	2.38	1.85
M	Management information systems: impact of external regulatory influences	2.31	2.23	1.69
M	Cash management	2.31	2.75	1.64
F	*Behavioral considerations in financial reporting	2.31	2.23	1.46
F	SEC reporting	2.31	2.38	1.54
A	Auditing procedures: working papers	2.31	2.46	1.69
M	Computer science	2.27	1.91	2.09
M	Performance evaluation: return on investment	2.23	2.31	2.00
M	Behavioral considerations	2.23	2.23	1.46
M	Management information systems: implementation	2.23	2.23	1.46
F	Partnership financial statements	2.15	1.91	2.00
F	*Fund accounting: governmental units	2.15	2.00	1.77
M	Information economics	2.15	2.00	1.08
M	*Performance evaluation: non-financial performance measures	2.15	2.31	1.69
A	Statistical inference in auditing: regression analysis	2.15	2.15	1.54
T	Complex tax provisions: individuals	2.08	1.67	1.83
T	*Theoretical framework of taxation: economic and social concepts	2.08	2.08	1.00
T	Accumulated earnings tax	2.08	1.83	1.27
M	*Corporate planning models	2.08	2.00	1.54
F	Fund accounting: financial statements	2.08	2.00	1.69
F	Installment sales	2.08	2.46	2.08
A	Audit administration: supervision	2.08	2.15	1.31

APPENDIX 7A
(continued)

Area	Topic	Importance	Conceptual Knowledge	Technical Ability
			Means	
A	Long-form audit report	2.08	1.85	1.31
F	*Fund accounting: types of organizations	2.00	1.69	1.46
A	Statistical inference in auditing: other statistical methods	2.00	2.00	1.55
A	*Special considerations in auditing not-for-profit organizations	2.00	2.08	1.67
T	Recognition of tax opportunities	2.00	1.67	1.50
T	Taxation of deferred compensation	2.00	1.83	1.42
A	Management letter	1.92	2.08	1.38
M	*Statistical cost estimation	1.92	1.92	1.62
F	*Full costing vs. successful effort costing	1.92	2.15	2.62
M	Consignments	1.92	2.15	1.92
M	*Simulation	1.92	2.00	1.25
M	*Sensitivity analysis	1.92	2.08	1.33
T	*Theoretical framework of taxation: alternatives to present framework	1.92	2.00	.92
T	Complex tax provisions: corporations and shareholders	1.91	1.73	1.82
M	*Zero base budgeting	1.85	2.00	1.38
M	*Performance evaluation: residual income	1.83	1.92	1.50
F	*Regulated industries	1.77	1.69	1.00
A	Audit administration: client relations	1.77	1.77	1.08
T	*Social security taxes	1.75	1.50	1.42
T	Complex tax provisions: partners and partnerships	1.75	1.50	1.58
T	Complex tax provisions: consolidated corporate returns	1.75	1.50	1.33
T	*Administrative processes in tax matters	1.75	1.58	1.27
M	*Social accounting	1.69	1.69	.92
M	*Linear programming	1.69	1.77	1.31
F	*Fiduciary accounting: bankruptcy	1.69	1.77	1.23
F	*Fiduciary accounting: receivership	1.69	1.69	1.23
F	*Fiduciary accounting: estates and trusts	1.69	1.85	1.38
M	*Network methods	1.67	1.83	1.33
M	Special considerations in non-manufacturing concerns	1.64	1.90	1.50
F	Foreign currency translation	1.62	1.54	1.31
M	Management information system: administration	1.62	1.69	1.08
A	*Historical development of auditing	1.62	1.62	.85
T	*Federal gift tax	1.58	1.25	1.18
A	*Audit administration	1.54	1.23	.92
T	*Judicial doctrines in tax disputes	1.50	1.33	.75
T	*Federal estate tax	1.50	1.42	1.18
M	*Learning curve models	1.46	1.62	1.15
T	*Complex tax provisions: subchapter S	1.42	1.17	1.33

APPENDIX 7A
(continued)

Area	Topic	Importance	Conceptual Knowledge	Technical Ability
			Means	
F	*National income accounting	1.38	1.58	.85
T	*State and local taxes	1.36	1.18	1.36
T	*Complex tax provisions: foreign tax credit	1.33	1.09	1.09
T	*Judicial processes in tax disputes	1.27	1.55	1.00
T	*Taxation for international operations	1.25	1.00	.92
T	*Personal holding company tax	1.25	1.25	.75
T	*Complex tax provisions: fiduciaries	1.25	1.00	1.00
F	*International accounting standards	1.23	1.46	.85
F	*Fund accounting: hospitals	1.23	1.42	1.00
F	*Fund accounting: colleges and universities	1.23	1.42	1.00
M	*Requirements for professional certification (CMA)	1.23	1.15	.77
A	*Auditing procedures: audit practice case	1.23	1.17	1.50
T	*Natural resource taxation	1.17	.92	.75
M	*Planning and control of international operations	1.15	1.00	.69
A	*Comparative accounting and auditing standards among nations	1.08	1.00	.69
A	*Human resource accounting	1.08	1.08	.69
F	*Development stage companies	1.08	1.15	.54
T	*Complex tax provisions: DISC	1.00	1.09	.91
T	*Tax practice procedures	.90	1.00	.80
T	*Preparation of tax communications	.80	.80	.90
A	*Audit administration: setting and collecting fees	.77	1.00	.46

* ➔ non-area core topic

APPENDIX 7B

RANK ORDERING BY IMPORTANCE MEANS:
AUDITING PRACTITIONERS

Area	Topic	Importance	Means Conceptual Knowledge	Technical Ability
A	Internal control: principles	3.75	3.63	3.29
A	Generally accepted auditing standards (GAAS)	3.71	3.69	3.33
A	Internal control: relationship of GAAS	3.70	3.59	3.21
F	Income statement	3.66	3.53	3.23
F	Balance sheet	3.64	3.49	3.17
A	Internal control: evaluation	3.57	3.54	2.95
M	Management information systems: internal control aspects	3.57	3.44	2.96
A	Internal control: audit exposure due to weaknesses	3.54	3.48	2.95
A	Internal control: modifications in audit program based on evaluation	3.54	3.41	2.86
F	U.S. financial accounting and reporting standards	3.53	3.13	2.77
A	Audit evidence: types	3.52	3.51	3.00
F	Double-entry system	3.49	3.34	3.38
F	Statement of changes in financial position	3.47	3.34	3.00
A	Internal control: in an EDP environment	3.46	3.38	2.84
F	Accruals and deferrals	3.46	3.42	3.34
A	Audit evidence: relative strength of types	3.43	3.42	2.96
F	Transaction analysis	3.42	3.43	3.22
F	Inventories	3.40	3.38	3.08
F	Revenue and expense recognition	3.38	3.57	2.88
F	Materiality	3.36	3.35	2.76
F	Theoretical framework: current structure	3.35	3.18	2.47
A	Statistical inference in auditing: statistical sampling	3.29	3.18	2.82
A	Professional rules of conduct	3.29	3.18	2.57
F	Regulatory influences	3.28	3.02	2.27
A	Auditing procedures: tests of transactions	3.28	3.24	2.89
F	Financial statement analysis	3.25	3.08	2.68
A	Standard short-form audit report	3.21	3.30	2.88
T	Fundamentals of Federal income tax determination	3.20	3.10	2.44
A	Auditing procedures: working papers	3.18	2.98	2.70
A	Auditing procedures: tests of account balances	3.18	2.98	2.70
F	Receivables	3.18	3.18	2.92
A	Auditing procedures: review of operations	3.14	3.09	2.66
A	Auditing procedures: compliance tests	3.14	3.16	2.86
A	Statistical inference in auditing: judgmental sampling	3.14	3.16	2.84

APPENDIX 7B
(continued)

Area	Topic	Importance	Conceptual Knowledge	Technical Ability
			Means	
A	Influence of professional and regulatory bodies upon auditing	3.11	3.02	2.02
A	Modifications of the standard short-form audit report	3.11	3.23	2.80
A	Audit evidence: post-statement events	3.05	3.13	2.55
A	Internal control: description based on flowchart	3.05	3.00	2.75
F	Business combinations: consolidation procedures	3.02	3.02	2.75
A	Internal control: description based on narrative	2.98	2.98	2.75
F	Long-term liabilities	2.98	3.06	2.71
F	Cash	2.96	2.98	2.83
F	Contingencies	2.92	2.94	2.35
F	Accounting for income taxes	2.92	3.02	2.57
F	Depreciation, depletion and amortization	2.91	3.02	2.77
F	Deferred taxes	2.90	3.04	2.52
F	Fixed assets	2.89	3.00	2.74
F	Short-term liabilities	2.88	2.98	2.63
A	User's expectations regarding the auditor's role	2.87	2.96	1.42
M	Management information systems: impact of external regulatory influences	2.84	2.65	1.94
M	Computer science	2.83	2.81	2.00
F	Investments in securities	2.83	2.89	2.62
A	Internal control: description based on questionnaire	2.82	2.82	2.41
F	Information needs of financial statement users	2.81	2.68	1.62
M	Accounting information requirements for management decisions	2.80	2.69	1.98
M	Standard costs	2.80	2.98	2.36
F	Leases	2.78	2.78	2.29
A	Legal responsibilities of auditors: at common law	2.70	2.87	1.93
A	Legal responsibilities of auditors: under the securities acts	2.70	2.78	2.00
F	Business combinations: purchase vs. pooling of interest	2.70	2.86	2.27
F	Business combinations: unconsolidated subsidiaries	2.69	2.80	2.43
M	Full costing	2.67	2.78	2.17
M	Tax considerations in managerial decisions	2.67	2.67	1.90
T	Capital gains and losses	2.67	2.52	2.10
F	Earnings-per-share	2.65	2.75	2.41
F	Corporate equity	2.64	2.85	2.38

APPENDIX 7B
(continued)

Area	Topic	Importance	Means Conceptual Knowledge	Technical Ability
M	Job order costing	2.63	2.84	2.09
M	Internal financial auditing	2.63	2.57	2.10
F	Present value and future worth concepts	2.62	2.77	2.15
A	Management letter	2.62	2.78	2.15
M	Process costing	2.61	2.80	2.09
A	Requirements for professional certification (CPA)	2.61	2.65	2.28
F	Pensions	2.60	2.57	2.16
F	Theoretical framework: alternatives to current structure	2.59	2.74	1.74
F	Interim reporting	2.58	2.61	2.04
F	Intangibles (excluding goodwill)	2.57	2.71	2.25
F	Goodwill	2.57	2.73	2.25
T	Recognition of tax opportunities	2.55	2.63	1.73
A	Operational auditing: objectives	2.54	2.57	1.73
A	Audit administration: client relations	2.50	2.54	1.77
A	Extensions of the attest function: possible areas	2.49	2.51	1.55
M	Cash management	2.49	2.33	1.80
M	Overhead control	2.48	2.46	1.83
A	Extensions of the attest function: associated audit risk	2.47	2.55	1.56
M	Internal operational auditing	2.47	2.51	1.84
A	Long-form audit report	2.46	2.55	1.95
T	Tax planning	2.45	2.35	1.48
M	Cost-volume-analysis	2.45	2.48	1.92
A	Audit administration: review	2.45	2.45	1.76
F	Error corrections	2.44	2.69	2.57
A	Legal responsibilities of auditors: responses of the auditing profession to classic cases	2.42	2.43	1.57
A	Legal responsibilities of auditors: classic cases	2.40	2.44	1.57
F	Convertible debt equity	2.40	2.52	2.25
M	Variable costing	2.40	2.65	1.91
A	Operational auditing: methodology	2.39	2.41	1.73
F	SEC reporting	2.34	2.37	1.85
F	Minority interest	2.36	2.59	2.25
A	Legal responsibilities of auditors: exposure to criminal liability	2.35	2.43	1.74
A	Audit administration: planning	2.32	2.54	1.67
A	*Auditing procedures: audit practice case	2.31	2.19	2.02
M	Direct costing	2.31	2.63	1.88
F	Installment sales	2.30	2.44	2.10

APPENDIX 7B
(continued)

Area	Topic	Importance	Conceptual Knowledge	Technical Ability
			Means	
F	Treasury stock	2.29	2.31	2.15
M	Spoilage, waste, defective units and scrap	2.27	2.45	1.89
M	Flexible budgets	2.24	2.31	1.54
M	Capital budgeting	2.23	2.28	1.67
M	Budgeted financial statements	2.22	2.34	1.68
M	Performance evaluation: return on investment	2.22	2.44	1.83
A	Audit administration: supervision	2.21	2.25	1.58
A	SEC filing requirements	2.21	2.38	1.78
T	Complex tax provisions: corporations and shareholders	2.20	2.17	1.44
T	Tax returns and accompanying schedules	2.19	2.00	1.73
A	Statistical inference in auditing: regression analysis	2.17	2.33	1.87
M	Management information system: design	2.16	2.10	1.55
M	Organization theory	2.15	2.17	1.40
T	*State and local taxes	2.14	2.17	1.58
A	Statistical inference in auditing: other statistical methods	2.14	2.33	1.92
F	Consignments	2.13	2.44	2.02
F	Research and development care	2.12	2.34	1.80
F	Segment reporting	2.12	2.21	1.76
F	Price-level adjusted financial statements	2.10	2.49	1.67
M	Short-range planning	2.08	2.20	1.48
T	Complex tax provisions: individuals	2.08	2.08	1.71
T	Complex tax provisions: consolidated corporate returns	2.08	2.19	1.42
M	Joint costs	2.07	2.33	1.69
M	Performance evaluation: responsibility accounting	2.06	2.32	1.57
T	Non-taxable exchanges	2.06	2.02	1.63
F	Statement from incomplete records	2.06	2.25	2.00
M	Long-range planning	2.04	2.22	1.36
M	Management information systems: implementation	2.04	2.00	1.47
M	Management information systems: administration	1.98	1.94	1.41
M	Performance evaluation: divisional performance	1.96	2.10	1.56
F	Partnership financial statements	1.94	2.29	1.94
M	Statistical decision theory	1.93	2.09	1.30
T	Taxation of deferred compensation	1.92	1.91	1.47
M	Information economics	1.88	1.93	1.28
F	Foreign currency translation	1.85	2.14	1.65
M	Performance evaluation: transfer pricing	1.83	2.04	1.38
M	Performance evaluation: common costs	1.83	1.98	1.35

APPENDIX 7B
(continued)

Area	Topic	Importance	Conceptual Knowledge	Technical Ability
			Means	
T	Tax research methodology	1.82	1.73	1.27
M	Statistical analysis of cost variances	1.80	1.96	1.40
F	Reporting forecasts	1.79	2.10	1.30
T	Complex tax provisions: partners and partnerships	1.78	1.77	1.40
T	*Complex tax provisions: subchapter S	1.76	1.75	1.19
T	*Complex tax provisions: foreign tax credit	1.76	1.77	1.15
T	Accumulated earnings tax	1.74	1.89	1.15
M	Special considerations in non-manufacturing concerns	1.73	1.88	1.27
F	Fund accounting: financial statements	1.73	1.92	1.42
F	*Full costing vs. successful effort costing	1.72	2.14	1.45
M	*Zero base budgeting	1.71	1.90	1.22
M	Behavioral considerations	1.71	1.76	.95
M	*Statistical cost estimation	1.71	1.89	1.32
F	*Fund accounting: types of organizations	1.70	1.90	1.28
F	Fund accounting: governmental units	1.69	1.80	1.29
A	*Audit administration: accounting firm organization	1.66	1.73	.96
A	*Special considerations in auditing not-for-profit organizations	1.66	1.91	1.07
F	*Fund accounting: hospitals	1.63	1.81	1.36
M	*Performance evaluation: non-statistical variance analysis	1.60	1.90	1.22
T	*Complex tax provisions: DISC	1.59	1.71	1.02
T	*Taxation for international operations	1.59	1.67	.98
A	*Historical development of auditing	1.59	1.75	.73
M	*Simulation	1.58	1.83	1.00
F	*Regulated industries	1.58	1.82	1.14
F	*Fund accounting: colleges and universities	1.55	1.75	1.30
M	*Performance evaluation: residual income	1.55	1.78	1.02
M	*Network methods	1.52	1.72	.90
F	*Development stage companies	1.52	1.78	1.20
F	*International accounting standards	1.51	1.55	.92
T	*Social security taxes	1.49	1.56	1.23
T	*Administrative processes in tax matters	1.49	1.58	1.02
M	*Corporate planning models	1.49	1.62	.93
M	*Sensitivity analysis	1.48	1.68	.93
A	*Audit administration: setting and collecting fees	1.45	1.38	.84
M	*Learning curve models	1.43	1.67	.98
M	*Performance evaluation: non-financial measures	1.42	1.70	.98
M	*Linear programming	1.40	1.74	.98

APPENDIX 7B
(continued)

Area	Topic	Importance	Conceptual Knowledge	Technical Ability
			Means	
M	*Planning and control of international operations	1.38	1.57	.91
T	*Theoretical framework of taxation: economic and social concepts	1.33	1.46	.69
M	*Social accounting	1.33	1.50	.67
F	*Fiduciary accounting: estates and trusts	1.31	1.80	1.32
T	*Federal gift tax	1.31	1.50	1.04
T	*Federal estate tax	1.31	1.50	1.04
T	*Natural resource taxation	1.31	1.35	.90
F	*Behavioral consideratons in financial reporting	1.30	1.51	.76
F	*Fiduciary accounting: bankruptcy	1.29	1.80	1.28
T	*Judicial processes in tax disputes	1.25	1.36	.85
A	*Comparative accounting and auditing standards among nations	1.25	1.44	.73
T	*Tax practice procedures	1.24	1.25	.98
T	*Theoretical framework of taxation: alternatives to present framework	1.24	1.42	.71
T	*Personal holding company tax	1.24	1.38	.92
T	*Complex tax provisions: fiduciaries	1.24	1.29	.92
F	*Fiduciary accounting: receivership	1.23	1.78	1.26
T	*Preparation of tax communications	1.15	1.22	.78
F	*National income accounting	1.13	1.40	.67
T	*Judicial doctrines in tax disputes	1.12	1.34	.81
F	*Human resource accounting	1.11	1.36	.71
M	*Requirements for professional certification (CMA)	1.09	1.26	.83

* ➞ non-area core topic

APPENDIX 8A

RANK ORDERING BY IMPORTANCE MEANS:
GENERAL EDUCATORS

Area	Topic	Importance	Conceptual Knowledge	Technical Ability
			Means	
F	Income statement	3.86	3.64	3.71
F	Theoretical framework: current structure	3.79	3.71	3.50
F	Revenue and expense recognition	3.79	3.77	3.50
F	Balance sheet	3.71	3.50	3.64
A	Internal control: principles	3.62	3.38	3.15
F	Statement of changes in financial position	3.57	3.43	3.57
A	Generally accepted auditing standards (GAAS)	3.54	3.38	3.17
F	Present value and future worth concepts	3.50	3.36	3.21
F	U.S. financial accounting and reporting standards	3.43	2.93	3.29
F	Transaction analysis	3.43	3.07	3.64
M	Capital budgeting	3.43	3.36	3.29
A	Audit evidence: relative strength of types	3.38	3.38	2.54
T	Fundamentals of federal income tax determination	3.38	3.00	3.17
F	Information needs of financial statement users	3.36	3.57	2.36
F	Double-entry system	3.36	2.93	3.79
M	Standard costs	3.36	3.07	3.07
M	Cost-volume-profit analysis	3.36	3.36	3.14
A	Standard short-form audit report	3.31	2.85	3.23
A	Internal control: relationship of GAAS	3.31	3.33	2.75
A	Audit evidence: types	3.31	3.38	2.38
F	Theoretical framework: alternatives to current structure	3.29	3.50	2.57
F	Accruals and deferrals	3.29	3.00	3.57
M	Flexible budgets	3.29	3.14	3.07
M	Performance evaluation: return on investment	3.29	3.14	2.93
M	Variable costing	3.23	3.14	3.07
A	Professional rules of conduct	3.23	3.15	2.85
F	Inventories	3.21	3.14	3.14
M	Accounting information requirements for management decisions	3.21	3.21	2.71
A	Internal control: evaluation	3.17	2.83	2.58
F	Regulatory influences	3.14	2.86	2.86
F	Receivables	3.14	3.07	3.07
F	Corporate equity	3.14	3.43	2.79
M	Full costing	3.14	3.07	3.00
M	Performance evaluation: non-statistical variance analysis	3.14	3.07	2.79
A	Internal control: audit exposure due to weaknesses	3.09	2.45	2.50

APPENDIX 8A
(continued)

Area	Topic	Importance	Conceptual Knowledge	Technical Ability
			Means	
A	Influence of professional and regulatory bodies on auditing	3.08	2.54	2.38
A	Internal control: in an EDP environment	3.08	2.62	2.82
A	Statistical inference in auditing: statistical sampling	3.08	3.15	2.31
F	Financial statement analysis	3.07	3.15	2.85
M	Short-range planning	3.07	3.07	2.57
M	Budgeted financial statements	3.07	2.79	2.86
F	Cash	3.00	2.71	3.00
F	Fixed assets	3.00	3.07	2.79
F	Depreciation, depletion and amortization	3.00	3.36	2.79
F	Intangibles (excluding goodwill)	3.00	3.14	2.71
M	Direct costing	3.00	3.00	3.00
A	Modification of the standard short-form audit report	3.00	2.85	3.15
A	Internal control: modifications in audit program based on evaluation	3.00	2.33	2.73
A	Statistical inference in auditing: judgmental sampling	3.00	3.15	2.31
A	Audit evidence: post-statement events	3.00	2.85	2.38
T	Capital gains and losses	3.00	2.62	3.08
F	Investments in securities	2.93	2.79	2.79
F	Materiality	2.93	2.92	2.54
F	Earnings-per-share	2.93	3.07	2.79
F	Accounting for income taxes	2.93	2.86	2.71
M	Process costing	2.93	2.79	3.00
M	Performance evaluation: divisional performance	2.93	3.00	3.00
M	Performance evaluation: common costs	2.93	2.86	2.57
F	Goodwill	2.92	3.31	2.77
A	Auditing procedures: review of operations	2.92	2.92	2.69
F	Long-term liabilities	2.86	2.93	2.71
M	Long-range liabilities	2.86	2.93	2.21
M	Cash management	2.86	2.43	2.64
M	Performance evaluation: responsibility accounting	2.86	2.93	2.71
M	Performance evaluation: non-financial performance measures	2.86	3.00	2.14
A	Auditing procedures: tests of transactions	2.85	2.69	2.54
T	Tax planning	2.85	2.85	2.67
F	Short-term liabilities	2.79	2.64	2.64
M	Job order costing	2.79	2.57	2.86
M	Tax considerations in managerial decisions	2.79	2.50	2.71
M	Computer science	2.79	2.21	2.29
M	Performance evaluation: transfer pricing	2.79	2.86	2.50

APPENDIX 8A
(continued)

Area	Topic	Importance	Means Conceptual Knowledge	Technical Ability
M	Overhead control	2.79	2.64	2.50
A	User's expectations regarding the auditor's role	2.77	3.08	1.85
A	Legal responsibilities of auditors: at common law	2.77	2.69	2.00
A	Legal responsibilities of auditors: under the securities acts	2.77	2.69	2.00
A	Statistical inference in auditing: other statistical methods	2.77	2.69	2.15
A	Auditing procedures: tests of account balances	2.77	2.69	2.54
T	Theoretical framework of taxation: economic and social concepts	2.77	3.17	1.46
F	Convertible debt or equity	2.71	2.79	2.50
F	Leases	2.71	2.79	2.57
M	Joint costs	2.71	2.86	2.21
M	Management information systems: internal control aspects	2.71	2.71	2.50
F	Price-level adjusted financial statements	2.69	3.15	2.38
A	Auditing procedures: compliance tests	2.69	2.69	2.62
F	Behavioral considerations in financial reporting	2.64	3.14	2.07
F	Deferred taxes	2.64	2.71	2.57
F	Business combinations: purchase vs. pooling of interests	2.64	2.86	2.43
F	Business combinations: consolidation procedures	2.64	2.71	2.71
M	Organization theory	2.62	2.92	1.92
M	Statistical cost estimation	2.62	2.62	2.38
F	Minority interest	2.57	2.71	2.21
M	Linear programming	2.57	2.57	2.36
M	Statistical decision theory	2.57	2.64	2.36
A	Internal control: description based on narrative	2.54	2.46	2.54
A	Internal control: description based on questionnaire	2.54	2.31	2.31
A	Statistical inference in auditing: regression analysis	2.54	2.77	2.00
A	Operational auditing: objectives	2.54	3.08	2.00
F	Pensions	2.50	2.85	2.77
F	Contingencies	2.50	2.71	2.23
M	Simulation	2.50	2.54	2.07
M	Behavioral considerations	2.50	2.77	1.85
A	Legal responsibilities of auditors: classic cases	2.46	2.50	1.75

APPENDIX 8A
(continued)

Area	Topic	Importance	Means Conceptual Knowledge	Technical Ability
A	Legal responsibilities of auditors: exposure to criminal liability	2.46	2.31	1.85
A	Internal control: description based on flowchart	2.46	2.23	2.38
T	Tax returns and accompanying schedules	2.46	1.69	2.33
F	Segment reporting	2.43	2.77	2.38
M	*Performance evaluation: residual income	2.43	2.54	2.46
M	*Social accounting	2.43	3.33	1.73
T	Non-taxable exchanges	2.42	2.45	2.33
T	Complex tax provisions: individuals	2.42	2.50	2.36
M	Statistical analysis of cost variances	2.38	2.31	2.08
A	Requirements for professional certification (CPA)	2.38	1.92	2.36
A	Extensions of the attest functions: associated audit risk	2.38	2.83	1.75
T	Tax research methodology	2.38	2.42	2.31
F	SEC reporting	2.36	2.36	2.07
F	Treasury stock	2.36	2.86	2.57
F	Reporting forecasts	2.36	2.92	2.15
M	Information economics	2.36	3.29	1.79
M	Sensitivity analysis	2.36	2.29	2.14
T	Recognition of tax opportunities	2.33	2.25	2.00
T	Theoretical framework of taxation: alternatives to present framework	2.33	2.91	1.55
F	Full costing vs. successful effort costing	2.31	2.85	2.08
A	Auditing procedures: working papers	2.31	1.92	2.00
A	Extensions of the attest function: possible areas	2.31	2.83	1.54
F	*Foreign currency translation	2.29	2.79	2.21
F	Error corrections	2.29	1.92	2.92
A	Legal responsibilities of auditors: responses of auditing profession to classic cases	2.23	2.08	1.75
A	Long-form audit report	2.23	2.15	2.00
A	Operational auditing: methodology	2.23	2.54	1.85
F	Business combinations: unconsolidated subsidiaries	2.21	2.69	2.54
M	Management information systems: impact of external regulatory influences	2.21	1.79	2.00
M	Spoilage, waste, defective units and scrap	2.15	2.15	2.23
A	Audit administration: review	2.15	2.00	1.67
F	Interim reporting	2.14	2.54	2.23
F	Research and development costs	2.14	2.43	1.93
F	Fund accounting: financial statements	2.14	2.46	2.15
M	Management information systems: design	2.14	2.46	2.23

APPENDIX 8A
(continued)

Area	Topic	Importance	Conceptual Knowledge	Technical Ability
			Means	
T	Complex tax provisions: subchapter S	2.09	2.18	2.00
T	Federal estate tax	2.08	2.09	1.82
T	Federal gift tax	2.08	2.00	1.73
T	Complex tax provisions: partners and partnerships	2.08	2.36	2.09
M	Corporate planning models	2.08	2.08	1.46
A	Management letter	2.08	2.08	1.92
A	Audit administration: planning	2.08	2.15	1.83
F	Installment sales	2.00	2.07	2.15
F	Statements from incomplete records	2.00	2.08	2.46
F	Partnership financial statements	2.00	2.38	2.54
A	SEC filing requirements	2.00	1.75	1.83
T	Taxation of deferred compensation	2.00	2.00	2.00
F	Fund accounting: types of organizations	1.93	2.08	2.08
F	Fund accounting: governmental units	1.93	2.08	1.69
M	Management information systems: implementation	1.92	2.08	1.92
A	Audit administration: client relations	1.92	1.50	1.58
M	*Special considerations in non-manufacturing concerns	1.91	1.73	1.45
M	Network methods	1.86	2.15	1.36
M	Internal financial auditing	1.85	2.00	1.69
M	Internal operational auditing	1.85	2.00	1.69
A	Historical development of auditing	1.85	2.25	1.25
T	Administrative processes in tax matters	1.85	2.00	1.58
F	*National income accounting	1.79	2.14	1.21
M	Zero base budgeting	1.79	2.17	2.00
M	*Learning curve models	1.79	2.00	1.57
A	Audit administration: supervision	1.77	1.77	1.50
T	Social security taxes	1.77	1.62	1.58
A	Special considerations in auditing not-for-profit organizations	1.69	1.77	1.33
T	Complex tax provisions: corporations and shareholders	1.67	2.18	1.73
F	Human resource accounting	1.64	2.14	1.07
T	Accumulated earnings tax	1.64	1.73	1.25
T	State and local taxes	1.62	1.33	1.58
M	*Planning and control of international operations	1.57	1.64	1.36
A	Audit administration: accounting firm organization	1.54	1.25	1.36
A	Auditing procedures: audit practice case	1.46	1.23	1.46
T	*Complex tax provisions: DISC	1.45	1.64	.91
F	*International accounting standards	1.43	2.25	1.75
F	Consignments	1.43	1.54	1.62

APPENDIX 8A
(continued)

Area	Topic	Importance	Means Conceptual Knowledge	Technical Ability
F	Fiduciary accounting: bankruptcy	1.43	1.85	1.46
F	*Fiduciary accounting: receivership	1.43	1.62	1.31
F	Fiduciary accounting: estates and trusts	1.43	1.77	1.69
F	*Regulated industries	1.43	1.92	1.42
F	Fund accounting: hospitals	1.43	1.50	1.50
F	Fund accounting: colleges and universities	1.43	1.50	1.50
M	*Management information systems: administration	1.38	1.42	1.42
A	*Audit administration: setting and collecting fees	1.38	1.17	1.55
T	*Natural resource taxation	1.36	2.20	1.20
T	*Judicial doctrines in tax disputes	1.33	1.82	1.00
T	*Complex tax provisions: consolidated corporate returns	1.33	2.00	1.55
T	*Personal holding company tax	1.33	1.82	1.00
T	*Tax practice procedures	1.33	1.09	1.64
T	*Complex tax provisions: foreign tax credit	1.18	1.64	1.00
T	*Judicial processes in tax disputes	1.17	1.45	1.18
T	*Complex tax provisions: fiduciaries	1.17	1.55	1.17
M	*Requirements for professional certification (CMA)	1.14	1.00	1.55
T	*Taxation for international operations	1.08	1.50	.92
F	*Development stage companies	1.00	1.54	1.00
A	*Comparative accounting and auditing standards among nations	1.00	1.42	.92
T	*Preparation of tax communications	1.00	1.40	1.10

* → non-core topic

APPENDIX 8B

RANK ORDERING BY IMPORTANCE MEANS:
GENERALIST PRACTITIONERS

Area	Topic	Importance	Means Conceptual Knowledge	Technical Ability
F	Balance sheet	3.68	3.56	3.37
F	Income statement	3.68	3.56	3.37
F	Statement of changes in financial position	3.64	3.52	3.33
A	Internal control: principles	3.63	3.46	2.96
A	Generally accepted auditing standards (GAAS)	3.59	3.65	3.12
F	Revenue and expense recognition	3.56	3.44	2.93
A	Internal control: relationship of GAAS	3.56	3.42	2.85
F	Financial statement analysis	3.54	3.37	3.26
F	Information needs of financial statement users	3.50	3.44	2.96
F	Accruals and deferrals	3.46	3.38	3.22
F	Regulatory influences	3.43	3.30	2.35
F	Inventories	3.43	3.22	3.11
T	Fundamentals of federal income tax determination	3.42	3.08	2.56
F	Theoretical framework: current structure	3.39	3.41	2.69
F	Materiality	3.39	3.44	2.69
A	Internal control: evaluation	3.38	3.48	2.88
A	Internal control: audit exposure due to weaknesses	3.36	3.35	2.78
A	Internal control: modifications in audit program based on evaluation	3.32	3.26	2.70
F	Transaction analysis	3.30	3.16	2.85
A	Standard short-form audit report	3.30	3.48	2.80
A	Modifications of the standard short-form audit report	3.30	3.15	2.81
F	U.S. financial accounting and reporting standards	3.29	3.00	2.58
F	Double-entry system	3.29	3.35	3.19
A	Internal control: in an EDP environment	3.28	3.30	2.74
A	Audit evidence: relative strength of types	3.23	3.21	2.71
A	Professional rules of conduct	3.22	3.23	2.77
A	Audit evidence: types	3.22	3.28	2.88
M	Management information systems: internal control aspects	3.19	3.00	2.27
A	Influence of professional and regulatory bodies on auditing	3.19	3.15	2.31
F	Depreciation, depletion and amortization	3.18	3.11	2.93
A	Legal responsibilities of auditors: at common law	3.15	3.24	2.44
F	Fixed assets	3.14	3.07	3.00
A	Audit evidence: post-statement events	3.11	3.16	2.60

APPENDIX 8B
(continued)

Area	Topic	Importance	Conceptual Knowledge	Technical Ability
			Means	
A	Legal responsibilities of auditors: under the securities acts	3.07	3.12	2.31
F	Receivables	3.07	2.96	2.96
F	Long-term liabilities	3.07	3.04	2.89
F	Deferred taxes	3.07	3.07	2.67
F	Earnings-per-share	3.07	3.04	2.70
F	Accounting for income taxes	3.07	2.96	2.50
M	Accounting information requirements for management decisions	3.04	2.92	2.24
T	Capital gains and losses	3.04	2.84	2.48
T	Tax planning	3.04	3.00	2.36
A	Statistical inference in auditing: statistical sampling	3.04	3.12	2.60
A	Auditing procedures: review of operations	3.04	3.24	2.60
F	Short-term liabilities	3.04	3.04	2.85
F	Corporate equity	3.00	2.96	2.56
A	Internal control: description based on narrative	3.00	3.04	2.65
A	Internal control: description based on flowchart	3.00	3.04	2.52
A	Auditing procedures: compliance tests	3.00	3.16	2.68
M	Standard costs	2.96	2.96	2.27
A	Auditing procedures: working papers	2.96	3.08	2.80
A	Auditing procedures: tests of transactions	2.96	3.16	2.68
A	Management letter	2.96	3.08	2.16
F	Cash	2.93	2.81	2.85
F	Investments in securities	2.93	3.00	2.67
M	Management information systems: impact of external regulatory influences	2.93	2.88	2.19
A	User's expectations regarding the auditor's role	2.92	2.92	1.75
A	Auditing procedures: tests of account balances	2.92	3.13	2.71
A	Internal control: description based on questionnaire	2.92	3.00	2.52
T	Recognition of tax opportunities	2.92	2.79	2.29
F	Business combinations: consolidation procedures	2.89	2.96	2.59
M	Tax considerations in managerial decisions	2.89	2.73	2.19
A	Requirements for professional certification (CPA)	2.89	2.92	2.08
A	Audit administration: planning	2.89	2.92	2.16
A	Statistical inference in auditing: judgmental sampling	2.88	2.96	2.50
M	Computer science	2.85	2.80	2.04

APPENDIX 8B
(continued)

Area	Topic	Importance	Means Conceptual Knowledge	Technical Ability
F	Theoretical framework: alternatives to current structure	2.82	2.93	2.04
F	Leases	2.82	2.93	2.41
F	Contingencies	2.82	2.93	2.26
M	Short-range planning	2.81	2.85	2.23
A	Audit administration: client relations	2.81	2.72	1.88
M	Budgeted financial statements	2.81	2.80	2.24
M	Flexible budgets	2.78	2.85	2.19
M	Cost-volume-profit analysis	2.78	2.73	2.31
A	Audit administration: review	2.78	2.92	2.16
F	Present value and future worth concepts	2.75	2.89	2.30
M	Cash management	2.74	2.69	2.15
M	Performance evaluation: return on investment	2.74	2.77	2.12
T	Non-taxable exchanges	2.74	2.56	2.24
T	Tax research methodology	2.72	2.75	2.25
F	Price-level adjusted financial statements	2.71	2.85	2.15
M	Long-range planning	2.70	2.88	2.12
A	Legal responsibilities of auditors: exposure to criminal liability	2.70	2.85	2.04
F	Error corrections	2.69	2.62	2.65
A	Long-form audit report	2.68	2.67	2.33
T	Complex tax provisions: corporations and shareholders	2.68	2.67	2.21
F	Goodwill	2.68	2.78	2.22
A	Statistical inference in auditing: regression analysis	2.67	2.70	2.17
A	Audit administration: supervision	2.67	2.72	2.04
F	Convertible debt or equity	2.64	2.70	2.19
F	Interim reporting	2.64	2.70	2.22
T	Complex tax provisions: individuals	2.64	2.46	2.29
T	Tax returns and accompanying schedules	2.64	2.50	2.38
M	Full costing	2.63	2.65	2.12
A	Legal responsibilities of auditors: classic case	2.63	2.72	2.12
A	Auditing procedures: audit practice case	2.62	2.76	2.48
F	Business combinations: purchase vs. pooling of interests	2.61	2.74	2.22
M	Performance evaluation: responsibility accounting	2.60	2.46	1.79
F	Reporting forecasts	2.59	2.85	2.23
M	Capital budgeting	2.59	2.77	2.08
F	Treasury stock	2.57	2.59	2.15
F	Business combinations: unconsolidated subsidiaries	2.57	2.67	2.22
F	Segment reporting	2.56	2.54	2.07

APPENDIX 8B
(continued)

Area	Topic	Importance	Means Conceptual Knowledge	Technical Ability
M	Overhead control	2.56	2.46	2.15
A	Extensions of the attest function: associated audit risk	2.54	2.43	1.57
F	Intangibles (excluding goodwill)	2.54	2.63	2.15
F	Pensions	2.54	2.70	1.93
M	Process costing	2.48	2.58	1.96
M	Management information systems: design	2.48	2.62	2.00
F	Minority interest	2.46	2.63	2.11
A	Statistical inference in auditing: other statistical methods	2.46	2.52	2.09
A	Extensions of the attest function: possible areas	2.46	2.35	1.48
M	Direct costing	2.44	2.69	1.92
M	Management information systems: implementation	2.44	2.38	1.72
T	Complex tax provisions: partners and partnerships	2.44	2.46	2.17
T	Taxation of deferred compensation	2.44	2.29	1.88
M	Job order costing	2.41	2.54	2.04
M	Variable costing	2.41	2.58	2.00
A	SEC filing requirements	2.41	2.38	1.77
A	Legal responsibilities of auditors: responses of the auditing profession to classic cases	2.39	2.44	2.11
F	Research and development costs	2.39	2.52	1.81
F	Statements from incomplete records	2.38	2.54	2.42
M	Organization theory	2.38	2.44	1.75
T	Federal estate tax	2.38	2.44	1.84
M	*Management information systems: administration	2.37	2.38	1.84
T	Complex tax provisions: subchapter S	2.36	2.33	1.96
F	Installment sales	2.36	2.62	2.19
T	Administrative processes in tax matters	2.35	2.43	1.48
T	Federal gift tax	2.35	2.44	1.84
A	Operational auditing: objectives	2.32	2.35	1.41
M	Spoilage, waste, defective units and scrap	2.31	2.40	1.92
T	Accumulated earnings tax	2.31	2.43	1.70
M	Information economics	2.28	2.33	1.72
M	Performance evaluation: divisional performance	2.27	2.40	1.80
F	Consignments	2.25	2.37	2.04
A	Operational auditing: methodology	2.24	2.22	1.36
T	*Complex tax provisions: consolidated corporate returns	2.24	2.33	1.75
F	SEC reporting	2.21	2.35	1.70

APPENDIX 8B
(continued)

Area	Topic	Importance	Conceptual Knowledge	Technical Ability
			Means	
M	Joint costs	2.21	2.30	1.65
T	State and local taxes	2.19	2.04	1.67
F	Fund accounting: financial statements	2.19	2.30	1.81
M	Statistical decision theory	2.17	2.45	1.77
M	Statistical cost estimation	2.17	2.32	1.77
M	Statistical analysis of cost variances	2.17	2.35	1.65
A	Audit administration: accounting firm organizatin	2.15	2.40	1.44
F	Behavioral considerations in financial reporting	2.14	2.35	1.70
T	*Tax practice procedures	2.12	2.26	1.52
F	Fund accounting: types of organizations	2.11	2.33	1.70
M	Zero base budgeting	2.09	2.32	1.64
M	Corporate planning models	2.09	2.23	1.43
T	Theoretical framework of taxation: economic and social concepts	2.08	2.26	1.04
T	*Complex tax provisions: fiduciaries	2.08	2.04	1.63
M	Internal operational auditing	2.08	2.20	1.72
F	*Regulated industries	2.07	2.11	1.59
T	Theoretical framework of taxation: alternative to present framework	2.04	2.22	1.09
A	*Audit administration: setting and collecting fees	2.04	2.04	1.36
F	Fiduciary accounting: estates and trusts	2.00	2.31	1.65
F	Full costing vs. successful effort costing	2.00	2.00	1.63
F	Fund accounting: governmental units	2.00	2.19	1.67
M	Performance evaluation: common costs	2.00	1.95	1.55
M	Internal financial auditing	2.00	2.00	1.54
T	*Preparation of tax communications	1.96	1.80	1.52
A	Special considerations in auditing not-for-profit organizations	1.96	2.00	1.33
M	Simulation	1.95	1.95	1.35
F	Fund accounting: hospitals	1.93	2.07	1.67
M	Performance evaluation: transfer pricing	1.92	1.91	1.52
M	Performance evaluation: non-statistical variance analysis	1.91	1.86	1.43
A	Historical development of auditing	1.88	2.20	1.08
T	*Judicial doctrines in tax disputes	1.84	1.72	1.28
F	Fund accounting: colleges and universities	1.81	1.93	1.50
F	*Development stage companies	1.81	2.12	1.50
M	Network methods	1.80	1.89	1.26
M	Sensitivity analysis	1.80	2.05	1.33
T	*Judicial processes in tax disputes	1.80	1.76	1.24
T	*Complex tax provisions: foreign tax credit	1.80	1.83	1.17

APPENDIX 8B
(continued)

Area	Topic	Importance	Means Conceptual Knowledge	Technical Ability
M	Performance evaluation: non-financial performance measures	1.78	1.86	1.23
M	Linear programming	1.77	2.00	1.19
T	Social security taxes	1.76	1.54	1.46
F	Human resource accounting	1.73	1.84	1.16
T	*Taxation for international operations	1.73	1.76	1.20
F	Fiduciary accounting: bankruptcy	1.71	2.11	1.44
M	Behavioral considerations (managerial)	1.70	1.85	1.15
T	*Personal holding company tax	1.69	1.84	1.28
F	*Fiduciary accounting: receivership	1.61	2.04	1.33
M	*Learning curve models	1.59	1.81	1.19
T	*Complex tax provisions: DISC	1.56	1.63	1.08
M	*Special considerations in non-manufacturing concerns	1.55	1.60	1.05
M	*Social accounting	1.54	1.71	1.00
F	*Foreign currency translation	1.54	1.81	1.19
F	*National income accounting	1.50	1.71	1.16
M	*Requirements for professional certification (CMA)	1.50	1.50	1.27
T	*Natural resource taxation	1.46	1.52	1.16
M	*Performance evaluation: residual income	1.44	1.67	1.11
F	*International accounting standards	1.39	1.56	1.00
M	*Planning and control of international operations	1.39	1.32	1.00
A	*Comparative accounting and auditing standards among nations	1.00	1.08	.63

* → non-core topic